The Indirect Effect of Direct Legislation

The Indirect Effect of Direct Legislation

How Institutions Shape Interest Group Systems

Frederick J. Boehmke

The Ohio State University Press
Columbus

Library of Congress Cataloging-in-Publication Data

Boehmke, Frederick J.
The indirect effect of direct legislation : how institutions shape interest group systems / Frederick J. Boehmke.
p. cm.
Includes bibliographical references and index.
ISBN 0-8142-0996-3 (cloth : alk. paper) — ISBN 0-8142-9074-4 (cd-rom)
1. Referendum—United States—States. 2. Direct democracy—United States—States. 3. Pressure groups—United States—States. 4. Lobbying—United States—States. I. Title.
JF494.B64 2005
328.273—dc22

2005002172

Paper (ISBN: 978-0-8142-5709-8)

Cover design by Dan O'Dair
Type set in Minion

Contents

List of Tables

List of Figures

Acknowledgments

The realization of this book is the product of two different processes. The first came during my years of graduate study at the California Institute of Technology when the faculty taught us how to ask questions and do the research necessary to answer them. Most important in this education was my dissertation adviser, R. Michael Alvarez, who taught me much of what I know about political science and helped instill my love of politics. Indispensable advice and feedback were provided by the other members of my dissertation committee; I thank Jeff Banks, Rod Kiewiet, and Bob Sherman. Other faculty at Caltech were helpful, including Lance Davis, Matt Jackson, Jonathan Katz, Richard McKelvey, Tom Palfrey, and Simon Wilkie. I had the great fortune of being surrounded by a particularly large group of graduate students who helped me navigate not only the program, but eventually the discipline as well. I thank all of them individually and collectively; specific thanks go out to John Patty, Valentina Bali, and Garrett Glasgow. My best friend from college, Chris Meissner, may have stuck with economic history but still provided much-needed inspiration and colloquy over the years.

The second stage of this project started when I arrived at the University of Iowa. In the Department of Political Science, I found excellent colleagues and students who offered a great atmosphere to rework my dissertation into a book. Discussions with Chuck Shipan and Doug Dion were essential over the course of this process. Shipan read through an entire draft of the manuscript and provided excellent comments. Additional feedback came from other members of the faculty and graduate students at departmental seminar presentations. I want to thank Gary Segura, Dave Redlawsk, Denise Powers, Chris Ball, Rick Witmer, Al D'Amico, Mike Lewis-Beck, John Nelson, and Kedron Bardwell for their advice. Throughout this project, Karen Stewart, Carole Eldeen, and Wendy Durant provided valuable secretarial assistance.

Along the way, I also had the assistance of various visiting faculty members at these two institutions who were willing to spend part of their time working with me. I had the rather propitious opportunity to walk down the hallway and talk to Frank Baumgartner for an entire year while I was planning and developing my survey of state interest groups. I thank him for all the time he spent guiding me through the process. Also at Caltech, Roger Klein provided invaluable assistance helping me work out the details of the statistical method that forms the basis for the analysis in chapter 7. At Iowa, I got to know Rick Witmer during the year he was visiting. His knowledge of Native American politics has been irreplaceable for all of the work we have done together and has made the analysis of Native American gaming activities in chapter 4 much more thorough and informed.

In addition to individuals at Caltech and Iowa, I also received valuable feedback at various professional presentations and seminars I have given. The comments of many individuals over this period were helpful, including Neal Beck, Shaun Bowler, John Brehm, Todd Donovan, Elisabeth Gerber, Jeff Gill, Paul Gronke, Brad Jones, Laura Langer, Beth Leech, David Lowery, John Matsusaka, Chris Mooney, Jonathan Nagler, Caroline Tolbert, and Dan Smith.

In more practical matters, a variety of scholars have provided data and assistance in gathering the data used in this book. Rod Kiewiet shared his data on state government finances used in chapter 4. All of the interest group data used in chapter 3 was graciously provided by David Lowery and Virginia Gray. Beth Leech was kind enough to allow me to use her survey of national groups as a starting point for my questionnaire and she and Frank Baumgartner answered numerous questions as I fine-tuned it. Resources and funding for the survey were provided by Mike Alvarez and the Division of Humanities and Social Sciences at Caltech. Organizing, formatting, printing, and mailing out the 2,000 surveys was tough going. I gratefully acknowledge the assistance of Laurel Auchampaugh and Gail Nash during that endeavor. In addition, I thank my dog, Quintin, for sacrificing much of the floor in my room during that period without engaging in any vengeful acts against the stacks of envelopes. I also thank the hundreds of groups that took the time to respond to the survey.

Some of the work done here was made possible by funding from other sources. Development of the survey was conducted while I received funding in 1998–99 from the John Randolph Haynes and Dora Haynes Foundation in the form of an intermediate graduate student fellowship. I was pleased to learn of Dr. Haynes's key role in bringing the initiative process to California almost a hundred years ago. Some of the work in developing the statistical model used in chapter 6 was performed with funding from an Old Gold Fellowship at the University of Iowa.

During the final step of turning my manuscript into a book, I received excellent comments and assistance from Malcolm Litchfield at The Ohio

State University Press. The comments of two anonymous reviewers were also very helpful.

Finally, none of this would have been possible without my family—Fred, Jen, Marcia, and Melissa—who provided love and support and helped keep me positive along the way. Because my father, Fred Boehmke, gave me everything, I dedicate this book to him.

1

Introduction

> The debate on direct legislation, by the press and from the platform, produced no lasting contributions to political theory. It consisted of pictures of the promised land by the advocates and forecasts of chaos by the opponents, and both prophecies were liberally spiced with personal denunciations approaching dangerously on libel.
>
> —V. O. Key Jr. and Winston W. Crouch (1939)

In many ways, little has changed in the sixty-six years since Key and Crouch wrote this in 1939. The debate about the initiative process, a form of direct democracy through which ordinary citizens can submit potential legislation to a state's voters for approval, still focuses on gloom and doom predictions about the end of democracy in books with titles like *Paradise Lost* (Schrag 1998), *Democracy Derailed* (Broder 2000), *Dangerous Democracy* (Sabato, Ernst, and Larson 2001), and *Democratic Delusions* (Ellis 2002). Yet at the same time, it is still staunchly defended by its supporters as the best remedy for the ills of state government. The critics generally argue that the growing importance of money in initiative campaigns restricts use of the initiative process to an elite set of interest groups. The ironic part of this criticism is that the Populist and Progressive reformers who fought for its adoption almost one hundred years ago intended it as a recourse against wealthy economic interests that had seized control of state legislatures. Even recent instances of grassroots uprisings like the hallowed tax revolt of the late 1970s and early 1980s have come under attack as a "*faux* populist moment" (Smith 1998).

In many ways, these negative assessments of direct legislation, specifically the initiative process, result from the failure of scholars to meet the first criticism leveled by Key and Crouch: there have been few advances in our theoretical understanding of how the initiative process influences politics. Evidence of the failure of the initiative process is often a handful of select initiatives chosen to highlight its shortcomings rather than systematic studies that assess the impact of the initiative on state politics. Observing that a few initiative campaigns are costly or that narrow interests occasionally prevail does not by itself constitute a valid reason to condemn the entire process.

Further, because most of the criticisms focus on specific initiative campaigns, they offer no sense of the extent of the problem. Notably, over the last century, the average initiative state passed about one initiative every two years. Even in California, the state now upheld as the poster child for the ills of the process, only two initiatives passed per year during of the peak usage decade of the 1990s. At the very least, these figures suggest that narrowly focusing on a few high-profile ballot measures may overemphasize the direct consequences of the initiative process.

Concomitant with an overemphasis on the potential negative consequences of direct legislation is an underappreciation of the many indirect effects that it has on state and interest group politics. Reformers saw the initiative process not just as a way to influence legislatures that they perceived as overly responsive to the interests of wealthy businesses, but they also expected it to spur the common citizen to increased levels of participation. Today, the emphasis has been predominantly on the negative effects, but there is no reason to expect that the hoped-for indirect effects have either failed to materialize or have since dissipated. An institution that allows ordinary citizens and interest groups the opportunity to propose legislation on their own, often with no input from the legislature whatsoever, should have myriad consequences for the political process. When groups seeking new policies are no longer at the mercy of elected officials, one would expect a collective change in how groups operate. Potential groups that before saw no hope for their proposals may now decide that they should become active. Legislators who thought they could keep a lid on the demands of some groups may now be faced by groups emboldened by the possibility of proposing an initiative. Legislators must take their potential irrelevancy into account when arbitrating between competing interests, leading previously unfavored groups to rise in prominence.

The initiative process is not just about what happens on election day; it is a fundamental twist on the institutions of representative democracy. To assess its impact, then, one must ask a broader question: how does the ability of citizens and organized interest groups to circumvent the legislative process alter traditional state and interest group politics? The answer to this question is crucial to understanding how the initiative process affects representation and influence in state politics. Changing the institutional structure that individuals and groups face alters which interests and characteristics are rewarded.

Because the initiative process does not function in the same way as the legislative process, the interests that benefit from its presence are different from those that thrive in the statehouse. Passing initiatives requires persuading a majority of voters to support the group's proposed policy over the status quo. Swaying voters is decidedly different from approaching legislators and lobbying them to introduce and vote for or against new bills. Legislatures are deliberative bodies with a host of checks and balances built in. This makes them conservative in terms of their tendencies toward policy change, particularly compared to all-or-nothing initiatives that are often conceived and drafted entirely by proponents. Groups with broad memberships and public support have a greater advantage with voters than with legislators, so the presence of the initiative process should increase their influence in state politics. And because legislators have to pay more attention to these groups in order to avoid losing their say on policy, the benefits to these groups extend beyond the ballot box.

The nature of the initiative process therefore suggests that it should continue to have multiple indirect effects on state and interest group politics. One of its most important indirect effects is to increase the influence of certain types of groups relative to others. This shift is particularly important because it works in favor of traditionally disadvantaged, broader-based membership groups that help represent a wider segment of the public interest. These groups have generally been less successful, compared with the narrow economic interest groups that find it easier to mobilize and represent their interests before government. As documenting and understanding this bias has been one of the major accomplishments of scholars of interest groups over the past half century, the fact that the initiative process ameliorates that bias increases its significance as a political institution.

The goal of this book, then, is to explicitly make the argument that the consequences of direct legislation extend far beyond the relatively few initiatives that make the ballot and the even fewer that actually pass. The incentives that access to the initiative process offers to existing and potential interest groups produce important differences between interest group populations in initiative and noninitiative states. Foremost among these differences, I show that initiative states have almost 30 percent more interest groups and over 40 percent more citizen groups, making them more representative than noninitiative states. In addition, groups in initiative states have more members and fewer financial resources, leading them to emphasize lobbying approaches that favor the former over the latter. Groups in initiative states are more likely to rely on membership-intensive lobbying tactics like organizing protests and electioneering rather than traditional approaches such as contacting legislators or agencies and testifying before committees. A complete evaluation of the initiative process must account for these indirect ways in which ballot access permeates and structures interest group politics.

To demonstrate the nature of the indirect effect, I rely on a model of interest group influence that incorporates both legislative lobbying and access to the initiative process. The model is used to predict specific ways in which the initiative process influences interest groups and state politics. The bulk of the book is devoted to testing these predictions and demonstrating the magnitude of the indirect effect of the initiative process. These tests are performed using a variety of different political phenomena, including policy adoption, policy diffusion, interest group mobilizations, interest group characteristics, and interest group lobbying behavior. That the initiative process influences each of these demonstrates the scope of its indirect effect on state politics.

Interest Groups and Initiatives

The Story of Medicinal Marijuana

The story of the recent successes of the medicinal marijuana movement is an excellent example of how the initiative process creates and influences interest groups. One of the objectives of this movement is to allow sufferers of chronic pain the opportunity to manage their discomfort by obtaining prescriptions for marijuana. The movement has met with widespread resistance from both state and federal governments. It has found some success in the last decade, however, by turning to the initiative process. So while the first statewide success of the movement occurred through the legislature in Ohio in 1995, almost every success since then has been through the ballot. In fact, even in Ohio the initiative process played an important role in keeping the legislation in place. In 1995, the legislature attached a provision to a state crime bill that allowed medicinal use of marijuana, which Governor George Voinovich apparently only discovered after the bill became law. When he found out, he declared that he would fight to repeal the provision. In response to his plan of attack, Americans for Medical Rights (AMR) threatened to place an initiative on the 1996 ballot if necessary (Americans for Medical Rights 1996). The threat of a ballot measure caused the governor to back down and helped secure the advocates' victory in Ohio.

Other groups were also involved in the drive for medicinal marijuana legislation in Ohio. One of these groups, Coalition for a Better Ohio, was formed in summer 1995. It started as a student group at Columbus State Community College, holding protests and using its expertise on the issue to get press attention (Coalition for a Better Ohio 1998). At the same time, similar groups in other states were also fighting for reform. In every case where the movement succeeded in passing medicinal marijuana legislation, the initiative process played a key role. Success at the ballot in many states demonstrates that political leaders in Ohio had to take AMR's threat to propose an initiative seriously; without this threat they may have felt comfortable overturning the law.

Besides its role in influencing policy, the initiative process also influenced interest group behavior, as evidenced by the history of Americans for Medical Rights. Originally, AMR did not begin with such a national focus. In fact, it started as Californians for Medical Rights and was more narrowly concerned with seeking reform in one state. Success came in 1996 when the group helped pass Proposition 215 in California, spending about $650,000 in the process. Only after early success in an initiative state did the group branch out and target other states. The campaign for Proposition 215 not only launched Americans for Medical Rights, it also served as a catalyst for other initiative mobilizations. The signature gathering campaign for 215 lead to the founding of the Sonoma Alliance for Medical Marijuana, a group that sponsors speakers and provides information at various public events (Miller 1997). Nor did these groups disband with the passage of Proposition 215. Many of them remained organized and battled to make sure it was implemented in the face of government resistance. Groups such as the Alliance for Medical Marijuana attempted to work with district attorneys and the police to establish cultivation and distribution systems (Miller 1997), which posed a challenge because of marijuana's federal status as a controlled substance with no therapeutic value.

With the success of Proposition 215, some of these groups decided to expand their focus beyond California and began to target other states. In 1998, for example, Americans for Medical Rights was behind the campaign for Amendment 19 in Colorado. In the process, it helped spur yet another initiative mobilization by helping to found another initiative state interest group, Coloradans for Medical Rights. Even though Amendment 19 was largely symbolic in nature, Coloradans for Medical Rights still fought for its passage to send what they believed would be an important message to state legislators (Colorado Citizens for Compassionate Cannabis 1998). Other groups had also formed around the issue in Colorado, including the Colorado Hemp Initiative Project. Although the group had been in existence since about 1990, it was not directly involved with Amendment 19.

Besides Colorado, many other states across the nation experienced similar campaigns in 1998, including Washington, Oregon, Nevada, Alaska, and the District of Columbia. As with the Colorado attempt, all of these passed.[1] AMR provided much logistic and financial support for many of these efforts, including $30,000 for the Washington campaign.[2] In many cases, AMR started state chapters for these campaigns in initiative states, including Mainers for Medical Rights, Coloradans for Medical Rights, Floridians for Medical Rights, Arizonans for Medical Rights, Oregonians for Medical Rights, and Alaskans for Medical Rights.

After the success of these efforts, many groups decided to push for even greater permissiveness in marijuana laws. In 2002, two initiatives sought to decriminalize possession of small amounts of the drug. In Nevada, citizens voted on a constitutional initiative, Question 9, to decriminalize possession of small amounts of marijuana for personal use. Nevada's regulations require constitutional initiatives to pass in two successive elections, but Question 9 failed to pass on the second vote. Arizona's failed Proposition 203 would have increased the ease of distributing medicinal marijuana and also would have reduced punishments for possession to a civil fine. So while voters appear to be sympathetic to medicinal uses for marijuana, attempts to expand its acceptance beyond such needs have met with much less success. This suggests that voters pay at least some attention to the substance of the issue at hand and are not duped by campaigns.

The story of medicinal marijuana provides excellent examples of the direct and indirect effects of the initiative process. The direct effect is manifested by the many states that adopted more lenient legislation through the ballot. The indirect effect includes the large number of groups that formed during the campaigns. These groups fought for the passage of specific ballot measures in the past, but they also continue to lobby for enforcement and additional reforms today. After Californians for Medical Rights formed to fight for the issue and pass an initiative in California in 1996, it became national in focus, as indicated by the name change to Americans for Medical Rights. The group then fought in other states and left established interest groups in its wake, including Coloradans for Medical Rights, Floridians for Medical Rights, Mainers for Medical Rights, and the Sonoma Alliance for Medical Marijuana.

What happens to groups such as these after they mobilize—either to win specific initiative campaigns or merely in response to the apparent increased potential for success that the initiative process provides? Is medicinal marijuana an unusual case, or are there other issues that involve similar stories of interest groups mobilizing, expanding, and continuing their work after successful initiatives? What, then, are the consequences of these indirect effects for interest group populations and state politics in initiative states? If there are more issues and groups like these, the indirect effects of the initiative process in terms of interest group mobilizations and lobbying behavior are likely large enough to warrant more attention than they currently receive. These are some of the questions and issues that I attempt to address in this book.

Initiative Mobilizations

The foundation for the differences between interest groups in initiative and noninitiative states can be summarized through the concept of initiative mobilizations. I use this term to mean the formation of interest groups that results directly or indirectly from the incentives that the initiative process offers. They occur directly when specific initiative campaigns lead to the formation of new interest groups. They occur indirectly when groups form because of the potential to propose an initiative, which might provide enough leverage to push the legislature into enacting their policy without actually resorting to a ballot proposal. These are groups such as the Sonoma Civil Rights Action Project, which most likely would not have successfully mobilized in noninitiative states because the incentives were not strong enough. Access to the initiative process, by offering an alternate avenue for policy influence, provides the additional incentives required to engender the group's mobilization. The process of initiative mobilization is the reason that direct legislation states have more interest groups.

The differences are likely to be much more than a simple increase in the number of interest groups. Because certain groups are better equipped to use the initiative process, groups that are born out of initiative mobilizations are different from groups that would have mobilized anyway. Thus, the process changes the mix of interests that are represented as well as the distribution of resources and legislative lobbying methods among state interest group populations. Additionally, since campaigning for initiatives is unlike lobbying the legislature directly, the experiences of groups in initiative campaigns shape their lobbying strategies. These groups may learn to rely on or discover that they are more successful with lobbying tactics that are emphasized in initiative campaigns and carry these approaches over even when lobbying the legislature.

Ultimately, the consequences of initiative mobilizations for state politics and representation depend crucially on which types of groups are better able to use the process to further their goals. In fact, recent theoretical and empirical work suggests that citizen groups are better suited to use the initiative process to change policy, whereas economic groups generally use it to preserve policy (Gerber 1999). Combining this important finding with the logic of initiative mobilizations allows one to more specifically understand the differences between initiative and noninitiative states and to more fully evaluate the consequences of direct legislation.

In short, the model's predictions can be summarized as follows. Because of initiative mobilizations, initiative states should have interest group populations that are larger and more representative. Given this shift in interest group composition, interest groups in initiative states should have different resources, including more members and less revenue, at their disposal. If groups base their lobbying decisions on the resources at their disposal, this shift in resources should be reflected by a related shift in the lobbying style of groups in initiative states. In general, scholars have made an important distinction between inside and outside lobbying (Walker 1991; Kollman 1998). Inside lobbying involves direct legislative contact on the part of interest groups through such tactics as testifying at hearings, organizing legislative coalitions, and providing information; outside lobbying consists of attempts to indirectly influence legislative action by shaping public opinion and grassroots activity. The model predicts two ways that interest groups' choice of which lobbying strategy to use are affected by the initiative process. First, because of the shift in group resources, initiative states experience a greater amount of outside lobbying than noninitiative states. Second, because of their experience in initiative campaigns, which tend to generate more experience with outside lobbying strategies than inside lobbying strategies, groups in initiative states rely more heavily on outside lobbying even when they are not involved in initiatives. This difference should hold even after controlling for resource differentials caused by distributional shifts.

Beyond interest mobilizations and lobbying strategies, the model also makes predictions about state policy adoption and how policies diffuse from state to state. Because the initiative offers groups an additional avenue of influence if they fail in the legislature, it should lead initiative states to adopt policies more quickly than noninitiative states. And because of the information that adoption in initiative states provides about voters' preferences, the model also predicts that initiative state adoptions should be more influential and informative when other states are considering adopting the same policy.

These findings have important implications for state politics. If systematically different interests are being represented in initiative states, then policy outputs should represent these differences. If different styles of lobbying are used and rewarded, then the process of determining policy outcomes may also be different. The indirect effect of the initiative process encompasses all of these changes in interest group characteristics and behavior. Studying it is necessary for evaluating whether the initiative process is beneficial in the main and for understanding how institutions shape interest group systems.

Critiques of the Initiative Process

Before moving on to demonstrate the broader effects of the initiative process, it is important to review some of the criticisms leveled against it. This offers a sense of some of the negative effects that direct legislation may have on state politics, which can later be compared to the indirect effects that I highlight. Perhaps because of the increased number of initiatives over the last three decades, the number of critiques of the process has grown.[3] Chief among these complaints is that the process has become yet another tool of wealthy economic interests that can merely buy legislation at the ballot box (Broder 2000; Smith 1998, 2002). Other concerns include the lack of flexibility that initiatives offer—once they are on the ballot it is impossible to make changes if potential problems or constitutional issues are raised. Furthermore, initiatives may attempt to deal with complex issues in an overly simplistic fashion (Zimmerman 1986). On the other hand, proposals may be so complicated that it is unreasonable to expect voters to comprehend what effect an initiative would have on policy if it were to pass.

Critics have also argued that the existence of too many initiatives in any one year leads to ballot clutter. In 1996, for example, California and Oregon had seventeen and sixteen citizen-initiated propositions on their respective ballots. This may make it more difficult for voters to understand each of them, reach an informed decision about how to vote, and then remember what conclusions they had arrived at when faced with the actual ballot. In addition, situations like this may merely create more opportunities for advertising by wealthy interest groups and individuals to affect the final vote.

Another objection to the process is that it leads to tyranny of the majority. Examples include California's Proposition 187, which sought to deny aid to illegal immigrants (although it passed, it was eventually ruled unconstitutional) and Proposition 209, which prohibited public universities from using race as a determining factor in admissions, thereby undermining affirmative action efforts.[4]

And, leaving all of these concerns aside, the argument has also been made that the initiative process stands in opposition to the form of representative democracy that the United States was founded on. Not only do successful initiatives take legislative power away from representatives, but they can often bind representatives' hands by making it harder to pass future laws. Such is the case with tax and expenditure limits set forth by Proposition 13 (which capped the rate at which property taxes could be increased and required the legislature to consult the voters for new levies and often created supermajority requirements), which has been blamed for the decline of California's educational system, among other things (Schrag 1998).[5] Haskell (2001) argues that direct democracy fails to provide a valid form of government because of difficulties in establishing the true will of the majority and, even if that could be established, because direct democracy institutions do not provide for the extensive array of checks and balances embedded in representative government.

Perhaps because of these criticisms, and perhaps because the initiative process takes power away from them, legislators have consistently attempted to make it harder for citizens to successfully place initiatives on the ballot. Various states have attempted to forbid groups from using paid signature gatherers (though the courts have ruled this unconstitutional—see Ellis [2003] or Lowenstein and Stern [1989] for discussion of this issue) and have also attempted to raise the signature requirements or impose harsh distribution requirements. In a report released by the National Conference of State Legislatures I&R Task Force on the current state of the initiative process (National Conference of State Legislatures 2002), the main conclusion was that states without the initiative process should not consider adopting it and that

> . . . [t]he initiative has evolved from its early days as a grassroots tool to enhance representative democracy into a tool that too often is exploited by special interests. The initiative lacks critical elements of the legislative process and can have both intended and unintended effects on the ability of the representative democratic process to comprehensively develop policies and priorities. (National Conference of State Legislatures 2002, vii)

Despite these criticisms and repeated attempts to make it more difficult to use the initiative process, public support for it is still high.[6] Surveys show that citizens in initiative states believe that they are competent to decide on ballot questions and that they believe that the initiative process is no less problematic or corrupted than the legislative process. Cronin found that 76 percent of respondents thought that voters should have a direct say on some public policy issues, whereas only 18 percent trusted elected officials to make laws (Cronin 1989, 80). Additionally, the initiative process creates the opportunity to regulate government activity in cases where elected officials might be resistant. Tolbert (1998) discusses the emergence of a New Populism since the tax revolt era in the late 1970s and early 1980s, when initiative states were more likely to adopt government reform legislation like term limits and restrictive tax increase regulations.

Interest Groups

The central argument of this book concerns the effect of the initiative process on interest groups' decisions regarding mobilization and lobbying. The initiative process is therefore the key variable that is used to further knowledge of interest groups. So while my findings have direct import for understanding direct legislation, they are primarily intended to advance understanding of how interest groups respond to incentives offered by political institutions.

The link between political institutions and structure and representation through organized interests has been discussed in previous work, particularly in Walker's important study (1991) of the effect of patronage on membership organizations. One of the few studies to follow up directly on Walker's speculation regarding the effect of political institutions on interest groups is Gais's study (1996) of the effect of government regulations on political action committee (PAC) formation. Neither of these studies, however, directly examines the role that variation in political institutions plays for interest groups. Yet it stands to reason that they would respond to differences in their environment as fundamental as direct legislation. In short, this book adds to the theoretical understanding of the initiative process by focusing on those that are most influenced by its presence: interest groups seeking to influence policy.

An important advantage of studying the effect of direct legislation on interest groups is that it is an avenue of approach available only in certain states, with almost half of them having some form of direct initiative provisions.[7] This variation allows me to study the differences in interest group populations and interest group behavior in these two types of states. Studies of the Washington, D.C., lobbying community, including those cited above, rarely have the opportunity to compare interest group behavior across different institutional arrangements. Additionally, while studies of state interest group populations, including Gray and Lowery's population ecology approach (1996), offer important theoretical and empirical insight into the factors that influence interest group populations, they do not consider the role of variation in political institutions.

A second advantage of studying state interest groups is that most of the groups that exist today were not around when direct legislation provisions were enacted. Almost all states that adopted institutions of direct democracy did so around the turn of the twentieth century. Because of this separation, I can reasonably treat the presence of these institutions as independent of the groups that exist today, meaning that I can reject the possibility that characteristics of state interest group populations determine which states have the initiative process rather than the other way around.

If there are, as I expect, important differences between interest group populations in initiative and noninitiative states, these findings are important for understanding how citizens' preferences are translated in public policy. If initiative mobilizations do lead to increased representation for broad-based citizen groups vis-à-vis narrow economic interests, then the type of policies that are brought up for debate and the ultimate decision on what policy changes to make are likely to differ as well. Similar differences could be brought about by changes in lobbying strategies caused by initiative mobilizations and the legislature's response to the threat of initiatives. Further, changes in interest group politics along these lines are likely to lead to increased opportunities for citizen participation in state politics, thus ameliorating decades of decline in citizen participation.[8] In the end, then, it may be that initiative state politics is closer to the Pluralist ideal of equal representation of all interests (Dahl 1961).

Plan of the Book

In this introduction, I have outlined the basic predictions of the theory that I develop fully in the next chapter. These theoretical results are used to generate three specific predictions about the effect of direct legislation on interest groups, and with the addition of three assumptions, I am able to generate additional implications. The second half of chapter 2 lays out the predictions of the model and explains how these three assumptions are incorporated to generate additional empirical implications of the model.

The remainder of the book tests the hypotheses derived from the model. Since the model generates predictions about many aspects of group behavior, different sources of data are required to test different predictions. Chapter 3 uses aggregate state-level data on total interest group mobilizations to test my model's prediction that access to the direct initiative process increases overall interest group mobilization. I then use data on the size of various interest group subpopulations in each state to show that these additional mobilizations are concentrated among traditionally underrepresented citizen groups, which are expected to benefit the most from direct legislation opportunities.

The next step is to analyze the extent to which groups are able to translate access to the initiative process into policy change. Chapter 4 therefore examines state adoptions of both capital punishment and Indian gaming agreements, demonstrating that interest groups can use the initiative process both directly and indirectly to effect policy change. These data are also used to test the model's prediction about the role of the initiative process in state-to-state policy diffusion.

Having demonstrated support for the model's predictions about both aggregate interest group populations and state policy outcomes, chapters 5 and 6 utilize survey data to evaluate the predictions of the model at the level of individual interest groups. In chapter 5, I use these data to provide another perspective on how initiative mobilizations change the characteristics of interest groups, including the size of their membership and the amount of financial resources available. These data are also used to test the model's predictions about the effect of access to the initiative process and the effect of involvement in specific initiative campaigns on interest group lobbying behavior.

While chapter 5 allows me to show the differences between interest groups and lobbying tactics in initiative states and noninitiative states, the model also has implications for how interest group lobbying strategies evolve in initiative states. Chapter 6 uses the survey data to construct indices of inside and outside lobbying, which are then used to test the effect of access to and involvement with direct initiatives on general lobbying strategies, controlling for resource differences. I find that interest groups in initiative states rely more on outside lobbying strategies and less on inside lobbying strategies, relative to groups in noninitiative states. I also find, however, that involvement in specific initiative campaigns increases the ability of groups to use inside lobbying strategies.

Overall, then, I find persuasive support for each of the model's predictions and implications. Although some can only be tested with one type of data, many are tested on multiple sources of data. The repeated support for many predictions using different types of data provides compelling evidence in favor of my theory of initiative mobilizations. It also makes a strong statement about the difference between interest group politics in initiative and noninitiative states. Interest groups in initiative states are more representative and rely less on inside lobbying and more on outside lobbying strategies. These findings demonstrate that direct legislation institutions have broader consequences for representation than earlier work suggests and that more work examining the indirect effects of institutions on interest groups is in order.

2

Modeling the Initiative Process

> The initiative and referendum process is an important means to bypass legislatures who refuse to vote on crucial issues. Initiative and Referendum reminds us the citizens of our republic are the rulers and elected officials are the servants.
>
> —Kip Fordice, governor of Mississippi[1]

Overview of the Initiative Process

In this chapter, I describe my model of the initiative process. The purpose of the model is to precisely lay out the relationship between interest groups, the legislature, and access to direct legislation institutions. From these relationships I use the model to derive specific predictions about how initiative state politics and interest group politics are affected by these institutions.

The method that I use to generate these predictions is a formal model of the initiative process. While formal modeling involves the use of varying levels of mathematical sophistication and generates a high degree of theoretical rigor, readers not familiar with this approach should not despair. As the primary objective of the model in this book is to generate empirically testable predictions about the effect of the initiative process, almost all of the mathematical detail of the model has been placed in a technical appendix. The presentation in this chapter relies almost entirely on a nonmathematical description of the model and its findings.

Before moving on to the development of the model and its predictions, I first outline many of the salient features of direct legislation and its history in the United States. After defining many of the key terms, I briefly discuss its history and current relevance and practice. Following this, I describe the model and then provide a description of how its predictions are generated and what they mean for initiative state politics. Lastly, I discuss three additional assumptions that I make and the resulting empirical implications that they generate.

Types of Direct Legislation

The process of direct legislation involves citizens voting directly on potential legislation. There are many different varieties within this broad definition, including statutory and constitutional direct initiatives, statutory and constitutional indirect initiatives, legislative referendums, and popular referendums. Understanding the differences among them is important for understanding the incentives that they offer to interest groups.

Perhaps the biggest distinction is between initiatives and referendums. Initiatives are put on the ballot by the public, often by interest groups. The proponents are able to draft the specific wording of their proposal and are responsible for qualifying it. Referendums, on the other hand, are votes on laws that the legislature has enacted or is considering enacting. In a popular referendum, citizens can attempt to overturn previously enacted legislation by submitting it to a popular vote, whereas in a legislative referendum, the legislature lets the public decide whether a specific statute should become law. Twenty-four states allow popular referendums, and every state permits legislative referendums. Initiatives therefore provide interest groups with a much greater deal of flexibility than popular referendums, since the group can pick any policy rather than merely having the opportunity to return to the previous status quo.

The difference between direct and indirect initiatives is much smaller than between initiatives and referendums and does not offer significantly different incentives for groups. Direct initiatives are referred directly to the people after qualification; indirect initiatives are first sent to the legislature for consideration. If the legislature chooses to enact the group's proposal, it becomes law and does not go to the ballot. If the legislature does not enact the proposal, it is put on the ballot for citizens to decide. In some states, such as Massachusetts, proponents only have to gather a portion of the signatures to put their proposal before the legislature; the rest are gathered if it is not enacted and the group wishes to put it on the ballot. In practice, the legislature almost never enacts indirect initiatives. In Utah it has never enacted one, in Massachusetts it has not enacted one in the last decade, and in Maine it has only enacted two in almost one hundred years.[2] Such infrequent use has lead some states to eliminate the indirect form of initiatives, including California in 1966 and South Dakota in 1988.

Overall, there are twenty-one states that allow some form of direct initiative and eight that allow for indirect initiatives, with some overlap between these two categories.[3] Both indirect and direct initiatives can be of the statutory or constitutional variety. Constitutional initiatives generally require more signatures for qualification (Ohio and Nevada are the exceptions). Sixteen states allow direct constitutional initiatives and two more allow indirect constitutional initiatives; sixteen states allow direct statutory initiatives and seven states allow indirect statutory initiatives.[4]

In this book, I focus almost exclusively on initiatives, whether direct or indirect, statutory or constitutional. This is because of the greater flexibility that they allow interest groups relative to referendums and also because of the greater frequency of use and broader public attention. Since interest groups are not required or generally involved in legislative referendums until possibly the campaign stage, it seems reasonable to exclude this type. Further, since all states save Delaware allow for them, it would be difficult to determine what effect they have on interest groups or state politics. Popular referendums are excluded since they offer minimal flexibility to groups and also since they are used less frequently.[5]

History

The history of direct democracy in the United States dates back at least as far as Massachusetts in the 1640s, when local towns used the referendum to decide important issues. The use of the referendum continued during the adoption of state and national constitutions at independence. Thomas Jefferson was one of the strong supporters of allowing citizens to vote on the adoption of state constitutions, though many of his contemporaries were concerned about allowing any form of direct democracy since it created opportunities for the "mischief of faction" in Madison's words and relied on the potentially unenlightened masses. Although Massachusetts and New Hampshire were initially the only states that submitted their constitutions to voters, the practice became quite common after 1800 (Cronin 1989).[6]

Toward the end of the 1800s during the Populist and then Progressive movements, many citizens became disenchanted with what they perceived as undue influence on state government by large businesses. The Populist movement was composed largely of farmers, though it also included miners, laborers, ranchers, and other occupations that were upset about the rise of an industrial society that they perceived as responsible for their increasing indebtedness. The Populists wanted to return to the agrarian society that put their concerns at the forefront of the political agenda. After attempts to make changes through the existing two-party system, these interests joined forces with various groups in different parts of the country, including socialist and semi-socialist movements and single-taxers, and formed the Populist Party in the late 1880s (Cronin 1989). Foremost among various reforms that the Populists desired were the initiative and referendum, which they felt would render unresponsive representatives helpless to the will of people, even in the face of pressure from industrialist interests (Cain and Miller 2001).

At first, the Populists had little success in gaining the initiative and referendum. Over time, however, their cause was endorsed by other groups, including prohibitionists, woman suffragists, and Progressives. In many cases, the latter group was especially critical. The Progressive movement focused on good-government reforms, including the initiative, referendum, recall, and direct election of U.S. senators. In California, it was not until the Progressive Party won control of the governorship under Hiram Johnson that the initiative was adopted. For Progressives, the goal of these reforms was to increase the responsiveness of state governments to broad interests. In contrast to the Populists' desire to deal with perceived corruption in state government via circumvention, the Progressives preferred reforms that promoted participation by informed and civic-motivated citizens.[7]

In 1898, South Dakota was the first state to add initiative and referendum to its constitution, though in 1904, Oregon achieved the distinction of being the first state with an initiative on its ballot. By 1918, a total of twenty-two states added one or both of these provisions to their constitutions. Most were in the western United States, but states in other regions were also adopting initiative provisions, including Arkansas (1911), Michigan (1913), Missouri (1908), and Ohio (1912).[8] After an extended period with no new adoptions, Alaska's 1956 constitution included provisions for the initiative and referendum. Wyoming and Florida then adopted them in 1968, followed by Illinois in 1970. The most recent adoption was by Mississippi in 1992.[9]

Some of the early reforms enacted once a state gained the initiative process fit into the categories of good-government reforms and anti-industrialist legislation. On the other hand, narrow economic groups, including gambling interests and the liquor industry attempted to use the new tool to their own advantage (Ernst 2001).

While the use of money and consultants and the rise of the "initiative industrial complex" in recent years has provided fuel for critics of the process, their involvement is not a recent phenomenon, as the following statement from B. J. Hendrick, quoted in Beard and Schultz (1912), regarding the initiative process in Oregon in 1911, attests:

> Young women, ex-book-canvassers, broken-down clergymen, people who in other communities would find their natural level as sandwich-men, dapper hustling youths, perhaps earning their way through college—all find useful employment in soliciting signatures at five or ten cents a

> name. . . . In [other] instances people sign petitions thoughtlessly—sometimes without reading the measures of even understanding their contents. "I could easily get ten thousand signatures to a law hanging all the red-haired men in Oregon," one cynic on popular government remarked to the writer. It is not at all unlikely that he could. The business of getting names, as everybody knows, depends more upon the individual than upon the merits of the particular case at issue.

Similar phenomena occurred in other states as well. Almost immediately after the adoption of direct legislation provisions in California in 1911, temporary consultants began to spring up to assist campaigns. While attempting to qualify a referendum in 1912, dairymen reportedly paid $0.10 a signature to gather twenty-three thousand signatures (Goebel 2002); a more typical rate at the time was about $0.05 per signature, corresponding to about $0.80 today (Ellis 2003). In 1922, seven initiatives in California produced aggregate expenditures in the neighborhood of $1 million, not adjusted for inflation. Early campaigns also featured media blitzes, including billboards, movie theater advertisements, automobile stickers, sound trucks, and skywriting campaigns (McCuan, Bowler, Donovan, and Fernandez 1998).

The first full-time, permanent firm, Whitaker and Baxter's Campaigns Inc., was established in 1930 and handled five or six initiatives per election (McCuan, Bowler, Donovan, and Fernandez 1998). The presence of initiative consultants was sufficiently widespread that many states responded by banning the use of professional circulators only a few years after adopting the initiative process. Oregon first attempted to ban them in 1909, and Washington, South Dakota, and Ohio followed suit about five years later.[10]

Current Importance

Although Mississippi is the only state to add initiative provisions in the last thirty years, many other states have considered them, including New York, Minnesota, Texas, Alabama, New Jersey, and Rhode Island.[11] In many cases, the governors of these states have been an important force behind the push for the initiative process. George Pataki, governor of New York, expressed the following sentiments:

> This initiative and referendum proposal is a cornerstone of our effort to ensure that the voices of all the people of New York are heard. This fundamental reform will empower all New Yorkers by enabling them to become an integral part of the lawmaking process and giving them the power to propose and approve new laws. By reforming the democratic

> process, we renew our allegiance to the sacred principle that all power ultimately rests in the hands of the people.[12]

Besides consideration by states that do not have the process, the initiative process has returned to prominence over the past quarter century. Much of this increase in use and visibility is credited to California's Proposition 13 in 1978, which set off the tax revolt of the late 1970s and early 1980s. Usage has continued to rise after a lull in the middle of the century, with the 1990s being the decade of greatest activity and 1996 being the high-water mark, with ninety-five statutory and constitutional initiatives on statewide ballots. Since that peak, usage has declined a bit in the last couple of election cycles, with 2002 seeing the fewest initiatives (fifty-three) on state ballots since 1986. In historical perspective, though, this is still an above-average number: during the twentieth century there was an average of 40 initiatives per two-year election cycle.[13] Given the average passage rate of slightly over 40 percent, this translates into less than one new law per year per state through the initiative process, not including those struck down by the courts after passage.

Many controversial policies have been dealt with through the initiative process in recent years. Some of these have had racial overtones, including attempts to deny social services to illegal immigrants, the banning of race-based policies for university admissions, and English-only laws. Others have dealt with important social issues, including the regulation of casino and Indian gaming, physician-assisted suicide, relaxing regulations on medicinal use of marijuana, and capital punishment laws. Another area showing recent activity is regulation of state governments, including imposing tax and expenditure limitations and imposing term limits on state representatives.

Despite the many important and controversial areas in which initiatives have been proposed, there are also lower-profile policies that have been voted on, including regulations governing cockfighting, exportation of horse meat, use of steel traps for hunting, daylight saving time, beverage container deposits, milk price controls, beginning of the school year, location of the state capital, and billboards.[14] So while critics often criticize the initiative process because of its involvement in a few hot-button issues, a large number of proposals—perhaps even a majority—deal with more mundane and occasionally esoteric issues.

Requirements for Proposing an Initiative

To get an initiative on the ballot, groups of voters have to overcome a variety of obstacles. In general, to propose a direct initiative, groups have to write legislation that meets certain guidelines and then gather a specified number of signatures. Once the proposal is on the ballot, groups must campaign until the election to persuade voters to vote "yes" on their legislation. If the initiative passes, the group can often expect a challenge in court or a battle to ensure that the spirit of the law is adhered to.

The preceding provides only a rough outline of the process, however, as there is a great degree of variation in requirements from state to state. The basic process starts with the drafting of the initiative's language, following which it is submitted to the relevant state official for certification. Some states provide a review process at this point to determine if the proposal is constitutional and if the language is reasonable and does not violate (increasingly stringent) single-subject rules and content restrictions. In most cases, these reviews are advisory, but in four states (Utah, Arizona, Oregon, and Florida) failed reviews can lead to the initiative's rejection.

Before circulation, the initiative must receive a circulation title. Usually, this is provided by the state, subject to challenge, but in a few cases, it is provided by the group, subject to state approval. The circulation title often becomes the official ballot title if the initiative makes it that far. The ballot title is reviewed in all states, and many provide for expedited challenges to the wording of the title and summary.

The next step is to circulate the petition and gather signatures. Some states limit the number of days a petition may circulate—150 in California, for example—but a few impose no time restrictions. While the average signature requirement for statutory initiatives is about 7.5 percent, usually defined in reference to turnout in the previous general or gubernatorial election, it varies from 2 percent of the state's population in North Dakota to 15 percent of votes cast in the previous general election in Wyoming. The other fourteen states that allow statutory direct initiatives have requirements between 5 and 10 percent. Nine of the eleven states that allow both statutory and constitutional direct initiatives require more signatures for constitutional proposals.[15]

Groups seeking to qualify measures for the ballot typically hire professional firms to actually gather the signatures. In California, there are about a half dozen full-time signature-gathering firms (McCuan, Bowler, Donovan, and Fernandez 1998), including Kimball Petition Management, National Petition Management, and smaller firms such as American Petition Consultants, National Voter Outreach, Masterton and Wright, and Progressive Campaigns (Broder 2000). These petition management firms typically hire independent contractors, often on a regional basis, to gather signatures. Contractors typically make $0.05 to $0.20 per signature. These "crew chiefs" then hire individuals to actually circulate the petitions, paying anywhere from $0.25 to $0.50 per signature (Broder 2000; McCuan, Bowler, Donovan, and Fernandez 1998). On a good day, a petition circulator can make $50 to $80 an hour, or even more when time is running out and groups are desperate to qualify their measure.

Besides being required to obtain a certain number of signatures, many states also have distributional requirements that dictate that a certain number of the signatures must come from a set number of counties. For example, Ohio requires signatures equal to at least 1.5 percent of the total votes cast in the previous gubernatorial election from at least forty-four of its eighty-eight counties. Wyoming requires at least one signature from at least eight of its twenty-eight counties (Tolbert, Lowenstein, and Donovan 1998).

After the signatures are gathered and submitted, all but four states require either full certification of all signatures or certification of a randomly selected subset of signatures. For example, in California county officials are required to check the larger of five hundred or 3 percent of the signatures submitted. State-level officials then calculate the predicted total number of valid signatures. If it exceeds 110 percent of the number required, the measure qualifies for the ballot; if it falls short of 95 percent, it fails to qualify; and if it is between these two percentages, county officials are directed to check all submitted signatures. This process is to ensure that only signatures from registered voters are counted and that there are no duplicate signatures. Combined with the fact that states vary with respect to how close a name must be to the voter's official registration, groups generally attempt to gather as many as 25 to 80 percent more signatures than they need to ensure qualification (Boehmke and Alvarez 2004a; Tolbert, Lowenstein, and Donovan 1998).

Because of the large number of signatures that must be gathered, most groups turn to paid professionals to do at least part of the job. Campaign consultants are also often brought in either to manage the initiative from the initial drafting through election day or else to oversee the media campaign. Based on their survey of initiative consultants in California, McCuan, Bowler, Donovan, and Fernandez (1998) report that while almost every group in California eventually uses a consultant, trade and well-organized interest groups do so earlier than more amateur and grassroots groups.

The costs of even getting an initiative on the ballot can be quite large, especially in states like California. Paid signature gatherers can charge anywhere from fifty cents to $2 per signature, depending on how much time remains before the qualification deadline and how many other petitions are still circulating. For some groups, the huge cost of qualification leaves them with no resources to fight the ensuing public opinion campaign. In extreme cases, the costs of an initiative campaign can reach astronomical heights: during a battle for Indian gaming in California in 1998, Indian nations spent over $60 million on Proposition 5, while the opposition, led primarily by Las Vegas gaming interests, spent about $30 million (Ellis 2002). Although the initiative passed with 65 percent of the vote, it was ultimately declared unconstitutional.[16] This was resolved in 2000, when the state legislature, attempting to negotiate a compromise, placed Proposition 1A on the ballot, which also passed.

It should be noted that these hurdles and costs have a great effect on the ability of groups and citizens to successfully qualify initiatives for the ballot. Specifically, signature and distribution requirements appear to have the biggest effect on the number of proposals that appear on the ballot (Boehmke 2003b). An indication of the difficulty in successfully qualifying measures is provided by the frequency of failed proposals in California. Since adoption of the initiative process in 1911, California has had 1,187 initiatives titled for circulation. Of those, only 290 actually qualified for the ballot, with 99 ultimately passing (Shelley 2002). This translates into a 75 percent attrition rate between the certification and qualification stages and means that less than 10 percent of submitted initiatives actually passed.

Finally, even when groups successfully pass their proposal, they must continue to work to make sure that it is properly implemented. During the campaign for a class-size initiative in Florida in 2002, Governor Jeb Bush was overheard saying that he had a "devious plan" for what to do if the expensive measure passed (Associated Press 2002), which it ultimately did with 52 percent of the vote. Comments like this may be extreme, but politicians often look for ways to reduce the effects of initiatives in the implementation stage.[17] Groups must be vigilant even after victory and continue to devote time and resources to make sure their policies are fully realized.

Outline of the Model

In this section, I attempt to distill all of the different aspects of the initiative process described in the previous section into a well-specified model that can be used to generate predictions about how interest groups respond to access to the initiative process. In making the transition from the real world of initiative politics to the abstract world of formal models, it is necessary to reduce the initiative process to its essential features; otherwise, as the model becomes increasingly complex, it becomes more difficult to make precise, testable predictions.

Using a formal model to generate predictions has many benefits, however. Foremost among them is the explicit link between the assumptions that the model makes and the results that are derived from these assumptions. This makes it relatively straightforward to ascertain whether the predictions are based on reasonable assumptions and to determine how sensitive the predictions are to each assumption.

While the details of the model and the derivation of the results will certainly be of interest to some readers, the basic logic of the model can be explained in a straightforward manner with a minimum of mathematical notation. So here, I present the model in words and with a minimum of technical detail, giving readers unfamiliar with the approach the opportunity to understand the logic of the model and the resulting predictions. The full model is presented in appendix B.[18]

The overview of the model and the development of its predictions proceed in four steps. First, I lay out the basic model of policymaking, following which I add the ability to propose initiatives and determine how the outcomes change. In the third step, I present the hypotheses derived directly from the model. Finally, I derive some additional hypotheses based on the implications of the model but requiring some additional assumptions. I take this step-by-step approach to underscore how the different components of the model lead to specific hypotheses and how the logic of the model can then be used to generate more general, intuitive predictions about how the initiative process influences interest groups.

Policymaking without the Initiative Process

To model the effect of the initiative process on interest groups, I have to start with a basic assumption about what groups are trying to achieve irrespective of institutional context. There are many possible objectives that a group could be trying to meet at any given time, including attracting members or donations, increasing or altering public perception of its concerns, or influencing election outcomes. Ultimately, however, it seems reasonable to treat these as means to an end: that of influencing public policy. The model assumes that the primary concern of interest groups is to achieve a specific policy reform. To meet this goal, they use whatever resources they have at their disposal in the most effective way they can.[19]

Since the central goal of the model is to determine the effect of the initiative process on interest groups and the goal of interest groups is to influence policy, the first step is to develop a model of policymaking in the absence of the initiative process. This requires introducing a legislative body that has complete control over state policy. As the traditional seat of policymaking, the legislature is entrusted with the ability to determine the exact content of policy outcomes, so the model allows the legislature to set policy as it desires. Of course, the legislature has to do this within certain constitutional boundaries and often with the threat of a gubernatorial veto, but in general it seems reasonable to assign the legislature monopoly control over selecting policy.[20]

Next, I assume the legislature, as well as the interest group, is motivated foremost by preferences over policy outcomes. I also assume that the legislature can be treated as a monolithic actor—policy preferences and the effects of interest group lobbying exist at the level of the legislature as a whole. Since the model focuses more on how the initiative process influences interest group behavior than on the internal functioning of the legislature, I use this simplified version of legislative politics. This assumption is justifiable through appeals to the median voter theorem, which says that the preferences of the legislature can be captured by considering only what the median legislator prefers, since her vote is necessary for any proposal to pass (Downs 1957; Black 1958). This assumption is common in other formal models of the initiative and referendum process (e.g., Gerber 1996; Matsusaka and McCarty 2001).[21]

To keep things simple, I also assume that both the legislature and the interest group are concerned about whether the state has a given policy or not. For example, the state can either have a lottery or not, or it can either permit capital punishment or not. Naturally, every policy has nuances about how it is implemented or when it applies, but I assume the all-or-nothing approach for many reasons. Most important, the greatest distinction between policies across states is likely to be which states have a policy, such as the death penalty or term limits, rather than the exact circumstances under which that policy applies. I am not claiming that statewide variation in policies is unimportant, just that it is secondary to having a policy in the first place. Because of the importance of the presence of a policy, this approach corresponds more directly to the structure of the empirical tests that will follow. Most studies of state policy adoption focus on whether a state has a given policy (e.g., Berry and Berry 1990; Mooney and Lee 1995). The upcoming chapter that tests the policy predictions of the model follows this approach, so it is reasonable for the model to make predictions that fit the features of the data. Additionally, treating policy in this way makes the model much easier to follow by greatly reducing its complexity.

To make the model interesting, I assume that the interest group and the legislature have opposite preferences for whether the policy is adopted.[22] An important consideration is how much the two actors value the policy change. Without loss of generality, I assign a value of zero to the most preferred outcome and negative utilities to other, less-preferred outcomes. Since the model here only has one other possible policy outcome, I only have to assign a value for not getting the most-preferred outcome. Further, since the predictions of the model depend on the relative valuations of these two outcomes, I fix the interest group's utility and allow the legisla-

Table 2.1
Summary of Utilities

	Policy Outcome	
	Do not Adopt	Adopt
Legislature	0	$-\beta$
Interest Group	-1	0

ture's to vary. For the interest group, then, the utility of not obtaining policy adoption is set at -1. For the legislature, the utility of adopting the policy is $-\beta$.[23] I treat the utilities in this fashion because it is more general and because the results of the model depend on whether the legislature loses more than the interest group gains when the policy is adopted. These utilities are summarized in table 2.1.

So far, the interest group has no means available to influence whether the legislature chooses to adopt the policy. To give the interest group a role in the policymaking process, I therefore allow it to directly lobby the legislature to implement the group's preferred outcome. In this case, direct lobbying by the interest group is treated as the making of a campaign contribution by the group to the legislature. If the contribution is large enough, the legislature is persuaded to respond to the group by implementing the policy.

The degree to which groups can influence legislators' votes through monetary contributions is an area of scholarly debate.[24] Empirical studies of specific votes are roughly evenly divided between those concluding that contributions influence votes and those concluding that they have no effect. In general, though, it is probably the case that contributions are most likely to affect votes on issues that are low in visibility and when legislators have no strong disposition to vote in a particular direction.[25]

Of course, votes are not the only thing that contributions can be intended to influence. The bulk of policymaking is over with long before a bill reaches a floor vote, and interest groups know this. Contributions can therefore be thought of as part of a broader lobbying strategy that includes direct interaction with key legislators, testifying before committees, and preparing policy statements. A well-timed contribution can be used to help an interest group gain access to convey its message (Wright 1990) or it can provide an incentive for a legislator to prioritize the group's issue. As Hall and Wayman (1990) argue, interest group money may be offered to key legislators at crucial points in the policymaking process to grease or sand the wheels by mobilizing support or demobilizing opposition.

These different interpretations just underscore the fact that legislatures are the seat of policymaking power and the focus of interest group activity. Besides contributions, groups can attempt to influence policy through various methods of persuasion, including testifying at hearings, generating grassroots public support, or by direct contacts with legislators or staff members. In the context of the model, then, the contributions variable can be thought of as a catch-all measure of direct lobbying by interest groups. Of course, when they are not successful, they may turn to other parts of government, including the courts or the governor's office, but for the purposes of the model developed here, all policymaking will be performed by the legislature, and interest groups will focus their lobbying efforts on that body.

In this preliminary version of the game, if the group does not have the ability to propose initiatives, the outcome is relatively simple to determine. Absent interest group influence, the legislature chooses not to adopt the policy, since it receives greater utility that way. Obviously the interest group is not happy with this outcome, and it can choose to lobby the legislature in order to persuade it to adopt the policy. If lobbied, the legislature adopts the policy only if the interest group provides enough in contributions to offset the utility lost to the legislature by adopting the policy. Because the interest group obtains a utility gain of 1 if the policy is adopted, it can successfully lobby only when the legislature values the policy loss at equal to or less than 1 ($\beta \leq -1$). In this circumstance, then, there is a mutually agreeable exchange that is made: the group contributes an amount t, for transfer, and the legislature adopts the policy. On the other hand, when the legislature values the policy loss at more than 1 ($\beta > 1$), the interest group is not willing to pay enough to persuade the legislature to adopt the policy.

One detail that must be worked out is exactly how much the group contributes to the legislature when it successfully lobbies. Since the group gains 1 and the legislature loses β, the transfer can be any amount between these two extremes. Thought of another way, successful lobbying generates a surplus—the net gain in utility for the legislature and interest group combined—of $1-\beta$. If the interest group pays $t=1$, then the legislature gets all of the surplus, whereas if the interest group pays $t=\beta$, it gets to keep the surplus, and the legislature does not gain or lose anything by adopting the policy. Since the focus of the model is not on the welfare of interest groups vis-à-vis the legislature, the ultimate allocation of the surplus is not extremely important. It is important, however, that the exact amount is specified, because the model is used to determine the effect of access to the initiative on interest group lobbying.[26] In the model, then, I let the legislature and interest group each keep half of the surplus.[27]

The equilibrium in the game without the initiative can be described as follows. When the utility loss for the legislature is less than or equal to the gain for the interest group ($\beta \leq 1$), the group successfully lobbies the legislature to move policy. The group makes a contribution to the legislature that evenly splits the surplus.[28] If the utility loss to the legislature is greater than the gain to the interest group, the group cannot successfully lobby, and the policy is not adopted. In the next section, I explain how adding the option of proposing initiatives affects the outcome of the model.

Adding Access to the Initiative Process

The next step is to determine how adding access to the initiative process affects the policy outcome and the interest group's behavior. By allowing the group to propose initiatives, the power of the legislature is reduced, since its monopoly on policymaking power is broken. As the legislature is aware of the potential for an initiative to be proposed, it has to account for this when it decides whether to respond to the group's lobbying attempts. In sum, then, adding the initiative process to the model helps the interest group while hurting the legislature. This may help explain why legislators are often opposed to the initiative process.

For the purposes of the model, the initiative process functions as follows. The interest group must expend resources to draft the initiative and to gather the signatures required to get it on the ballot. The cost of this endeavor is assumed to be some fixed amount c. This amount can also be thought of as including the cost of campaigning for the initiative once it is on the ballot, but these costs are assumed to be fixed and do not depend on the expected amount of voter support.

Once the interest group pays this cost and the initiative is on the ballot, if a majority of voters support the initiative it passes; otherwise it fails, and the game is over. Since the group and the legislature may not be certain as to whether voters are in favor of adopting the policy, the model assumes that there is some chance the initiative will pass and some chance it will fail. The influence of the initiative process is likely to depend on whether voters will pass the group's proposal: the legislature responds much differently to an interest group that has overwhelming public support for its goals than it does to a group that does not speak for the public interest. Rather than examine one particular case, I allow the probability of passage to be a variable in the model. Specifically, both actors believe the probability of the initiative passing is λ, which may vary across policy areas but is the same for both players for any single policy.

There are many reasons to think that the players are uncertain as to whether an initiative proposal will pass. First, voters might not yet have made up their minds about which policy outcome they prefer when the interest group qualifies the initiative. Initiatives often deal with complex issues, which many critics of the process assert voters are not qualified to evaluate. Cronin (1989) summarizes the situation that voters, especially the less educated and less prosperous, face in ballot issue elections: "'[I]nformation costs'... are generally even higher than in candidate elections. Legal and technical language on ballot issues sometimes causes confusion, and the absence of party labels usually attached to candidates denies a majority of these voters a familiar cue" (Cronin 1989, 67). He reports that more than one-quarter of voters say that they have difficulty choosing wisely on ballot issues. Magleby (1984) reaches even more dramatic conclusions, describing voters as facing an "informational vacuum," leading to votes that are essentially "electoral roulette."[29]

Second, there might be uncertainty about exactly which voters will turn out to vote on election day: this uncertainty could be related to the ballot item in question or to spillover effects from other races. Smith (2001) finds that voter turnout is increased as the salience of initiatives on the ballot increases. Since the number and salience of other initiatives on the ballot, as well as the characteristics of candidate races, cannot be known when a group attempts to qualify an initiative, it is reasonable to assume that the sponsors cannot be sure of the outcome. Third, opinions could shift during the campaign period. As Magleby (1984) observes, support for initiatives generally starts out above 50 percent but gradually decreases over time as election day approaches. The shift in opinion may be caused by many factors, including campaigns by opponents and proponents, undecided voters making up their minds, and the perceived tendency of voters to vote no when they are unsure about an initiative.

All of these arguments therefore point to the same fact: nobody can be sure whether an initiative will pass until the votes are counted. Despite this uncertainty, the interest group and the legislature probably have some information about what might happen, possibly through polls, experience from previous initiatives, campaign consultants, or studying similar initiatives that may have been proposed in similar states. The model summarizes this information through λ,which is the expected probability that the initiative will receive a majority on election day. In a later section of the model, I discuss a specific mechanism through which actors can formulate their expectations of this probability.[30]

The solution to the game is reached by starting at the end and working backward: when deciding whether to accept the group's contributions, the legislature first determines what the interest group will do if it rebuffs its lobbying efforts. If the group is not successful with the legislature, the group has two options: it can propose an initiative or do nothing. If it does nothing, the game ends and the policy is not adopted. If it proposes an initiative, however, the policy may or may not be adopted, depending on the outcome of the vote. Since it has to pay a fixed cost *c* just to get the initiative on the ballot, the interest group will only do so if the expected gain is greater than this cost. As the probability that the initiative passes (λ) increases, the expected gain from the proposal increases as well. At some point, the likelihood that a proposal will pass becomes great enough that the group is willing to pay the cost to get it on the ballot and risk having it fail. I label the threshold above which the expected utility of proposing the initiative is greater than 0 as λ^*. When the probability of an initiative passing is greater than λ^* the group proposes an initiative if it is not successful in the legislature. When the probability of an initiative passing is less than λ^* the group does not make a proposal.

So even if the legislature does not consider how the group will respond if it refuses to adopt the policy in question, it is apparent that the ability to propose initiatives benefits the group, as it gives the group another option if its proposal fails in the legislature. In the model, however, the legislature does take into account what the group will do if it is turned away. This ends up benefiting the group even more, since the legislature becomes more receptive to the group's direct lobbying efforts in order to avoid the possibility of an initiative's passing. When an initiative passes, the legislature loses utility because the policy is adopted, but it gets nothing in return from the group. This means that the group can often convince the legislature to move policy for a smaller contribution, which the legislature may prefer to an initiative, because it at least gets some compensation.

So how exactly does the ability to propose initiatives influence legislative behavior? When the probability of an initiative passing is large enough ($\lambda \geq \lambda^*$) the legislature must decide whether to take a calculated gamble by ignoring the group's lobbying attempts and hoping the ensuing initiative fails. This is the critical difference between the model with the initiative process and the version developed without it: without the initiative, there is no risk to the legislature from ignoring the group. Because the legislature's power is reduced with the initiative process, it cannot demand as sizable a contribution at the lobbying stage of the game. Likewise, the interest group is aware of its increased bargaining position and does not offer as large a contribution. Because the cost to the group of unsuccessful lobbying goes down and the gain to the legislature also goes down, the amount of money the group offers the legislature decreases.

To be precise, the group knows that proposing an initiative requires a cost *c* but offers a potential gain of 1 with probability λ. Thus the group's utility when lobbying fails is λ-1-c, whereas without the initiative it was stuck with a utility of -1. Recall that the group only proposes an initiative when $\lambda \geq c$, which implies that the group's utility is larger when it is able and willing to propose an initiative. Likewise, the legislature's expected utility of unsuccessful lobbying is its utility loss multiplied by the probability that the initiative passes: $-\beta \times \lambda$ With the initiative process, the cost to the legislature of adopting the policy decreases from β to $\lambda \times \beta$, which is smaller because λ is between 0 and 1.

The change in both parties' expected utility of failing to negotiate alters the outcome of the bargaining process. In appendix B, I explicitly derive the equilibrium contribution amount with the initiative process and show that it is less than the amount transferred without the possibility of initiatives.[31] The reason for this change is relatively straightforward: since the group gains less by lobbying the legislature rather than proposing an initiative, it is not willing to contribute as much. Likewise, since the legislature loses more if it refuses the group, it is willing to accept less. Combining these two changes, then, it is intuitive that the group will end up contributing less.

Even though the group does not have to contribute as much, this does not imply that it always prefers to go through the legislature rather than propose an initiative. The initiative may be so attractive that the group is better off taking a chance with voters than lobbying the legislature. In the appendix, I show that this can only happen when the utility loss to the legislature is greater than the gain to the group ($\beta > 1$). Otherwise, the interest group and the legislature can always reach a lobbying agreement that they prefer to an initiative proposal. When the legislature's loss is large, however, the group's ability to lobby the legislature depends on the probability that an initiative would pass. When the probability of an initiative's passing is relatively low, the group proposes an initiative. As the probability of an initiative's passing increases, the legislature becomes increasingly pliable until the necessary contribution amount decreases enough that the initiative is no longer more attractive than lobbying. I call the critical point at which the interest group switches from proposing an initiative to lobbying the legislature λ^B.[32]

The results of the model are summarized in figures 2.1 and 2.2. Figure 2.1 shows the interest group's expected utility and the action it takes as a function of the probability that an initiative would pass when the legislature's utility loss from adopting the policy is small ($\beta \leq 1$). When the group cannot propose an initiative, its only option is to make contributions to the legislature. The legislature accepts these contributions, since the fact that $\beta \leq 1$ implies that the group will offer at least β in contributions and make the legislature (weakly) better off. The contributions made are such that the group and the legislature split the gains generated by the exchange, which translates into a contribution $t=(1+\beta)/2$. The interest group's final utility is its policy utility, 0, minus the cost of the contributions made. This utility is represented by the dashed horizontal line at $-(1+\beta)/2$.

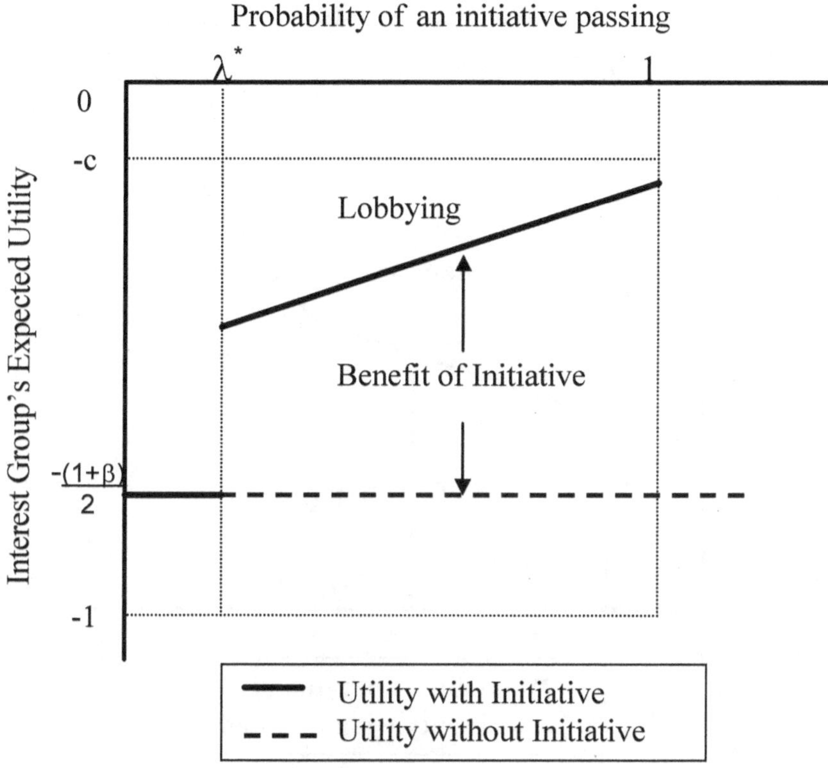

Figure 2.1
Equilibrium Outcome and Interest Group's Utility (Case 1: $\beta \leq 1$)

In initiative states, however, the ability to go to the ballot can affect the size of the contribution made. This only happens when proposing an initiative is a credible threat, or when $\lambda \geq \lambda^*$. When an initiative proposal is not a credible threat, the outcome and the group's utility are the same as when there is no initiative process: the group and the legislature bargain, and the group makes a contribution of size $t = -(1+\beta)/2$. Once the probability of an initiative's passing becomes large enough, though, the threat of the group's proposing one reduces the size of the contributions made by the group. In the figure, this is demonstrated by the jump in the group's utility when the solid horizontal line reaches λ^* and becomes the solid diagonal line. As the probability of an initiative's passing increases, the equilibrium contributions become smaller, since the group's utility of proposing an initiative increases

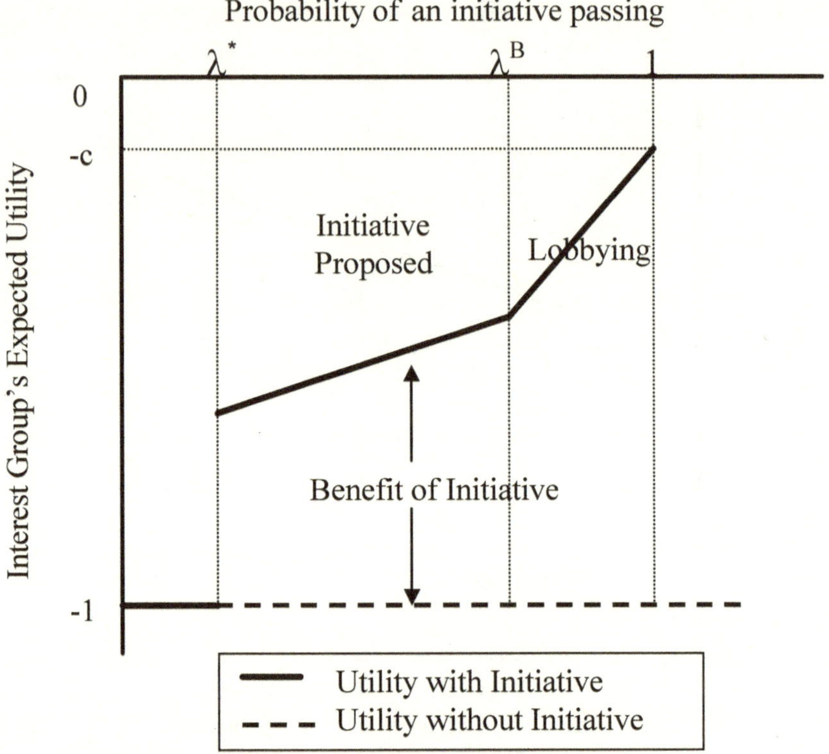

Figure 2.2
Equilibrium Outcome and Interest Group's Utility (Case 2: $\beta>1$)

and the legislature's utility of ignoring the group decreases. The increase in utility to the group from access to the initiative process is represented by the distance between the dashed line for its utility without initiatives and the diagonal line for its utility with initiatives. Most important, note that the utility with the initiative is always greater than the utility without it.

Figure 2.2 contains the same information for the case when the legislature has a large utility loss from adopting the policy ($\beta > 1$). When there is no initiative process, the group is not willing to compensate the legislature for its utility loss of adopting the policy, so nothing happens and the group's utility is -1. When the group has the option of proposing an initiative but is not willing to do so, the outcome does not change, and its utility stays at -1 when $\lambda<\lambda^{*}$.

Once the group is willing to propose an initiative, however, its expected utility increases immediately. To illustrate the full set of possible outcomes, the example lets $\lambda^B > \lambda^*$. Recall that this inequality implies that the legislature is not always willing to move policy for contributions even when the group is willing to propose an initiative. So when the expected probability of an initiative's passing is in the middle range, the group proposes an initiative. Its utility in this range is indicated by the diagonal line between λ^* and λ^B. Once this line reaches λ^B, the legislature is no longer willing to risk the chance that initiative will pass, so it agrees to move policy in exchange for contributions. So when the probability of an initiative's passing is very high, the group does not have to propose one, and its utility increases relative to proposing (otherwise it would not agree to the contributions). As in the previous figure, the distance between the dashed line at -1 and the solid line indicates the increase in utility for the interest group from access to the initiative process; again, the group is always better off with the initiative process that without it.[33]

These two figures highlight the two different ways that the initiative process benefits interest groups. The first one is the direct benefit that it provides, which is manifested in initiatives on the ballot. The direct benefit corresponds to the section of figure 2.2 where the probability of an initiative's passing is between λ^* and λ^B. In this case, the group proposes an initiative.[34]

While the direct benefit is easily observable, the second, or indirect, benefit may be harder to ascertain. The indirect benefit is the effect that the ability to propose initiatives has on the ability of the interest group to persuade the legislature to move policy in exchange for contributions. This corresponds to the section of figure 2.2 where the probability of an initiative's passing is greater than λ^B and to the entire section of figure 2.1 where the probability of an initiative's passing is greater than λ^*. Note that this area is greater in the first figure, as the legislature is always willing to bargain. In fact, when the legislature's utility loss from adopting the policy is small, which is the case represented by figure 2.1, it is only the indirect effect of the initiative process that is felt.

The indirect effect is harder to detect for two reasons. First, and most obviously, there are no initiatives on the ballot. Second, figure 2.1 shows that the policy outcome may not be different. In this case, the legislature moves policy with or without the initiative process, but with the initiative process it does so for less in contributions. This means that observing an interest group making contributions and the legislature adopting a policy is not necessarily evidence of the indirect effect of the initiative process. Of course it can be, as figure 2.2 shows, since in that case policy would not have moved without the threat of an initiative.

Even looking at the amount of interest group contributions made is not sufficient evidence to know if the initiative had an effect, either on average or in total. The model as formulated does not, therefore, make any specific predictions about the effect of the initiative process on campaign contributions in a state. This may seem counterintuitive, so a quick explanation is in order. The presence of the initiative process does decrease the amount of contributions that a group makes, but only if it was going to make contributions at all. Some groups merely make smaller contributions, while other groups stop making contributions altogether and instead propose initiatives. There is, however, an opposite effect: some groups switch from making no contributions to making some contributions. This happens because the threat of an initiative may decrease the amount that the legislature requires to the point where it becomes worthwhile for the group to take this route rather than remain inactive. This situation corresponds to the part of figure 2.2 where the probability of an initiative's passing is greater than λ^B: without the initiative, no contributions are made, whereas with the initiative, the group does make contributions. So while one consequence of the initiative is to reduce contributions that would have been made without it, another effect is to induce contributions that otherwise would not have been made at all. The net effect depends on the distribution of groups.[35]

The indirect effect of the initiative process described above is slightly different from that discussed in previous work on the initiative process. Based on the use of a spatial model that allows for a continuum of different policy outcomes, Gerber (1996) finds an indirect effect consisting of policy moderation on the part of the legislature. To avoid the utility loss associated with the group's proposing an initiative, the legislature responds by picking policy points that are just close enough to voters to preclude an initiative proposal by the group. Thus, the indirect effect described by Gerber's model is in terms of policy moderation, whereas the indirect effect in this model is on the presence and amount of campaign contributions made by the group to the legislature. Of course, the logic behind the two is analogous: the legislature offers concessions due to groups' ability to propose initiatives.

One difference between the two models, however, is in the effect of the initiative process on voters' welfare. In models with no uncertainty about whether an initiative will pass, the legislature can always perfectly respond to the threat of proposal. Because of the precision afforded by this case, voters are always better off with the initiative process.[36] When the probability of an initiative's passing is between 0 and 1, however, the legislature sometimes responds to the threat of initiatives that might fail. This can lead to outcomes where voters are potentially worse off with the initiative process than they would have been without it.[37] By creating circumstances in which the legislature accepts contributions to avoid initiatives that have less than a 50 percent chance of failing, the initiative process may systematically hurt voters. Note, however, that this only happens in the case where the legislature's utility loss from adopting the policy is large ($\beta > 1$) and even then only when the probability of an initiative's passing is greater than λ^B but also less than 50 percent.

The Model's Predictions

In this section, I use the results of the model just developed to generate specific predictions about the effect of the initiative process on state interest groups and state politics in general. By comparing the results of the model with and without the initiative process, I can determine whether and how its presence influences the interest group, the legislature, and the final policy outcome. The predictions and implications of the model presented in the rest of this chapter are crucial, as they represent the end product of my formal model and define the empirical tests that comprise the rest of this book. The presentation of my hypotheses proceeds in two steps. Here, I discuss those that derive directly from the model. Then in the following section, I discuss additional hypotheses that follow from the logic and spirit of the model, but are not explicitly derived from it.

An important distinction is made in this section between direct predictions of the model and implications that can be drawn from it. Predictions are results that are derived directly from the model presented in the previous section—they are precise mathematical statements that follow directly from the assumptions of the model. Implications are based on the results of the model as well, but require additional assumptions.[38] Thus, they do not obtain directly from the model. Yet these implications follow quite closely from the model and generally require only one or two additional assumptions. Because these extra assumptions might appear to be ad hoc in the context of the model, I separate them from the formal model.[39] All of these extra assumptions are relatively reasonable and allow me to generate a wider variety of implications to test. Further, I present evidence for the validity of two of these three assumptions later on in the book. First, however, I start with one of the model's direct predictions.

Prediction 1. (Utility) *An interest group's expected utility is the same or better when it has access to the initiative process.*

This prediction is easy to understand. If the group is not willing to propose an initiative, its utility does not change—either it does nothing, or it makes the same size contribution as it would without the initiative.[40] If it is willing to propose an initiative, however, its expected utility increases. This happens in one of two ways. If the group proposes an initiative, it must have greater expected utility than not proposing one. On the other hand, if the interest group successfully lobbies the legislature, I have shown that the size of the contribution made is decreased by the threat of an initiative: the group accomplishes its goal, but for a reduced price. In either case, the group is better off because of access to the initiative process.

This prediction is the most important one that the model makes because of the implications it has for interest group behavior in initiative states relative to noninitiative states. Since the utility to groups is greater, groups should be more likely to mobilize to seek their policy goals. They may also be more likely to get involved in policy areas that they would not have attempted to influence before. The history of the medicinal marijuana movement is just one example of the consequences of this prediction.

Mobilization and interest group formation are not costless activities, however, and the model does not address these costs. Examples of these costs include the administrative costs of setting up and running an interest group, the costs of searching for and attracting members, and the costs associated with attempting to overcome the collective action problem. While the costs of formation and mobilization may be sizable for certain types of interest groups, there is no reason to think that they are greater for potential groups in initiative states. In their studies of state interest group populations, for example, Gray and Lowery (1996, 1998) find that registration costs do not vary enough from state to state to systematically affect interest group lobbying registrations. Other costs, such as the costs of communication and the costs to individuals of joining are also unlikely to differ. To be explicit, however, I make the following noncontroversial assumption:

Assumption 1. (Costs) *The costs of mobilization are not systematically different in states with the initiative process relative to states without the initiative process.*

When this assumption is combined with prediction 1, the model has implications for interest group mobilizations. Given a specific cost of mobilization, groups for whom the benefit of organizing exceeds the cost successfully mobilize. Other groups remain latent, or unorganized, since it is not worth the trouble. Because the initiative process increases the utility of mobilization without affecting the cost of doing so, some of the latent groups perceive it to be in their interest to mobilize. Since all groups that mobilize without the initiative process continue to do so and some groups that would not are spurred to organize because of the initiative, this results in more groups mobilizing in initiative states. This consequence is summarized in the following implication.

Implication 1. (Mobilization) *Initiative states have more interest groups than noninitiative states.*

Adapting prediction 1 in this way has important consequences for how I test the model. Foremost among these is the relative ease of measuring interest group mobilizations rather than interest group utility. Although the link between the two is straightforward—if access to the initiative process increases a group's expected utility, some groups should form that would not have formed without it—the ability to observe mobilization makes it a much preferred phenomenon of study. Further, an increase in the number of interest groups has a more important impact on politics than an increase in the utility of preexisting groups, because it is groups that are conduits for citizens' interests.[41]

The results of the model also indicate that there may be policy consequences of having the initiative process. From the point of view of an interest group, such as Californians for Medical Rights, the presence of the initiative increases the incentives to get active. The group mobilizes knowing that even if it fails in the legislature, it has another recourse. For a group seeking the adoption of a new policy, mobilization is more likely in an initiative state. Sometimes, policy success will follow. By encouraging the involvement of change-seeking groups, the initiative process may lead states to adopt policies that they would not have adopted without it.

Alternatively, a group that has had some success in its state of origin may not be satisfied with merely influencing policy in one state. Groups may want to move on to encourage citizens and legislators in other states to follow suit and adopt the group's policy. The model predicts that these groups, all else equal, prefer to seek policy change in states that have the initiative process. Not only would it be less expensive to lobby the legislature, but in the cases where that does not happen, the group can propose an initiative.

As an example, consider Scientific Games of Atlanta, which funded more than 99 percent of California's 1984 lottery initiative's qualifying fees in the hope that once the measure passed, it would become the supplier of lottery materials and make a hefty profit (Tolbert, Lowenstein, and Donovan 1998). Similar stories derive from the expansion of casino gaming: groups such as Bally's and MGM Grand have been involved in initiative campaigns to legalize casino gaming in other states (Dombrink and Thompson 1990). The process through which Californians for

Medical Rights became Americans for Medical Rights and helped found Coloradans for Medical Rights, Floridians for Medical Rights, and Mainers for Medical Rights, among others, is yet another version of this phenomenon.

The consequence of these two processes is captured by the following prediction:

Prediction 2. (Policy) *Policy adoption occurs under a wider range of circumstances in initiative states.*

The derivation of this prediction is straightforward. The only time that policy change occurs without the initiative is when the interest group can successfully lobby the legislature to move policy on its behalf. This is only the case when the legislature's utility loss from adopting the policy is small ($\beta \leq 1$). Adding the initiative to these circumstances does not change the outcome—policy still moves—it only changes how much it costs the interest group. And since the interest group never has to resort to proposing an initiative, there is no opportunity for one to fail. This is the case depicted in figure 2.1.

In some cases ($\beta > 1$), however, the group cannot persuade the legislature to adopt the policy without the ability to propose an initiative. As figure 2.2 shows, adding the initiative process can lead to policy change in two ways. First, when the group is willing to propose an initiative, the legislature may respond by reducing its demands to the point where the group will meet them. Second, if the legislature is not sufficiently threatened, the group can still propose an initiative. While policy change occurs with certainty in the first case, in the latter case it only happens when voters pass the initiative. The possibility of an initiative failing does not undermine the prediction, however, since initiatives are only proposed in circumstances under which policy would not have changed otherwise.

Not only does the presence of the initiative make existing groups more likely to be successful, but it also encourages latent groups to seek change. There are two different ways this can occur. First, as prediction 1 states, the initiative process can provide enough additional incentive for a latent interest group to mobilize. This group then has the opportunity to effect policy change that would not have happened without it. Second, interest groups wishing to alter policy are more likely to target initiative states rather than noninitiative states, because the expected utility of operating there is greater.

Americans for Medical Rights demonstrates both aspects of this prediction: before its name change, this group was known as Californians for Medical Rights as it pushed for legalization of medicinal marijuana in its home state before finally succeeding with Proposition 215 in 1996. After becoming Americans for Medical Rights, the group became involved in campaigns for medicinal marijuana in other states and helped form Coloradans for Medical Rights, which fought for the passage of Amendment 19. Another example is the American Civil Rights Institute, formed by Ward Connerly after the passage of Proposition 209 in California.[42] Connerly and his group attempted to replicate their success in California by making similar proposals in Colorado, Ohio, Washington, and Florida.

The model makes another prediction about policy adoption, but this one focuses on the role of the initiative process in information diffusion. One of the central variables in the model is the belief that the legislature and interest group have about the probability that an initiative will pass if it is proposed. This influences not only the interest group's willingness to propose an initiative but also affects the willingness of the legislature to adopt policy for the group in exchange for contributions. To contextualize this uncertainty, I argue that because initiatives are generally lower-information environments for voters, it may be hard to predict what will happen on election day. To determine the likelihood that an initiative will pass, interest groups and politicians may conduct polls or examine results from similar policy areas.

Another place that they can look for information is in other states. If the characteristics of voters in other states are similar, then whether those states already have the policy might provide some clues as to how voters in the group's state might respond to an initiative. To determine how this might effect policy diffusion, I allow the probability that voters in one state would pass an initiative to be related to the probability that voters in another state would support an initiative. When the interest group and legislature are estimating the chance that an initiative in their state will pass, they can use information from what happens in the other state to get a better estimate.

Consider an example with a group and legislature in Arizona. Assume that the game has already been played in California and that California has adopted the policy that the group in Arizona is seeking. And assume that greater probabilities of voting for the policy in California are associated with greater probabilities of voting for the policy in Arizona.[43] What can the players in Arizona learn from California's experience? If, for example, there is an initiative proposed in California, they can infer that the probability of California's voters passing the initiative must have been above the minimum probability required for the California group to propose an initiative. Given this knowledge and the positive relationship between voter's preferences, the group and legislature in Arizona would expect that an initiative in their state would be more likely to pass than they would if California had not had an initiative proposed and had not adopted the policy. In appendix B, I show that even if California adopts through the legislature, the group's and the legislature's beliefs about the probability of such an initiative passing in Arizona increase.

The previous paragraph argues that there should be policy diffusion between states with the initiative process. The model also has something to say about diffusion from and to states without the initiative process. Recall that in the version of the model that does not allow the group access to the initiative, the outcome depends on whether or not the group can compensate the legislature for its utility loss when it adopts the policy. Since there is no initiative process, the outcome does not depend on how likely voters are to pass an initiative. This means that groups in Arizona cannot learn anything about their voter's preferences from what happens in New Mexico. It also means that even if groups in noninitiative states can learn from initiative states, the information is not of any use to them, since they do not have the option of proposing an initiative. This implies that information about voter's preferences should diffuse only between initiative states. This is summarized in the following prediction.

Prediction 3. (Diffusion) *Information diffuses only from initiative states to other initiative states.*

This prediction asserts that policy decisions in states with the initiative process are influenced by the same decisions in other initiative states. When one initiative state adopts a policy, similar initiative states become more likely to follow suit. This is a more explicit model of diffusion than that provided by previous examinations of policy adoptions. In the recent policy adoption literature that uses the event history approach, diffusion is assumed to be an "I want one too" phenomenon, with one state's adoption somehow increasing the propensity of a neighboring state to adopt (e.g., Berry and Berry 1990). While there are certainly reasons why this might be the case—diffusion can have different patterns if it results from economic competition rather than from social learning—these studies have not sought to incorporate a theoretical underpinning for their notions of diffusion.[44]

The model does not consider forms of diffusion based on other forces, only diffusion caused by information. These other forces probably exist, however, suggesting that there is some constant, baseline rate of diffusion among all states. The most common explanations for policy diffusion include social learning and economic competition. Social learning theory explains diffusion as a consequence of political decision makers' efforts to solve various public policy problems. In attempting to solve these problems, they may be more likely to consider potential solutions already implemented in nearby states, for reasons of political and demographic similarity, convenience, political networking, and overlapping media markets (Mintrom 1997; Mintrom and Vergari 1998; Mooney 2001; Rogers 1995; Walker 1969). Nearby states are likely to be more similar, allowing elected officials to introduce policy reforms that are better suited to their specific circumstances. These explanations lead to a prediction of a regional diffusion effect that is not contradictory to the one in my model.[45] As long as these other influences on policy diffusion are constant, the prediction of the model can be interpreted that diffusion between pairs of initiative states should be stronger than among other state dyads.

Further Implications of the Model

In the previous section, I presented the core hypotheses of the model: the mobilization hypothesis (implication 1), the policy hypothesis (prediction 2), and the diffusion hypothesis (prediction 3). Two of these three hypotheses follow directly from the model, and one uses the assumption that the costs of mobilization are not different in initiative states to restate the other prediction (prediction 1). In this section, I complete the presentation of the model and its predictions and implications by making two additional assumptions and deriving five additional implications. Both of these assumptions are relatively intuitive, and their validity is bolstered by previous work on the initiative process. The first two implications that result are about the types of interest groups that are created by initiative mobilizations. The final three concern the effect of the initiative process on how interest groups lobby the legislature.

The Asymmetry of Interest Group Mobilizations

The first additional assumption concerns the type of group that benefits the most from the ability to propose initiatives. Groups that are likely to be more successful at qualifying and passing initiatives should benefit more from access to the initiative process than groups that would not be as successful. This implies that the additional mobilizations engendered by the initiative process are not proportionately distributed across all types of groups. For a variety of reasons, I expect that broad-based citizen groups are better suited to propose initiatives than narrow economic groups.

The first argument is based on the nature of the introduction of the initiative process itself. One of the intentions of early supporters of the initiative process was to help wrest control of state governments from powerful business interests and increase the involvement of average citizens. In California, for example, the Southern Pacific Railroad earned itself the nickname "the Octopus" for its ability to reach into and influence all sorts of government decisions. Southern Pacific was one of the chief targets of Progressive reformers at the time, who also favored the initiative process (Mowry 1951). While there is still great concern and evidence of the dominance of economic interest groups in politics (Baumgartner and Leech 2001; Salisbury 1984; Schlozman 1984; Schlozman and Tierney 1986), their modern counterpart is more likely to be organized citizen groups. Thus, if the Progressive goal of increasing the influence of citizens vis-à-vis economic interests has been successful, the benefits of the initiative process should accrue more among broad-based citizen groups.

Progressive intentions aside, there are many reasons to believe that today's citizen groups are better positioned to avail themselves of the initiative's benefits than economic groups. To achieve success with the initiative, a group has to be able to muster majority support for its proposed policy change, a task which is probably somewhat easier for a group that already represents a broader public interest than for a narrow economic interest. Although money is required for any type of group to prevail at the ballot, groups that have large, voluntary membership bases can often substitute their own workforce for tasks that economic groups must contract out for.

Previous work has already theorized and provided evidence that this is the case. In an important study of how different types of interest groups use the initiative process in different ways to achieve their objectives, Gerber (1999) concludes that citizen groups are better positioned to succeed at modifying policy through the initiative process. This is because they are likely to possess both of the necessary resources to do so: revenue and members. Economic groups, on the other hand, have the money but lack the personnel to use the initiative to modify policy. Instead, they use the initiative process to stop policy change. The empirical evidence confirms that this is in fact the case: whereas economic groups can use direct legislation to stop policy change, citizen groups are much more effective at using it to promote policy change. This argument is summarized in the following assumption.

Assumption 2. (Asymmetric Benefit) *Broad-based membership groups are more effective at using the initiative process than wealthy economic groups.*

An alternate form of evidence in favor of assumption 1 comes from studies that show that citizen groups may be more skilled at the type of lobbying strategies that initiative campaigns require. In general, scholars divide interest group lobbying into two distinct strategies: inside lobbying and outside lobbying. Citizen groups tend to engage in more outside lobbying, and economic groups engage in more inside lobbying. This difference is due both to the greater amount of conflict that citizen groups face and the resources available to the two types of groups. As Walker and Gais argue (Walker 1991), there are "sharp differences in tactical priorities between citizen groups, whose preference overwhelmingly is for outside strategies, and those groups whose members come mainly from the profit sector, which lean heavily toward inside strategies . . ." (Walker 1991, 113). Since outside strategies are probably more useful for mobilizing public support and attracting attention in an initiative campaign, citizen groups are better equipped to take advantage of the opportunities offered by the initiative process.

There are other reasons to expect that citizen groups might benefit more from the initiative process. First, they might more often find themselves in a position where the status quo is not their preferred policy outcome. Second, the added benefits of the initiative might be more valuable to large broad-based groups that suffer most from the collective action problem. By providing a salient opportunity to mobilize, initiatives can offer a distinct tool for groups to use to attract members. After the initiative has passed or failed, many of the supporters may stay involved with the group. Through this process, new citizen groups may emerge from specific initiative campaigns and subsequently remain active in state politics.

Given these different justifications and the existing empirical evidence, discussed in further detail in the following chapter, in favor of some of them, assumption 1 is almost certainly correct. This assumption can be used to extend the model and draw implications about how access to the initiative process will affect citizen groups differently than economic groups. The first implication I generate is possibly the most important of the four, since it concerns representation in the interest group system and speaks to the success of the initiative process in achieving its founders' goals. This implication lies at the heart of my argument that the initiative process has an important and beneficial indirect effect on state politics that should be accounted for when assessing its value. The three implications that follow, however, also have important ramifications for interest groups and who is represented in state politics.

The first prediction is about how access to the initiative process affects interest group mobilizations. In light of assumption 1, implication 1 can be modified to distinguish between the effect of the initiative on citizen and economic groups. If the increase in utility is greater for citizen groups than for economic groups, its impact should be greater among the former.

Implication 2. (Representation) *The increase in interest group mobilizations caused by the initiative process is greater for citizen groups than for economic groups.*

This implication of the model is important for understanding interest group representation. Empirical studies of interest group systems in the United States, both at the federal and state level, have consistently demonstrated that there is a powerful bias toward economic groups. Every systematic study of interest group populations has found that business groups and corporations are overrepresented and broad-based membership groups are underrepresented.[46] This bias is a result of the collective action problem inherent in mobilizing broader-based groups: while the benefits of their actions can be enjoyed by anyone, the costs are borne solely by the members (Olson 1965). Although some studies have investigated the different methods groups can use to encourage people to join (Moe 1980; Chong 1991; Rothenberg 1992), they have rarely studied how political institutions can serve in this capacity.[47] If implication 2 is true, then, the initiative process can be viewed as a powerful tool that can increase the representativeness of interest group populations. Given broad concerns about bias in the representativeness of the interest group system, as well as about recent declines in democratic and social participation, the initiative process can be viewed as one important tool through which both can be ameliorated.

Besides relative numbers of economic and citizen groups, there should also be important differences in the types of resources that mobilized interest groups possess. Since success in using the initiative process to change policy requires both members and revenue, the additional groups that mobilize in initiative states should reflect this requirement. Implication 2 formally states that initiative states have a greater proportion of broad-based membership groups, one consequence of which is that the average number of members for a group in initiatives states is larger. Similar shifts should be observed in other resources, including revenue, staff size, and so forth. Besides this direct shift in resources resulting from initiative mobilizations, there may be an indirect effect among existing groups as well. Groups that would have mobilized even without the initiative process should have an incentive to acquire more members, who are useful for legislative lobbying and initiative proposals.[48] The following implication states this formally.

Implication 3. (Resources) *The groups that mobilize in initiative states are characterized by resources that are more likely to be useful in initiative campaigns than groups in noninitiative states.*

Interest Groups and Lobbying Tactics

In this section, I present the final three hypotheses, which focus on how the initiative process influences interest group lobbying behavior. Since lobbying behavior is determined in part by groups' resources, and since there are more broad-based membership groups in initiative states, the average lobbying approach should also differ. In addition to this distributional shift in lobbying, the model also implies behavioral differences: even after accounting for resource differences, groups in initiative states emphasize different lobbying approaches.

If, as scholars have argued (e.g., Walker 1991; Gerber 1999), interest group lobbying tactics are a function of the resources at their disposal, changes in resources should lead to changes in lobbying tactics. Thus, the shift in resources predicted by implication 3 should be reflected by a concomitant shift in lobbying tactics. The natural question is: which lobbying tactics are used more and which are used less? The resources that are possessed by membership groups and that are useful in initiative campaigns are more appropriate for lobbying tactics that rely more on widespread citizen action and on mobilizing and influencing public opinion. While having more members may be useful for obtaining access to legislators, they are less important for preparing research reports and testifying at hearings or organizing legislative coalitions. In general, then, citizen groups are less successful at strategies of this type. This fits nicely with previous studies of lobbying tactics (Walker 1991; Kollman 1998), which tend to group them into inside and outside categories. Given that the types of resources that are useful in initiative campaigns are more likely to be useful for tactics in the outside lobbying category rather than those in the inside lobbying category, I expect that groups in initiative states engage in more outside lobbying.

Besides providing evidence for my model of interest group response to initiative access, differences in the balance of lobbying tactics employed in initiative states are important for understanding representation in interest group systems. Discussing the importance of interest group lobbying tactics, Walker highlights the relationship between which strategies are used and who is represented:

> Questions about interest group strategies become particularly significant when we consider their aggregate effects. A political system in which inside strategies are predominant is likely to be quite different from one in which outside strategies are common or even the primary method of advocating interests—different in the interests represented, in the systems' capacity for comprehensive change, in the autonomy of elective and

> executive institutions, and in the precision and types of political issues raised. (Walker 1991, 104)

A political system that favors outside lobbying might be expected to produce policy decisions that more closely reflect the interests of groups that are successful at outside lobbying. This would include groups that are accustomed to and capable of engaging in such tactics as organizing protests or demonstrations, mobilizing grassroots support, and utilizing the media. To the extent that these and similar lobbying tactics are useful in initiative campaigns and that they can readily be adapted to outside lobbying of the legislature, and to the extent that the primary benefactors of the initiative process are citizen groups, this means that policy in initiative states is more representative of citizen groups' preferences. This issue is explored in more detail in chapter 4, along with tests of predictions 2 and 3.

Implication 4. (Lobbying Tactics) *Because of the differences in resources predicted by implication 3, interest groups in initiative states rely more on outside lobbying tactics than groups in noninitiative states.*

Another reason that groups in initiative states may rely more on outside lobbying is to signal support for a potential initiative proposal. Whereas in the model the legislature knows precisely under which conditions the interest group will propose an initiative, in reality it may be harder for the legislature to know. For example, the legislature may have doubts about whether the interest group is capable of raising the resources necessary to pay the cost of proposing an initiative or, even it can afford to, whether the group values the policy change enough to expend its resources on an initiative.[49] Alternatively, the legislature and the group might have different expectations about the likelihood that an initiative will pass.

In all of the scenarios outlined above, it might be in the group's best interest to send a signal to the legislature that it is willing to expend resources or that it can generate sufficient public support to pass an initiative.[50] Given that public support is more aptly indicated through outside lobbying tactics than inside lobbying tactics, groups in initiative states may utilize outside lobbying tactics to demonstrate the strength of their position to the legislature. If groups do engage in signaling by tailoring their lobbying strategies to take advantage of the threat of an initiative, groups in initiative states should rely on outside lobbying more than groups in noninitiative states, even after accounting for differences in organizational resources.

Implication 5. (Lobbying Strategies) *Interest groups in initiative states rely more on outside lobbying strategies, even after controlling for resources.*

It is important to note that implication 5 is fundamentally different from implication 4. The latter is a statement motivated by shifts in interest group resources caused by initiative mobilizations. Given the greater preponderance of personnel relative to monetary resources, these additional groups engage in lobbying tactics that put their resources to their best effect. Thus, there is a greater use of outside lobbying tactics in initiative states. Implication 5 states that even after controlling for the distributional shift in groups and resources in initiative states, a group in an initiative states resorts to more outside lobbying than it would in a noninitiative state. This implication is therefore about the behavioral response of individual groups to the initiative process and indicates that the initiative process increases the reliance on outside lobbying above and beyond the increase due to the shift in resources.

Besides the potential for sending a signal to the legislature about the strength of its position as described above, there is another reason why groups in initiative states might use more outside lobbying. This explanation focuses on the role of the initiative in how interest groups learn to lobby. If groups mobilize because of the incentives offered by the initiative or to get involved in a specific initiative campaign, then their early experiences with lobbying will be focused more on mobilizing public support, working the grass roots, placing advertisements, and generating press releases. Groups that have success with these tactics in their formative years are likely to ingrain them into their normal lobbying practices and will return to them in the future, either in subsequent initiative campaigns or possibly even when they are directly lobbying the legislature.

> The choice between [inside and outside] strategies is a fundamental one usually made early in a group's history that orients the organization's tactical decisions throughout much of its life. This stability grows out of the strong roots of these strategic choices, which are intertwined with the group's constituency and resources, as well as with crucial aspects of its political environment. The political strategies of interest groups . . . are not adopted or changed by interest leaders at will but, rather, depend on previous decisions and the particular institutional and political environment they face. (Walker 1991, 103)

Returning to the potential importance of signaling support, the last assumption and implication focus on how the initiative process increases the ability of interest groups to directly lobby the legislature. Recall that the ability to propose initiatives decreases the amount that a group has to contribute to the legislature to secure policy change. This implies that interest groups should be able to get more bang for their buck in initiative states: the same gain can be achieved, but for a reduced price.

In the context of the model, campaign contributions were intended to be an abstraction for many different types of direct lobbying: contact with legislators, testifying before committees, building legislative coalitions, and convincing legislators to spend more time on a group's issue. So taking a broad interpretation of the model means that the threat of an initiative should increase the effectiveness of any form of inside lobbying. Groups in initiative states should therefore be able to obtain policy change through the legislature with the expenditure of fewer resources than in noninitiative states.

While this statement should hold for all interests that can propose an initiative with any chance of passing, it depends critically on the legislature's perceiving that the group can credibly threaten an initiative. Whereas the model assumes that the legislature knows exactly under what conditions the threat is credible, in the real world there may be more uncertainty. For example, the legislature may doubt whether the group has sufficient resources to pay the cost of getting the initiative on the ballot. Once the group has begun to circulate its petition and gather signatures, however, the legislature may begin to see the threat as real and begin to respond more favorably. The final assumption states this more formally.

Assumption 3. (Legislative Responsiveness) *The legislature is more responsive to the threat of an initiative when groups have explicitly begun the process of drafting and qualifying an initiative.*

While the threat of an initiative should always make the legislature more responsive to inside lobbying, in the sense that the group can achieve its goals for less resources, the legislature should probably worry more once the group has demonstrated that it is serious. This is summarized in the following implication:

Implication 6. (Threat of Use) *The threat of an initiative makes the legislature more responsive to an interest group's inside lobbying efforts.*

Another reason to consider the importance of involvement in a specific initiative campaign is that the incentives offered by the initiative should lead to the mobilization of groups that are, all else equal, less effective at inside lobbying. This is, to some extent, the converse of implication 5, which says that groups in initiative states rely more on outside lobbying. If this is at the expense of their inside lobbying skills, then initiative state groups are less effective at inside lobbying. The threat of the initiative may be sufficient to overcome these deficiencies, but it may take more than just an idle threat to make an initiative-mobilized group more effective at inside lobbying. As with campaign contributions, the model (with the additional assumptions) does not predict more or less inside lobbying in initiative states. If the legislature does respond to the threat of an initiative, however, groups that are involved in initiatives should see an increase in the responsiveness of the legislature to their inside lobbying efforts.[51]

Conclusion

Interest groups' responses to the incentives that direct legislation offers them lead to important differences in interest group mobilizations and behavior. While most research on the initiative process focuses on how groups can use it to influence policy or which groups benefit the most from it, the model developed here shows that its consequences extend beyond the immediate realm of initiative politics. Initiative states have interest group populations that consist of a greater number of broad-based membership groups, leading to a shift in interest group resources toward personnel and away from monetary resources. Combined with the fact that the initiative process leads groups to utilize more outside lobbying, even when the target is the legislature, this means that the style of lobbying, and thus whose interests are ultimately represented, is different in initiative states.

The purpose of the model discussed in this chapter is to provide an analytical foundation for making specific predictions about how the initiative process influences interest groups and state policy outcomes. The rest of the book is devoted to empirically testing two of the three predictions and the six implications derived in this chapter. When possible, data are also used to validate the additional assumptions made. Because of the differences between the model's predictions, different types of data are required to test different sets of predictions, with some of them tested in multiple data sources.

The next chapter explores the mobilization and diversity hypotheses (implications 1 and 2) by using aggregate state data on the number and type of registered interest groups. Following that, in chapter 4, I use data on state policy outcomes to test the policy and diffusion hypotheses (predictions 2 and 3). Lastly, I use survey data to test the hypotheses about representation, resources, lobbying tactics, and lobbying strategies. Chapter 5 tests the effect of the initiative process on representation and group resources (implications 2 and 3) by comparing the average resources of groups in initiative states with those in noninitiative states. A similar comparison is performed to test the effect of the initiative process on interest groups' lobbying tactics (implication 4). These data are then used in chapter 6 to compare and explain the choice of lobbying strategies and to test whether groups in initiative states rely more heavily on outside lobbying (implication 5) and the effect that the initiative has on their ability to inside lobby (implication 6).

3

Interest Group Mobilizations

> Every political system is organized around a distinct constellation of interests that is the product of its rules, processes, and institutions, none of which are products of natural forces beyond our leaders' control.
>
> —Jack L. Walker (1991), 17

In this chapter, I begin to test the predictions and implications of the model that were derived in chapter 2.[1] Because of the diverse nature of these hypotheses, a variety of data is needed to test all of them. Here, I use data on aggregate state interest group populations to test the mobilization and representation hypotheses. Recall that the mobilization hypothesis (implication 1) states that because of the additional incentives created for mobilization, initiative states have more interest groups than noninitiative states. Furthermore, the representation hypothesis (implication 2) predicts that these additional mobilizations are disproportionately engendered by broad-based membership groups, since they are better positioned to take advantage of the initiative process's benefits than more narrow economic interests.

I begin by discussing the issue of bias in interest group systems and the data that are used to test the mobilization hypothesis and how they are adapted to test the representation hypothesis. I then discuss other theories of interest group mobilization that must be incorporated into my empirical model to ensure that any confounding factors have been accounted for. Following these discussions, I present the empirical results, first for the mobilization hypothesis and then for the representation hypothesis. Finally, I present some additional results that evaluate the main findings of the chapter using an alternative categorization of interest groups into institutions, associations, and membership groups. Overall, the empirical results provide strong support for both of the model's predictions.

Aggregate State Interest Group Populations

The focus of the two hypotheses tested in this chapter is the number and composition of interest groups in a state. This topic has received widespread attention from interest group scholars, because the consequences of lobbying and otherwise influencing government and elected officials depend crucially on whose interests are represented among interest groups that form. If there are particularly onerous burdens to mobilization, whether arising from government regulations or characteristics of potential members, then certain segments of society may not be equitably represented in the interest group system.

Not surprisingly, the evidence clearly indicates that not all interests are equally represented. Study after study has found that economic interests are overrepresented, whereas broader interests are underrepresented.[2] The reason for the skew toward economic groups is generally thought to lie in the collective action problem inherent in mobilizing large numbers of dispersed individuals. As developed by Mancur Olson in *The Logic of Collective Action* (1965), the problem is as follows. Groups that produce public goods, which provide benefits that can be enjoyed by everyone, including nonmembers, have trouble convincing potential members to pay the cost of signing up. The individuals each realize that if enough other people join, they will get to enjoy the fruits of the group's efforts without paying the cost of joining—the classic definition of a free rider. When the involvement of only a few people is necessary for the group to be viable, it may be possible to convince people to join, but as the number of members required for success increases, it becomes increasingly difficult. In the end, this logic implies that as the size of the potential group increases, the ability to successfully mobilize the group decreases.

There are ways, however, that larger groups can attempt to overcome the collective action dilemma. Olson's theory argues that groups can attract members by offering selective incentives—benefits that are only available to people who join—such as magazines, discounted travel and towing, or cheap insurance. According to Olson, people join solely for these benefits, and the group then uses their contributions to advance its political agenda: lobbying is a by-product of what is essentially a business organization. This theory of interest group mobilization has met with mixed responses.[3] It is quite clear that there are in fact a fair number of large membership groups such as the National Rifle Association and Common Cause, but it is also quite clear that many obvious interests have not been able to successfully mobilize.

Besides selective incentives, scholars have sought other motivations for individuals to join interest groups (Moe 1980). These generally fall into two categories: purposive (sometimes referred to as expressive) and solidary benefits. Purposive benefits are the good feeling that accrue to individuals when they take action, such as joining or contributing to an interest group, to support a cause that they believe in. Additionally, scholars have suggested that interest groups provide a way for people to encounter individuals with similar interests; these are known as solidary benefits.[4] In his study of Common Cause members, Rothenberg (1992) finds that while individuals join groups out of curiosity about what the group stands for, they tend to remain members because of purposive benefits.

The vast majority of studies that attempt to explain how groups can overcome the collective action problem and create a more representative interest group system focus on individual-level incentives for joining groups. My theory concerns characteristics of the political system the groups operate in, but it also offers a way to reduce the bias in interest representation. Given that reducing this bias is probably desirable, institutional choices such as the initiative process offer political leaders an opportunity to reduce the consequences of the collective action problem. Thus, one of the most important indirect effects of the initiative process is to increase representation in interest group systems.

To test for this effect, I use data from Gray and Lowery's *The Population Ecology of Interest Representation* (1996), which sought to explain variation in the size and composition of state interest group populations. These data are ideal for testing the effect of the initiative process on interest group mobilizations, but have not been used for that purpose previously. Specifically, the data include the total number of interest groups that registered to lobby in each state in 1975, 1980, and 1990. Additionally, the total number of groups is broken down into ten subcategories, which permits me to separate them into economic and citizen groups to test the representation hypothesis.

While these data constitute the most complete picture of state interest group populations and offer an excellent opportunity to test my hypotheses, it is important to consider the role of lobbying registration in determining how many groups are observed in each state. Whereas the hypotheses generated by the model are about mobilization, the data only count groups that mobilize and register in a given year. Certainly some groups will be overlooked, but how does this affect the results? One of the advantages of using registered groups is that in most cases, groups are required to register before they can lobby the legislature and attempt to influence policy outcomes. Groups that do not register to lobby are essentially putting themselves on the sidelines, at least temporarily. Given the assumptions of the model that groups are interested in policy outcomes and lobby the legislature to achieve their goals, the registration requirement seems appropriate.

Furthermore, it is also likely that this requirement biases the data against my hypotheses. This is because of the differences between registration requirements for lobbying the legislature and getting involved with statewide initiatives, particularly due to the relative lack of reporting requirements for groups that contribute to ballot initiatives. Since groups can be involved in initiatives without registering, the ones that are most likely to be overlooked are those that are the product of initiative mobilizations.

Gray and Lowery's study also provides some support for assumption 1, which states that the costs of mobilization do not systematically vary between initiative and noninitiative states. By requiring groups to register to lobby, states are influencing the cost of mobilization. While similarities in this one cost do not demonstrate that the assumption is valid, a lack of differences at least indicates that it is not invalid in regard to this one specific type of cost.[5] While Gray and Lowery (1996) note that there are "variations in the restrictiveness of lobbying registration laws as well as variations in the rigor of their enforcement" (8), they conduct tests (appendix 1) and conclude that "the impact of lobbying regulation on registrations appears to be minimal and of uncertain direction" (257). Further work also indicates that various measures of the restrictiveness of lobbying regulations do not influence the size of interest group subpopulations (Gray and Lowery 1998). Given these findings, then, I can at the minimum state that the assumption is still reasonable.

Given that the data provide a strong measure of the quantity of interest for the mobilization hypothesis, I now explain how I use them to test the representation hypothesis as well. Since the focus of the Gray and Lowery study was differences across interest group subpopulations, the data for their study are broken down into ten different categories. For the purposes of testing my theory, I only need to consider the effect of the initiative on economic and citizen groups. I therefore partition the total number of groups into these categories based on the ten original subpopulations.[6] Although this partitioning is somewhat subjective and there are undoubtedly some groups within these categories that are misplaced, it is the most appropriate division of the ten categories, and any miscategorizations across the two subpopulations are likely to bias the results against my hypothesis of an asymmetric effect.[7]

The total number of groups and the number of groups in the two subpopulations are presented in table 3.1.[8] Overall, the average number of groups in a state over the three time periods is 384. This increases from 196 in 1975 to 342 in 1980 and 587 in 1990. Turning to the two subpopulations,

Table 3.1
Average Size of State Interest Group Populations and Subpopulations

	Initiative States	Noninitiative States	All States	*t* statistic (w/Florida)	*t* statistic (w/o Florida)
All Groups	427	346	384	-1.41†	-0.94
	(430)	(239)	(340)		
All Groups, 1975	226	172	196	-1.56†	
	(147)	(89)	(122)		
All Groups, 1980	352	333	342	-0.35	
	(178)	(178)	(176)		
All Groups, 1990	681	507	587	-1.35†	-0.80
	(581)	(302)	(456)		
Economic Groups	287	249	267	-1.00	-0.47
	(257)	(184)	(221)		
Citizen Groups	141	96	117	-2.14**	-2.00**
	(161)	(75)	(125)		

Source: Gray and Lowery (1996).
Standard errors in parentheses.
** Significantly different from zero at the 0.05 level; † significantly different from zero at the 0.10 level (one-tailed test)

there are, on average, 267 economic groups and 117 citizen groups. Note that this proportion of citizen groups, 70 percent, is about the same as studies of the Washington, D.C., lobbying community have found (Schlozman 1984, Baumgartner and Leech 2001).[9]

So what effect does the initiative process have on interest group mobilization? Comparing the average number of groups across years and categories indicates that it has a consistently positive effect, providing evidence consistent with the mobilization hypothesis. Over the entire time period, initiative states have 427 groups compared with 346 for noninitiative states, making them about 22 percent larger. In 1975, the numbers are 226 to 172; in 1980, the gap decreases a bit—352 compared with 333; and in 1990, the gap increases—681 compared with 507. Not only are some of these increases politically large, but many are statistically significant as well, as indicated by the values of the test statistics reported in the last two columns. The fourth column presents the *t* statistic for a difference in means test.[10] The tests provide preliminary support for the mobilization hypothesis, as the total number of groups in initiative states is significantly greater than in noninitiative states at the 0.10 level with a one-tailed test. This result also holds in 1975 and 1990 individually, though it does not hold in 1980.

One concern exists about these numbers, however. As Gray and Lowery (1996) note, "Florida proved to be an outlier in the 1990 sample, with nearly twice as many registered interest organizations as any other state" (86). While Florida has the largest interest group population in all three years, with 596 registered organizations in 1975 and 872 in 1980, its total of 2,969 in 1990 is much further out of line compared with other states. A more detailed examination of Florida's interest group system (Brasher, Lowery, and Gray 1999) indicates that its status in 1990 is due more to political conflict than to changes in registration requirements. The late 1980s saw an extreme budget crunch that resulted in many proposals for new or greater taxes; this debate, along with other issues, fueled a steady increase in Florida's interest group population from 1980 to 1990. This expansion then reversed itself in the early 1990s until registrations returned to their mid-1980s level. Furthermore, the growth in organizations is almost certainly not caused by changes in lobbying registration requirements, as they occurred almost exclusively during the period from the end of 1990 until 1993.[11]

Because Florida allows constitutional initiatives, my results could be inflated by the size of its 1990 interest population, so to be conservative the last column repeats the *t*-tests without Florida's 1990 numbers. Given that its interest group population is so great, removing it from the calculation reduces the average number of groups in initiative states from 681 to 577 and makes the difference insignificant. This indicates that Florida is influencing the findings and should be controlled for in subsequent analysis.

Turning now to the representation hypothesis, I compare the relative size of the economic and citizen subpopulations. If the initiative process does asymmetrically benefit broad-based membership groups, I expect their relative increase to be greater than for economic groups. This expectation is supported by the data: there are 287 economic groups in initiative states compared with 249 in noninitiative states, an increase of 15 percent, whereas there are 141 citizen groups in initiative states compared with 96 in noninitiative states, an increase of 47 percent. Comparing the results of the difference in means tests indicates that the increase is only significant, and at the 0.05 level with a two-tailed test, for citizen groups. This result holds with and without Florida in 1990.

Overall, then, this first look at state interest group populations provides support for the mobilization hypothesis and the representation hypothesis. Yet the conclusion regarding the mobilization hypotheses is influenced by the presence of Florida in 1990. When it is excluded, there is not a statistically significant difference in the number of interest groups in initiative states, though initiative states still have more groups. The 1975 numbers, since they are not affected by this problem, do provide support for the hypothesis, as does the comparison between economic and citizen groups. While there are more of both types of groups in initiative states, the difference is only significant for citizen groups, and it is not affected by the exclusion of Florida in 1990. This last result not only provides support for the mobilization hypothesis, but also provides strong support for the representation hypothesis: initiative states' interest group populations are more representative of broad-based membership groups.

With preliminary support for my hypotheses, I now turn to specifying a regression model that allows me to control for other factors that influence interest group mobilizations. In the next section, then, I discuss previous theories that seek to explain the size of interest group populations and use them to identify key control variables. I then estimate the models to isolate the effect of the initiative process on the total number of interest groups as well as on the number of citizen and economic groups. This analysis solidifies the support for both hypotheses.

Theories of Interest Group Populations

Most of the theories about interest group mobilization that I discussed in the previous section focus on individuals' incentives for joining groups and how those incentives influence whether specific groups form. While they serve as an important part of understanding the bias in the interest group system, they are less helpful for understanding variation across states—the collective action problem is essentially the same in every state. At this point, then, I turn to three theories that seek to explain the total number of interest groups in a given political system.

The first theory again comes from Olson. Following up on his earlier book, he sought to address the issue of what effect interest groups have on nations. In *The Rise and Decline of Nations* (1982), he argued that interest groups tend to accumulate over time; once a group has solved the collective action dilemma, it is likely to remain in existence for a while. In a stable society, then, the size of the interest group population gradually increases. Although Olson argued that the consequence of this build-up of groups is to throw sand in the wheels of government and lead to inefficiency and reduced economic growth, the important point for this study is that any empirical model of interest group populations needs to account for time. To do this, I include indicator variables for 1980 and 1990.

Shortly after Olson's work, the Virginia School (Mueller and Murrell 1986; Coughlin, Mueller, and Murrell 1990; Mitchell and Munger 1991) began modeling the incentives for government officials to attract groups and their money. Gray and Lowery (1996, 18) refer to this as the "hey kid, wanna buy some drugs?" model of interest group mobilization: legislators offer policy concessions to groups in exchange for votes and electoral resources to ensure they remain in office. States that have a greater amount of resources should entice more groups to mobilize and seek those resources. To account for this relationship, I include a variable for state and local government expenditures as a percentage of gross state product (GSP).[12]

The final theory of aggregate interest group populations is from Gray and Lowery themselves. In *The Population Ecology of Interest Representation* (1996), they adapt biological theories of species' diversity and density to interest group populations. This model, dubbed the Energy-Stability-Area (ESA) model, posits that the number and type of interest groups in a state are a function of three key components: the energy available for consumption, which they interpret as government output; the stability of the environment, or how similar the political landscape looks from year to year; and area, a state's carrying capacity or total economic activity. Since government spending has already been considered to test the Virginia School's hypothesis, to measure carrying capacity I include real gross state product (GSP) and its square. The square is included to account for the possibility of density dependence, which, as Gray and Lowery argue, occurs because it is harder for additional groups to mobilize when there are already a lot of groups competing for and consuming existing resources. Density dependence implies that states with larger economies have more interest groups, but that the rate of increase is smaller for larger states. To account for energy, I include an indicator variable for divided control of state government.[13]

While all three of these theories are useful for explaining aggregate populations, to test the representation hypothesis I need to explain the number of economic and citizen groups as well. Since there is no reason to expect any of the predictions of these theories to be different for these two subsets of groups, I maintain the same theoretical arguments and thus the same variables.

One additional variable that I include in the model is ideology. This variable is intended to control for the possibility that more liberal states may have a more politically active citizenry and thus more citizen groups. I expect this variable to have its greatest effect on citizen groups, which tend to be more liberal and perhaps more driven by ideology than economic groups. Additionally, this variable may help account for differences in lobbying environment or registration laws.[14]

Methodology

Combining my predictions with the theories outlined in the previous section suggests the explanatory factors that will be used to predict the number of interest groups in each state in 1975, 1980, and 1990. Because the dependent variable is the number of interest groups and can only take on positive num-

$$E\left[\textit{Population Size}_{i,t}\right] = \exp\Big(\alpha + \beta_1 \times \textit{Initiative}_i + \beta_2 \times 1980_t + \beta_3 \times 1990_t + \beta_4 \times \frac{\textit{Government Spending}_{i,t}}{\textit{Gross State Product}_{i,t}} + \beta_5 \times \textit{Real Gross State Product}_{i,t} + \beta_6 \times \textit{Real Gross State Product}^2_{i,t} + \beta_7 \times \textit{Ideology}_i + \beta_8 \times \textit{Divided Government}_{i,t}\Big)$$

bers, estimating the preceding equation using standard linear regression models can produce incorrect findings (King 1988). Models for counts are more appropriate for these data.[15] This leads to following empirical model: where i indexes states and t indexes years. Besides this basic model, I also estimate an alternative model with an indicator variable to account for Florida's possible outlier status in 1990.[16]

Unfortunately, I am not able to include a variable that measures the cost of proposing an initiative in direct legislation states. While the model predicts that initiative states have more interest groups no matter what the cost of placing a proposal on the ballot (if the costs are infinite, this essentially renders the initiative process nonexistent), recall from the previous chapter that the benefit of the initiative accrues only to groups who are willing to pay the costs of proposing one. As these costs decrease, more potential groups will decide to mobilize, since the benefits have become available to them. The problem with including a variable that measures the costs of proposal is that it is highly correlated with the initiative indicator (ρ = 0.89), making it impossible to sort out the individual effects of the two variables, especially with relatively few observations.[17] The coefficient on the indicator variable should therefore be considered an estimate of the average effect of the initiative process on interest group mobilizations.[18]

These estimation issues aside, however, the empirical model should still provide an accurate estimate of the average effect of direct legislation on the number of interest groups in a state. This allows me to test both the mobilization and representation hypotheses.

The Initiative Process and Mobilization

The results for the models of the total number of interest groups with and without the Florida in 1990 variable are presented in table 3.2. A quick glance at both of the models demonstrates consistency in the results. Most important, the initiative indicator is positive and significant in both models, providing strong evidence for the mobilization hypothesis (implication 1). Because of nonlinearities in the count model, the coefficients are not directly interpretable in terms of magnitude. Yet because the initiative variable takes on only values of 1 and 0, the exponentiated coefficient corresponds to the percentage increase in the number of groups as a result of the initiative process. Thus, the initiative process increases the number of groups by 34 percent in the first model and 28 percent in the second model. The effect decreases a little because the second model removes the effect of Florida in 1990. In political terms, then, these effects are large: a 28 percent increase corresponds to 49 more groups in 1975, 85 more groups in 1980, and 136 more groups in 1990.

Turning to the other variables, the results are also similar across the two models. There is a significant increase in the number of groups over time as the two year variables are positive and strongly significant in each model. This is consistent with Olson's theory of interest group accumulation. The results for government expenditures, which are included to test the Virginia School's model of interest group enticement by legislators seeking reelection, are not as supportive. In both models, the coefficient is wrongly signed and is nowhere near traditional significance levels.

The next two variables, real GSP and its square, test the ESA model's concept of area and its related density-dependence argument. The linear component is, as expected, positive and significant in both regressions, offering support for the ESA's concept of area. The squared term is negative and significant in both models, providing evidence for the ESA model's concept of density dependence—as the carrying capacity of a state increases, the number of interest groups increases, but at a declining marginal rate. There is no apparent relationship between divided control of state government and interest group mobilizations in any of three models. These results are consistent with those of Gray and Lowery (1996).

Lastly, the ideology variable produces mixed results. While the estimated coefficient does not vary much across the models, it is only significant in the second model. The positive coefficient indicates that liberal states have more interest groups than conservative states. I expect that this relationship is driven more by citizen group mobilizations than economic group mobilizations. This will be determined in the next section, which studies these two groups separately to test the representation hypothesis.

The Initiative Process and Representation

In the previous section, I showed that states with the initiative process have

Table 3.2
Negative Binomial Regression Results for Total Registered Interest Groups per State in 1975, 1980, and 1990

	Model 1	Model 2
Initiative State	0.29**	0.25**
	(0.12)	(0.11)
1980	0.52**	0.52**
	(0.06)	(0.06)
1990	0.98**	0.94**
	(0.08)	(0.08)
Real GSP	0.78**	0.70**
	(0.17)	(0.15)
Real GSP squared	-0.11**	-0.09**
	(0.03)	(0.03)
Government Expenditures	-0.91	-1.09
	(3.16)	(3.13)
Divided Government	-0.08	-0.05
	(0.10)	(0.08)
Florida in 1990		1.07**
		(0.15)
Ideology	0.01	0.01*
	(0.01)	(0.01)
Constant	4.95**	5.03**
	(0.39)	(0.39)
$\ln(\alpha)$	-1.88**	-1.96**
	(0.17)	(0.17)

N=134.
Robust standard errors (clustered by state) are reported in parentheses.
** Significantly different from zero at the 0.05 level; * significantly different from zero at the 0.10 level (two-tailed test). Overdispersion measured by $\alpha=\exp(\ln(\alpha))$. Due to missing data, results are based on multiple imputation using Amelia (Windows version). See Honaker, Joseph, King, Scheve, and Singh (2001) for more information.

more interest groups. The next test of the model is whether these additional groups are more likely to be broad-based membership groups rather than economic groups. So in this section, I test the model's representation hypotheses, implication 2. I do this by running the model for the economic and citizen group subpopulations, as described above. The preliminary evidence from table 3.1 shows that while there are significantly more citizen groups, the difference in the number of economic groups is not significantly greater. The conclusions are now subjected to a more detailed regression analysis. First, however, I discuss some evidence in favor of assumption 1, which is the lynchpin for the representation prediction.

Assumption Test: Benefits of Access to the Initiative Process

The key link between prediction 1 and implication 2 is that the ability to propose initiatives is relatively more beneficial for citizen groups than for economic groups. Without this assumption, the model would not predict that initiative mobilizations have a greater influence on the number of citizen groups. Given the importance of this assumption for the representation hypothesis and some of the other implications that are developed from the model, it is worthwhile to consider evidence about whether it is true. I therefore mention some relevant results that offer support for this assumption.[19]

Recall from the previous chapter that I suggested three different reasons why the initiative process might be more useful for citizen groups than for economic groups. First, citizen groups might be better suited to meet the challenges of proposing and passing an initiative. Second, if economic groups are more successful in the legislature than citizen groups, then the ability to have a way to avoid the legislature may be more valuable to citizen groups. Finally, since economic groups do not have as much difficulty overcoming the collective action problem, the additional benefits and immediate salience of proposing an initiative may be more valuable to citizen groups, as it can help ameliorate the collection action problem.

The first argument has been explored in detail by Gerber in *The Populist Paradox* (1999). The central question in that book is whether economic interest groups have co-opted direct legislation for their own benefits, contrary to the original intent of Populist and Progressive reformers. After examining which types of groups are involved in favor of and in opposition to initiatives and whether those initiatives passed, Gerber concludes that "direct legislation outcomes show that economic groups find it very difficult to pass new initiatives, whereas citizen groups are much more successful at modifying policy through the direct legislation process. Economic groups are more successful at blocking measures through opposition spending" (119). Thus, the evidence from this extensive study is clearly in support of my assumption of an asymmetric benefit in favor of citizen groups.

This has also been studied in Donovan, Bowler, McCuan, and

Fernandez (1998), which examined a sample of all California general election initiatives from 1986 to 1996 and coded the type of groups that were in favor of each initiative and those that were opposed to it. Breaking groups into either diffuse or narrow interests, it found that thirty-nine of the fifty-three initiatives during this period were supported by diffuse interests, while narrow interests supported the other fourteen. This evidence also indicates that broad-based groups are more likely than narrow interests to use the initiative process to seek policy change, even ignoring the fact that broader interests are consistently found to represent a significant minority of the interest group universe. This provides support for the veracity of the first or second justifications for my assumption—if the first is not true, and economic groups are at least as well situated to propose initiatives, then the fact that citizen groups still do it more often would indicate that they have a disproportionate number of opportunities to do so. Additional support for the first assumption is provided by the finding that initiatives supported by narrow interests are less likely to pass than those supported by diffuse interests, independent of opposition.[20]

In a similar study involving all initiatives on statewide ballots from 1898 to 1995, Ernst (2001) uses a coding scheme that divides proponents and opponents into "narrow-material interests" and "other interests." He then divides the data into three time periods and compares the sources of support and passage rates within the four categories. While the results from all three periods are consistent, those for the period 1981–95 are perhaps most relevant. Similar to the previous study, a majority of initiatives (56 percent) receive support from his "other" category, whereas the "narrow-material" category supports the other 44 percent. Once again, initiatives supported by "narrow-material" groups were less likely to pass than those supported by groups from the "other" category.

Although these last two studies provide support for my assumption by looking at sources of support and opposition for initiatives that are on statewide ballots, I have elsewhere used the survey data that is utilized in chapters 5 and 6 to study which groups attempt to use the initiative process to effect policy change (Boehmke 2003a). The crucial difference in that study, relative to the two just mentioned, is that it includes a random sample of groups in initiative states rather than starting with initiatives that have already made the ballot and then determining which groups were on which side. The survey asked the groups to discuss a specific public policy that they had been involved with recently and then asked whether they had attempted to use the initiative process to achieve their goals.[21] These data have the advantage of indicating which groups try to use the initiative process, even though some of them will ultimately fail to get their proposal on the ballot (or may withdraw it as a result of legislative action). If the financial burdens of proposing initiatives are more difficult for citizen groups to bear, they may be less well represented in a sample that only includes initiatives that make the ballot.

By examining which groups become involved in supporting a potential initiative, this study also offers support for the assumption being tested. First, groups with more revenue are significantly less likely to get involved in favor of potential initiatives. Second, groups with larger memberships are significantly more likely to get involved, especially when they have the financial resources to qualify an initiative. The model also finds that groups that lobby more often and those that are in more conflictual environments are significantly more likely to turn to the initiative process.[22] The profile of a group that attempts to use the initiative process would therefore appear to be more consistent with broad-based membership groups than narrow economic groups.

Finally, there is also evidence that states with more citizen groups experience greater initiative usage (Boehmke 2003b). In fact, this study also finds that states with more economic groups actually experience fewer ballot measures. While this study does not link specific groups to each measure, in conjunction with the earlier studies just outlined, it indicates that citizen groups are responsible for initiative proposals.

The evidence from all five of these studies is consistent with assumption 1, thereby bolstering the foundation for the representation hypothesis. Of course, demonstrating that the assumptions used to derive a prediction are reasonable is not the same as demonstrating the accuracy of that prediction. It is to that task that I now turn.

Analysis of Interest Diversity

The results for the analysis of the two subpopulations are presented in table 3.3.[23] In both models, the effect of the initiative process is both positive and significant. Translating the coefficients into numbers of interest groups indicates that there are about fifty-three more economic groups and thirty-nine more citizen groups in direct legislation states.

While these findings essentially reconfirm the mobilization hypothesis, to test the representation hypothesis I need to determine whether the increase in the number of groups is proportionately greater for citizen groups compared with economic groups. Comparing the exponentiated coefficients indicates that the percentage increase among economic groups as a result of the initiative process is 22 percent. For citizen groups, the increase is 45 percent. So while the increase is substantial for both categories, the relative effect is twice as large for citizen groups. Thus, the evidence strongly indicates that the relative effect of the initiative process is

Table 3.3
Negative Binomial Regression Results for Total Economic and Citizen Groups per State in 1975, 1980, and 1990

	Economic	Citizen
Initiative State	0.20**	0.36**
	(0.10)	(0.14)
1980	0.50**	0.57**
	(0.05)	(0.08)
1990	0.92**	0.98**
	(0.07)	(0.09)
Real GSP	0.75**	0.58**
	(0.14)	(0.17)
Real GSP squared	-0.10**	-0.07**
	(0.03)	(0.03)
Government Expenditures	-0.19	-3.09
	(2.95)	(3.65)
Divided Government	-0.03	-0.06
	(0.08)	(0.11)
Florida in 1990	0.91**	1.38**
	(0.13)	(0.20)
Ideology	0.01	0.02**
	(0.01)	(0.01)
Constant	4.54**	4.13**
	(0.37)	(0.44)
ln(α)	-2.05**	-1.58**
	(0.17)	(0.17)

N=134.
Robust standard errors (clustered by state) are reported in parentheses.
** Significantly different from zero at the 0.05 level; (two-tailed test). Overdispersion measured by α=exp(ln(α)). Due to missing data, results are based on multiple imputation using Amelia (Windows version). See Honaker, Joseph, King, Scheve, and Singh (2001) for more information.

much greater for citizen groups than for economic groups, providing strong evidence for the representation hypothesis.

Having demonstrated support for both the mobilization and representation hypotheses, I now briefly address how the findings in the two subpopulations relate to the other theories previously discussed. Again, there is strong evidence of interest group accumulation over time, and the coefficients indicate that the relative increase is the same for both types of groups. Also, there is no evidence that either government expenditures or divided government influence the number of interest groups in either subpopulation. Finally, both subpopulations exhibit significant evidence of density dependence.

Lastly, it is interesting to note that while ideology has a significant effect on the number of citizen groups, it does not have one in the model for economic groups. Whereas citizen group mobilizations are greater in more liberal states, the number of economic groups is independent of a state's liberalness. In terms of actual mobilizations, the coefficient of 0.02 for citizen groups implies that a two standard deviation increase in state ideology (equivalent to going from California to Louisiana) adds about thirty citizen interest groups.

An Alternative Test of Representation

The previous section provided strong evidence in favor of the representation hypothesis, but the data offer another way to investigate this question. The Gray and Lowery study (1996) also includes a different breakdown of the data, but only for 1990. This alternative coding includes the percentage of groups in each of three categories: institutions, associations, and membership groups.[24] By multiplying the percentages for each type of group by the total number of groups used in the previous section, I can generate totals for each of these three interest group subpopulations. Institutions include groups like hospitals, universities, and other public and private corporate entities. These correspond mainly to economic groups. Membership groups generally have individuals as members and correspond most strongly to the citizen group category. While associations have members, they are collections of other groups or institutions, and it is not obvious which category they fall into. According to the representation hypothesis, then, the membership categories should be increased the most, though each category should be affected to some degree. Unfortunately, the first two categories include groups with autonomous individuals, organizational representatives, and other groups, which may reduce any observed effect.[25]

The average number of interest groups in each of the three categories for both initiative and noninitiative states are presented in table 3.4. On average, institutional interests comprise about 46 percent of a state's interest group populations, whereas membership groups are 23 percent of the total. The number of groups of each type is greater in initiative states, as the mobilization hypothesis predicts: 344 versus 234 institutions, 171 ver-

Table 3.4
Average Number of Groups by Alternate Categorization in 1990

	Noninitiative States	Initiative States	*t* statistic	
			w/ Florida	w/o Florida
Institutions	233.82	344.26	-1.46†	-0.95
Associations	156.04	171.14	-0.52	0.23
Membership	111.86	156.22	-1.67*	-1.27

Source: Gray and Lowery (1996).
N=50.
* significantly different from zero at the 0.10 level (two-tailed test); † significantly different from zero at the 0.10 level (one-tailed test).

sus 156 associations, and 156 versus 112 membership groups. The *t* statistics indicate that these differences are significant at the 0.10 level for a one-tailed test for institutions ($p = 0.08$) and for a two-tailed test for membership groups ($p = 0.10$). The removal of Florida makes these results insignificant, though only narrowly so for membership groups ($p = 0.11$). As proportions of the population, membership groups make up 25 percent of the total in initiative states and 23 percent in noninitiative states. So a first look at the data provides evidence consistent with the mobilization and representation hypotheses.

As in the previous sections, I ran regression analyses for each of the three subpopulations, using the same variables. Table 3.5 presents the results for the negative binomial regression model that includes the Florida indicator variable. For both institutions and membership groups, the coefficient on the initiative indicator is positive and highly significant. The results indicate that there are ninety-four more institutions, on average, in initiative states and thirty-seven more membership groups. While the coefficient among associations is positive, it does not approach traditional significance levels.

The conclusions for the other theories are essentially the same as before. While the GSP variables and the Florida indicator are significant in all three models, the ideology variable only has a significant effect for associations and membership groups. More liberal states have more of these larger, membership-based groups but do not have more groups that represent institutions.

Although the positive and significant coefficients for membership groups and institutions provide more support for the mobilization hypothesis, they provide less support for the representation hypothesis.

Table 3.5
Effect of the Initiative on Alternate Categorization of Groups in 1990

	Institutions	Associations	Membership Groups
Initiative State	0.36**	0.05	0.29**
	(0.12)	(0.08)	(0.12)
Ideology	0.01	0.01**	0.02**
	(0.01)	(0.01)	(0.01)
Real GSP	0.83**	0.52**	0.46**
	(0.13)	(0.09	(0.13)
Real GSP squared	-0.09**	-0.05**	-0.05**
	(0.02)	(0.01)	(0.02)
Government	-0.28	-1.66	-3.47
Expenditures	(3.31)	(2.38)	(3.40)
Divided Government	-0.08	0.05	0.01
	(0.12)	(0.09)	(0.12)
Florida in 1990	0.95**	0.93**	1.04**
	(0.39)	(0.27)	(0.39)
Constant	4.87**	4.87**	4.87**
	(0.42)	(0.30)	(0.43)
$\ln(\alpha)$	-2.10**	-2.93**	-2.15**
	(0.20)	(0.23)	(0.22)

N=48.
Robust standard errors are reported in parentheses.
** Significantly different from zero at the 0.05 level (two-tailed test).

Despite the fact that table 3.4 indicates that the proportion of membership groups is larger in initiative states compared with noninitiative states, the increases implied by the regression coefficients are 33 percent for membership groups and 44 percent for institutions.

The evidence from this analysis suggests that the increase is actually greater for institutions than for membership groups and that it is statistically nonexistent for associations. The inclusion of membership groups and associations with organizational members may be decreasing the percentage growth in the latter two categories, however. Additionally, these results are based on only one year of data: although the percentage increases are reasonably similar here, the proportionate increase among citizen groups was found to be much larger than for economic groups in the previous section.

Conclusion

The empirical tests in the chapter provide strong support for two of my model's predictions. Analysis of the total number of interest groups in a state demonstrates that the initiative process increases the incentives for interest groups to form, leading to an aggregate increase of about 28 percent. Focusing on different subsets of these groups also leads to the same conclusion: there are significantly more citizen groups, economic groups, membership groups, and institutions. These results confirm the mobilization hypothesis.

These data were also used to test the representation hypothesis. Using the full data set and examining the numbers of citizen and economic groups provides evidence in favor of this hypothesis as well. The initiative process increases the number of citizen groups by 45 percent, whereas it increases the number of economic groups by only 22 percent. The initiative process therefore levels the political playing field somewhat and reduces bias in interest representation by offering broad-based membership groups an alternative means of policy influence. Using a different categorization of groups available only in 1990 leads to a less consistent conclusion, however. Whereas the number of membership groups is significantly greater in initiative states, the increase in the number of institutions is sufficiently large enough that the overall proportion of membership groups does not go up. Given the smaller number of observations and the fact that the percentage increases are closer in these data, on balance it seems fair to conclude that the results provide support for the representation hypothesis, though not as strongly as for the mobilization hypothesis. This implication is revisited in later chapters, which use survey data to compare the average membership of groups in initiative states and noninitiative states.

The main results from this chapter are summarized in figure 3.1, which clearly depicts how the initiative process changes the composition of state interest group populations. Among the first three categories, the larger growth among citizen groups compared with economic groups means that direct legislation states have more representative interest group populations. This reduction in bias may have important consequences for state politics as the balance of power is slightly shifted and different voices may have an opportunity to make their position known. The increases among citizen and membership groups also suggest that initiative states may experience greater citizen participation through group involvement.

Since one of the biggest concerns about interest group representation is its skew toward business and economic interests, the fact that the initiative process decreases this bias may provide a clue as to other changes

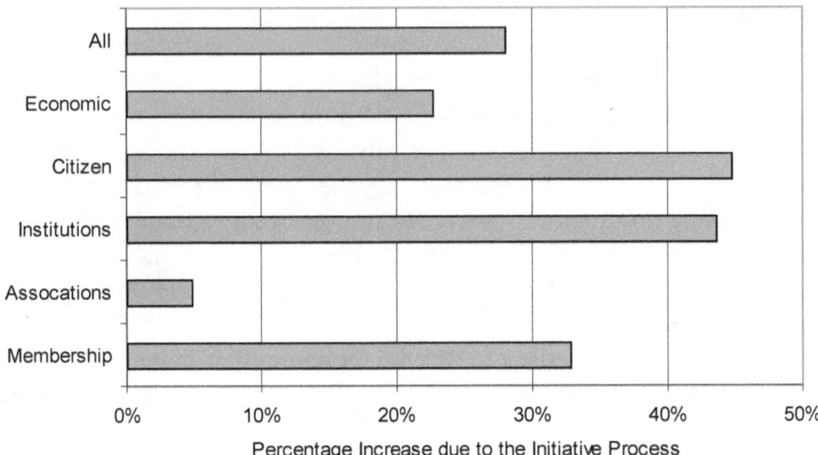

Figure 3.1
Estimated Increase in Interest Group Populations Due to the Initiative Process

in government institutions that could also assist in ameliorating bias. Of course, this chapter does not address whether there are any costs associated with the increase in a state's interest group population that the initiative process brings, which is crucial to determining whether a more representative interest group system is preferable. As Olson (1982) argues, more groups may mean slower policymaking and less effective results.

The results in the next chapter are related to this concern, as it deals with state policy adoption. The main objective, however, is to test the model's policy and diffusion predictions. This is accomplished by examining states' adoptions of capital punishment and Indian gaming operations.

4

State Policy Adoptions

> I love it when the people go to the polls and flex their muscles and let their voices be heard!
>
> —Arnold Schwarzenegger, *The Economist* (2004)

In the preceding chapter, I found evidence in favor of my mobilization and representation hypotheses. This support is consistent with the model's prediction that the expected utility to interest groups is greater in states with the initiative process. In this chapter, I explore whether the incentives offered by the initiative allow groups to engender policy change more often than they could without the initiative process. In addition to the policy adoption hypothesis (prediction 2), I also test the diffusion hypothesis (prediction 3) that policies should diffuse from initiative states to other initiative states.

These two predictions are important because they demonstrate that groups can and do influence policy through the initiative process, both directly and indirectly. It is this influence that provides the incentives for additional groups to mobilize and for existing groups to go to the ballot when they are unsuccessful in the legislature. To propose initiatives and even to credibly threaten to propose them, interest groups must have the resources and political skills required for success. This need, coupled with the experience groups obtain in initiative campaigns, alters the overall lobbying style of groups in initiative states, as outlined in chapter 2. Thus, demonstrating that groups can use the initiative to influence policy is important for establishing the argument that groups in initiative states exhibit different characteristics and behavior.

To test these two predictions, I first review each of them and discuss how to best translate the theoretical predictions into empirical tests. I then discuss related theories of state policy adoption and discuss the appropriate empirical model, an event history analysis. I then provide a brief overview of the two policy areas I study—capital punishment and Indian gaming. Finally, I present the results of the empirical models and evaluate the performance of my two predictions through a series of simulations. I then offer discussion and conclusions.

The Initiative and Policy Adoption

While the previous chapter demonstrates that groups respond to the presence of the initiative process through increased mobilizations, it remains to be seen whether the impact of the initiative process is great enough to allow these groups as well as those that would have mobilized anyway to successfully achieve their policy goals. The model predicts that under certain conditions the initiative process produces different policy outcomes than would obtain without it. Specifically, prediction 2 asserts that direct democracy states adopt policies under a broader set of circumstances than noninitiative states. Furthermore, prediction 3 states that policy diffusion should occur between initiative states but not between other state dyads.

The first of these two predictions is a direct consequence of access to the initiative process for interest groups. Its presence has two effects distinguished by the model. First, if groups are able to lobby the legislature without the initiative process, it reduces the size of the contributions that the group makes. This effect has no direct policy consequences—policy moves with or without the initiative process—it merely makes the group relatively better off while making the legislature relatively worse off. The second circumstance occurs when the group cannot effectively lobby the legislature without the initiative process. When the probability of passing an initiative is sufficiently large, the threat of the group's proposing an initiative may induce the legislature to accept contributions and move policy itself rather than risk a vote. In this case, policy is certain to move, whereas without the initiative, it would not have changed. When the probability of an initiative's passing is lower, but not too small, the legislature takes a chance, and the group must propose an initiative. Under these circumstances, policy moves only if the initiative passes, whereas it would not have moved for certain without the initiative. Thus, policy always changes in initiative states whenever it would have moved without the initiative, and sometimes it alters when it otherwise would not have.

One of the important aspects of this prediction is that it does not say that policy change that occurs because of the initiative is through the ballot. Recall from chapter 2 that the legislature accounts for the group's ability to propose an initiative when deciding whether to change policy in exchange for campaign contributions. This consideration decreases the amount that the legislature demands, since if it asks too much, the group may balk and propose an all-or-nothing initiative. The legislature's decreased demands may therefore allow the group to make contributions and generate policy change via legislative action, whereas without the initiative, the legislature's monopoly control on policymaking would have allowed it to demand more than the group could offer. This implies that it is not necessary to observe initiatives on the ballot for the possibility of proposal to affect policy outcomes. This point is crucial because it implies that we must look at policies in initiative states in general rather than focusing on initiatives on the ballot.

Evidence of the indirect effect of the initiative process is necessarily harder to come by since it is often unobserved and represents shifts in strategies and negotiations over policy, but in some cases, proponents of policy change have proposed initiatives only to withdraw them once the legislature responds. These events are consistent with the initiative process's potential to provide leverage for individuals and groups seeking to influence policy. An example of the indirect effect occurred in 1998 when Silicon Valley entrepreneur Reed Hastings set out to expand the charter school system in California. State law limited the number of charter schools to one hundred, but Hastings was a strong advocate for greatly expanding this number. Leading a coalition of high-tech companies, Hastings gathered more than one million signatures to qualify a measure for the November 1998 ballot.

The proposed ballot measure would have removed the limit on the number of charter schools, but it was withdrawn after the legislature responded with a compromise bill. The new regulations passed by the legislature and signed by Governor Pete Wilson increased the cap from 100 to 250 charter schools in the following year and allowed for an additional 100 schools each year subsequently. Once the legislature saw that the proposal had strong support and sufficient backing to make the ballot, it chose to respond with legislation that would preempt the measure by expanding the charter school system while still imposing a cap. In response to the legislature's actions, Hastings promised to burn the signature petitions once the bill was signed by Wilson (Billingsley 1998).

Besides these direct and indirect effects on policy wrought by existing groups, the initiative process may also produce different policies through the process of initiative mobilization. As shown in the previous chapter, the incentives the initiative process adds for potential interest groups can often be sufficiently large that a group that otherwise would not have mobilized decides to coalesce and become politically active. The addition of these groups should also have policy effects, since they can help other groups lobby for policy change or may become active on an issue that would otherwise not receive attention from previously mobilized groups. This is precisely the role that Americans for Medical Reform played in many states where groups were attempting to legalize medicinal marijuana. Thus, the mobilization effect may also lead to circumstances in which policy changes because of the presence of the initiative process.

Since this prediction is tested in specific policy areas, it is important to account for how the effect of the initiative process varies from state to state. As the model shows, for a specific policy area, the effect of the initiative depends on how likely a state's voters would be to pass an initiative if one were proposed. For policies that are unlikely to receive majority support, the model predicts that the initiative process has no effect. Because of this, it is important to account for voters' preferences when formulating the empirical test of this prediction. In states where voters are in favor of the policy, the initiative has a positive effect, whereas in states where voters do not favor the policy, it has a small or nonexistent effect.

Turning to the model's second prediction about policy adoption, I expect the initiative process to play an important role in the diffusion of policy between states. Policy diffusion is the process whereby one state's adoption of the policy influences whether another state also adopts that policy. In general, scholars have focused on regional policy diffusion, motivated by theories of social learning (Walker 1969; Glick and Hays 1991; Mooney and Lee 1995; Mooney 2001). The model developed here builds on social learning theory by modeling one specific piece of information that may be useful to state officials when considering whether to adopt a specific policy and by suggesting a mechanism through which one state's adoption can influence another state's decision. Specifically, the information that policy outcomes in a state with the initiative process provide about its electorate's preferences allows interest groups and legislators in states with similar electorates to formulate a more precise estimate of the probability that an initiative proposed in their state would pass. Because policy outcomes in noninitiative states depend only on the legislature's preferences and the lobbying ability of the interest group, outcomes in these states are not affected by outcomes in other states and provide no information to other states. Thus, the model predicts that information should diffuse only from initiative states to other initiative states.

This process helps explain why groups that succeed with initiatives in California often proceed to attempt to replicate their success in Oregon, Colorado, Nevada, and Arizona. After term limits were successfully adopted in California and Colorado in 1992, Arizona, Oregon, Utah, and Washington were among the next batch of states to adopt in 1994. Certainly the process does not always work this quickly, but similar patterns emerge if one examines the diffusion of other policies like medicinal marijuana and anti–affirmative action policies.

To test whether diffusion is a systematic process requires determining if past adoptions by initiative states influence other initiative states' present decisions about whether to adopt. It also requires ascertaining which states decision makers look to for cues about their voters' preferences. If all states are similar, then adoptions by any state are informative. If some states are more similar than others, then adoptions by these states are the most informative. There are many arguments for why neighboring states may play a more prominent role in decision makers' search for information, including engaging in "satisficing" (Simon 1976) to simplify the decision process and for reasons of political and demographic similarity, convenience, political networking, overlapping media markets, and economic competition (Boehmke and Witmer 2004; Rogers 1995; Mintrom and Vergari 1998; Mooney 2001; Walker 1969).

Of course, similarity and nearness are not necessarily enough, as decision makers have to be aware of these facts for them to be informative. For the purpose of testing the diffusion prediction, then, I make the assumption that decision makers are more familiar with the relationship between their voters' preferences and those of voters in nearby states. This assumption also makes sense because states in the same region more often than not will tend to have greater correlations between their voters' preferences. Using nearby states also reduces the risk that an arbitrary "similarity" rule imposed by the researcher will affect the results.

Determining the Effect of the Initiative on State Policy Adoptions

Previous research has utilized many different approaches to test whether the initiative process influences policy adoptions and has reached various conclusions about its impact.[1] Some studies have started by comparing the current frequencies of adoptions by policy area at a given point in time; when initiative states have a higher adoption rate, the difference is attributed to that institution (e.g., Gerber 1999). More detailed analyses let adoption at a given point in time depend on many characteristics of a state, including whether it has the initiative process.[2]

This approach may be problematic conceptually as well, however, since the dependent variable is whether a state has adopted the policy in question and the independent variables are all measured in the current year. The problem is that enhanced explanatory variables change over time: using current values to explain a phenomenon that may have occurred more than twenty years ago generally produces incorrect results. Many of the variables that may affect the timing of adoption, including state finances, income, and partisan control of state government fall into this category. Additionally, my model's diffusion hypothesis is inherently dynamic and requires a model that measures the number of neighbors that have adopted each year.

The appropriate model to use with data where states can adopt the policy at any point over some period of time and at least some of the characteristics of the state vary over that time period is an event history model. This is a special type of duration model for data in which the adoptions can take place in discrete intervals, such as years. These models are commonly used in studies of state policy adoption in areas such as lottery adoptions (Berry and Berry 1990; Pierce and Miller 1999a), casino gaming adoptions (Pierce and Miller 1999b), abortion regulations adoptions (Mooney and Lee 1995), and English-only laws (Schildkraut 2001). Only the last of these studies considers the role of the initiative process in influencing the timing of adoption.

Mooney and Lee (1999b) do suggest one additional issue when they examine repeal of capital punishment in the states: what about the potential for policy repeal? This is important to consider in the context of my model, because if groups can use the initiative process to implement policy change in one direction, their opponents could turn the tables to undo the change. The effect of this is unlikely to wash out the initial effect of the initiative on adoption for two reasons. First of all, initiatives that have passed and have received a majority of votes are obviously going to be hard to repeal in the near future, as the majority would have to reverse itself. If groups were uncertain about how likely an initiative would be to pass beforehand, they will be very unoptimistic about their chances for a reversal immediately after one succeeds.[3]

There are cases where groups have tried to revisit a recent initiative, such as Proposition 28 in California's 2000 election. This measure sought to overturn Proposition 10, which was passed in 1998 and placed a fifty cent tax on cigarette packs. It would also have eliminated the California Children and Families First Trust Fund, which was created to disburse the funds raised by the new tax. In addition, Proposition 28 would have denied voters the right to subsequently impose additional surtaxes on cigarettes through the initiative process, while leaving the legislature free to do so at any time.

Although this measure failed to receive a majority, successful attempts to overturn recent, successful initiatives might require a group with the stature and wealth of the tobacco industry. Their failure also demonstrates how unlikely these about-faces might be to happen within short periods of time. That being said, there is no reason to think that after enough years, perhaps once the initiative's policy has become the new status quo across the country, that groups cannot return to the initiative process to restore the previous status quo. Capital punishment provides one such example (Mooney and Lee 1999b). Second, in many states it is harder to repeal an initiative than to pass a new law. In California, for example, the legislature is unable to rewrite laws that result from initiatives. Other states more typically maintain waiting periods of up to five years before the legislative branch can revise or repeal initiatives. In fact, groups often write ostensibly statutory changes in the form of constitutional revisions to avoid future legislative action (Ellis 2002).

To study these adoptions and test the predictions derived from the model, the approach taken here uses event history analysis to study states' adoptions of capital punishment and Indian gaming operations and to test the model's policy and diffusion predictions. This method allows me to study the effect of both internal state characteristics and external factors, such as other states' adoptions, on a state's choice of whether to adopt. Event history analysis is better suited to testing my hypotheses because of the importance of over-time dynamics such as state-to-state policy diffusion. This method allows me to gain more information than cross-sectional approaches by constructing a data set that measures the characteristics of the unit of observation, in this case a state, in all years in which it could experience a change in the relevant state, or policy.[4]

The dependent variable for this analysis is whether a state adopts casino-style Indian gaming in one case or capital punishment in the other case in the current year. Since the probability of adoption is not observable, I use an indicator variable that is zero until a state adopts, when it is coded as a one. After adoption, a state is dropped from the analysis. This leads naturally to a logit or probit regression model—I use the latter.

The event history model that I estimate takes on the following basic form:

$$\begin{aligned}\Pr(adopt_{i,t}) = F(&\alpha + \beta_1 \times Initiative_{i,t} + \beta_2 \times Signature_{i,t} \\ &+ \beta_3 \times Voter\ Preferences_i \times Initiative_{i,t} \\ &+ \beta_4 \times Initiative\ to\ Initiative\ Diffusion_{i,t} \\ &+ \beta_5 \times Initiative\ to\ Non\text{--}Initiative\ Diffusion_{i,t} \\ &+ \beta_6 \times Non\text{--}Initiative\ to\ Initiative\ Diffusion_{i,t} \\ &+ \beta_7 \times Non\text{--}Initiative\ to\ Non\text{--}Initiative\ Diffusion_{i,t} \\ &+ \beta_8 \times Control\ Variables_{i,t}),\end{aligned}$$

where i indexes states and t indexes time. The first four variables are used to test whether initiative states are more likely to adopt each of the two policies.

The next four variables are used to test for various patterns of state-to-state diffusion.[5] I will detail how these tests are performed in a moment. The control variables will be different for the two different policy areas considered, but they are needed to account for state-specific variation in the probability of adoption. These include factors such as partisan control of government, regional variables, variables to account for time trends, and policy-specific effects such as, for the gaming model, the number of Indian nations in a state and, for the capital punishment model, the state's per-capita murder rate.

An important aspect of testing the model's predictions is to determine which variables are relevant for each of the two predictions and then combine the results before conducting the statistical test. Testing the diffusion hypothesis is relatively straightforward: the coefficient for *Initiative to Initiative Diffusion*$_{i,t}$ should be significantly different from 0. While the theory does not state whether the relationship between neighboring states' voters' preferences is positive or negative, if (as I suspect), it is positive, the coefficient will also be positive. Since the model predicts a lack a diffusion between the other three dyads, these coefficients should be 0.

Testing the policy prediction is a bit more complicated. To test this hypothesis, I will have to combine the effects of the first four variables to determine if the overall effect is significant. The direction of the individual variables is certainly relevant—the signature variable should have a negative coefficient, and the voter preference variable should demonstrate that states where voters are more likely to support the policy are more likely to adopt.[6] Unfortunately, though, even if all of these variables are correctly signed, the overall effect once they are combined could indicate that initiative states are less likely to adopt the policy. A precise test of the prediction therefore involves examining changes in the probability of adoption and not focusing on the individual coefficients.[7]

Policy Adoptions Data

One of the important considerations in testing the model's policy predictions is which policy areas to use for the analysis. In some cases, it is relatively straightforward to think of policy areas where the initiative process has almost certainly played a leading role in determining which states adopt. Examples include medicinal marijuana, term limits, and anti–affirmative action adoptions. In each of these cases, almost every state that has adopted has done so through the initiative process and almost no states without the initiative have adopted. While this does not, of course, guarantee that the presence of the initiative process is the deciding factor in adoption, empirical evidence to this effect could be contested on the basis that the policy areas were selected to give the theory the best chance of success.

Thus, while it would be useful to actually demonstrate the influence of the initiative process on the tax revolt, it seems to be a policy area where it must matter. Likewise, in some recent policy adoptions, the initiative has played a central role. The Americans for Medical Rights group has used the initiative process to legalize use of medicinal marijuana. After their successful campaign for Proposition 215 in California in 1996 and a similar one in Arizona, they also assisted in successful initiative campaigns in 1998 in Oregon, Washington, Nevada, and Alaska. Ballot measures also passed that year in Colorado and the District of Columbia, but were nullified for procedural reasons.

Given that the only states that adopted medicinal marijuana reforms are initiative states, it seems almost certain that the initiative played an important role. Furthermore, that all but one adopted through the initiative itself suggests that legislators could not be persuaded with direct lobbying and campaign contributions. If this is true for all of these initiative states, then perhaps other states are unlikely to adopt through the legislature.

Another policy area where the effect of the initiative process is well documented is term limits (Tolbert 1998). As of 1996, all initiative states but one had passed some form of term limits, whereas no noninitiative states had term limits. This is not surprising since this is a policy area where action through the legislature is extremely unlikely—legislators would experience a relatively large loss in utility, so they are loath to pass these reforms themselves. Interest groups seeking changes are forced to circumvent the legislature by resorting to ballot initiatives. This corresponds quite well to the situation described by my model: the legislature prefers not to adopt the policy, its utility loss (β) from doing so is large, and the probability of passage is reasonably high. This corresponds to situations where the legislature refuses to negotiate and initiatives are proposed, which is consistent with what happened. Thus, term limits is clearly another policy area where the initiative process has had a huge impact.[8] Rather than rely on policies that have predominantly been enacted through initiatives, it is preferable and probably a more challenging test of the model to examine policy areas where the use of the initiative process is less ubiquitous. It is also beneficial to select policies that have relatively different political dynamics.

To study the effect of the initiative on adoptions, therefore, I have selected two notably different policy areas: capital punishment adoptions and adoption of Indian gaming. Capital punishment is a social policy with strong overtones of morality politics, whereas Indian gaming is generally viewed as a tool of economic independence and a question of sovereign rights for Native Americans. These differences are beneficial because different political processes may be at work: if the initiative process matters in these two distinct areas, then I can have more confidence in my conclusions about the accuracy of the model's predictions.

Another advantage of these two policy areas is that they both offer specific starting dates for when states can begin to consider adoption. This is useful in an empirical sense because it leaves no doubt about which year in which to begin the analysis. Capital punishment has been sought by social groups and legislators in response to the Supreme Court's 1972 decision in *Furman v. Georgia,* which declared current versions of capital punishment unconstitutional. This left interest groups and legislators in a position to work quickly to examine public opinion in their state and move forward once a constitutional version of capital punishment was found. Similarly, the rise of Indian gaming began after another Supreme Court decision, *California v. Cabazon Band of Indians* in 1987, which declared that Indian nations have the right to conduct gaming activities on tribal land. In response to this decision, Congress passed the Indian Gaming Regulatory Act in 1988 to set up a framework for states and tribes to establish the parameters for such gaming operations.

Besides being relatively distinct policy areas, capital punishment and Indian gaming adoptions also took place in relatively different eras. Capital punishment adoptions occurred in the 1970s and early 1980s, whereas gaming adoptions did not begin until the 1990s. The political impact of the initiative process has changed significantly between these two time periods, symbolically marked by the passage of Proposition 13 in California in 1978 which set off the tax revolt through the early 1980s.[9]

The post–Proposition 13 era has been characterized by expanded usage, funding, and attention to the initiative process. By the late 1990s, sovereign Indian nations in California were proposing initiatives to expand their gaming rights and spending about $67 million to convince voters to support their cause (Ellis 2002).

The years of adoption for each state and policy are show in table 4.1, which confirms that these policies were adopted in different eras. The most recent capital punishment adoption occurs in 1982, whereas the first Indian gaming adoption occurs eight years later in 1990. Before moving ahead to the two empirical models, I first discuss each of these policy areas in more detail to set the context.

Capital Punishment

Capital punishment adoption is an interesting area to study because of the relative familiarity that most states had with it. Many states had previously adopted capital punishment before the Supreme Court declared it unconstitutional in 1972 in its *Furman v. Georgia* decision. The ruling was

Table 4.1
Years of Policy Adoptions by State

	Indian Gaming	Capital Punishment		Indian Gaming	Capital Punishment
AL		1976	NE	1990	1973
AZ	1992	1973	NV	1990	1973
AR		1973	NH		1974
CA	1990	1974	NJ		1982
CO	1992	1975	NM	1995	1973
CT	1991	1973	NY	1993	1974
DE		1974	NC	1994	1974
FL		1972	ND	1992	
GA		1973	OH		1974
ID	1993	1973	OK	1994	1973
IL		1974	OR	1992	1978
IN		1973	PA		1974
IA	1992		RI	1994	1973
KS	1995		SC		1974
KY		1975	SD	1990	1979
LA	1992	1973	TN		1974
ME			TX		1973
MD		1975	UT		1973
MA		1979	VT		
MI	1993		VA		1975
MN	1990		WA	1991	1975
MS	1993	1974	WV		
MO		1975	WI	1992	
MT	1992	1974	WY		1973

Sources: Indian compacting data taken from list compiled from the Federal Register by the Office of Indian Gaming Management, Bureau of Indian Affairs (last updated July 6, 2000). Capital punishment data from Mooney and Lee (1999a).

based on the majority's belief that in its then-present form, capital punishment constituted cruel and unusual punishment. "All five agreed that the 8th Amendment prohibited capital punishment when it was imposed so rarely that it could not serve any valid social purpose, be it deterrence or retribution" (Meltsner 1973).

While this decision rendered the states' current laws unconstitutional, it was not clear whether the death penalty could be reinstated if the states avoided the constitutional problems found by the Supreme Court. States then had the opportunity to reconsider whether to adopt it in an acceptable form. This created the opportunity for a new policy innovation process and allows me to analyze adoptions after the decision, since all states were forced to enact new capital punishment legislation.[10] In addition, this facilitates the choice of a starting date after which states can be considered potential adopters.

Indian Gaming

The history of Indian gaming follows a much different trajectory, though it also involved a key decision by the Supreme Court. In this case, the Court's decision followed on the heels of a rise in high-stakes bingo and unregulated gaming on tribal lands that was intended to help Indian nations increase their tribal sovereignty and combat budget cuts made during the Reagan administration.

As the scope and stakes of this gambling continued to increase, states began to take measures to try to limit or halt gaming on tribal lands (Mason 2000). This led to the Supreme Court's 1987 ruling in *California v. Cabazon Band of Indians* that the state of California could not prohibit Indian nations from operating gaming establishments on their reservations. This opened the door even wider for the expansion of gaming as a form of economic development for the nations. The Cabazon decision did, however, leave the door open for federal regulation of such gaming.

After much debate concerning the role of Indian nations versus the states in determining what this gaming would entail, Congress responded with the passage of the Indian Gaming Regulatory Act (IGRA) in 1988. IGRA was an attempt by Congress to balance states' rights to regulate the type of gaming their citizens can access with Indian nations' rights as sovereign entities (Mason 2000; McCulloch 1994). One of the key components of IGRA is that states are required to negotiate in good faith to allow tribes to engage in any form of gaming that the state currently regulates; they do not have to allow forms of gaming that are expressly prohibited.[11]

Since its first appearance after passage of the Indian Gaming Regulatory Act in 1988, casino-style Indian gaming has become a nearly $14 billion part of the U.S. and Native American economy.[12] The consequences of this transformation are many, including improving standards of living and increasing the self-reliance of Native American tribes (Cornell, Kalt, Krepps, and Taylor 1998; McCulloch 1994), a dramatic expansion in the availability of casino gaming to many Americans, and the emergence of Native Americans as a powerful force in state politics and, to a lesser degree, federal politics.[13] One avenue of political influence that the nations have pursued since the mid-1990s is the use of the initiative process to help secure gaming. When the governor of Arizona refused to negotiate additional compacts, many of the tribes worked to place Proposition 201 on the 1996 ballot, which passed with 64 percent of the vote. Two years later, tribes in California followed suit with Proposition 5, which not only passed with 62 percent of the vote, but also resulted in one of the most costly initiative campaigns ever, with Indian nations spending about $67 million to counter almost $30 million spent by the opposition, a large portion of which came from Nevada's commercial gaming industry (Ellis 2002).[14]

So although this might seem an unlikely policy issue through which to study the effect of the initiative process given Native Americans' historically low involvement in state politics and lack of financial resources to sponsor an initiative, recent experience indicates that once initial gaming revenues began to grow, Indian nations behaved in much the same way as other interest groups that met with legislative resistance and turned to the initiative process.

Findings for the Effect of the Initiative on Policy Adoption

The trend in adoptions is best seen in figure 4.1, which shows the total number of initiative and noninitiative states that had adopted by each year. All of the capital punishment adoptions occur during the period 1972–82, and 18 of the 34 total are in noninitiative states. While initiative states start out slightly ahead of noninitiative states (7 to 5 in 1973), noninitiative states are ahead with 16 adoptions compared with 14 in initiative states in 1977. It is important to keep in mind that there are only twenty-two initiative states and twenty-six noninitiative states in the sample.[15] This means that even in 1977, 64 percent of initiative states had adopted compared with 62 percent of noninitiative states. The difference in adoptions remains one state until one more noninitiative state adopts in 1982.

The Indian gaming adoptions are more pronounced in terms of initiative state leadership. All but one of the first five adoptions in 1990 were in initiative states. By 1993, there were thirteen initiative states with Indian gaming, but only six noninitiative states had signed compacts. Four more noninitiative states adopt by 1995. to leave the current proportions at 58 percent for initiative states and only 38 percent in noninitiative states. Since initiative states are more likely to have federally recognized Indian nations, it is important to determine whether the different adoption rates are caused by the initiative or the presence of tribes.[16] This suggests that there may be a variety of other factors to control for. Following other studies of state policy adoptions

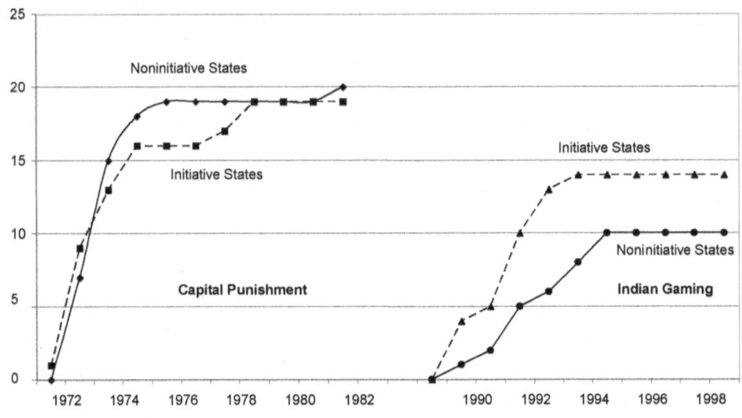

Source : Table 4.1.

Figure 4.1
Total Capital Punishment and Indian Gaming Policy Adoptions by Year

(Berry and Berry 1990; Mooney and Lee 1995), I include controls for state economic performance, state budget performance, the partisanship of state government, and whether the state is in the South.[17]

Besides these general controls, there are specific items that ought to be included in two different areas. For capital punishment adoption, I also include lagged state murder rates per capita to measure the level of violent crime in a state. States with greater levels of violent crime should be more likely to adopt capital punishment as a deterrence. For gaming adoptions, I include the number of federally recognized Indian nations with reservations within a state's borders, whether the state permits commercial casino gaming, and whether the state is one of the six Public Law 280 states.[18] Commercial casino-style gaming is included, because IGRA mandates that states must negotiate for gaming that is not prohibited under state law. Lastly, states with more federally recognized tribes may have greater demand and opportunity to negotiate for gaming.[19] I now discuss the results of the event history analyses for these two areas.

Capital Punishment

The estimates from the event history analysis of state capital punishment adoptions are presented in table 4.2. Given the number of interactions involving the initiative process, it is difficult to immediately assess its overall impact on the probability of adoption. A few observations on the coefficients are in order, though. First, neither the initiative indicator nor the

Table 4.2
Event History Analysis of Timing of Capital Punishment Adoptions

	Coeff.	S.E.
Initiative	-1.317	(0.901)
Signature Requirement	0.069	(0.068)
Religion in Noninitiative States	-0.018	(0.023)
Religion in Initiative States	0.035**	(0.013)
Ideology in Initiative States	-0.075**	(0.031)
Ideology in Noninitiative States	-0.051	(0.050)
Initiative to Initiative Diffusion	0.305**	(0.129)
Noninitiative to Initiative Diffusion	0.466**	(0.180)
Initiative to Noninitiative Diffusion	0.030	(0.254)
Noninitiative to Noninitiative Diffusion	0.144	(0.117)
South	0.726	(0.642)
Murder Rates per Capita	0.060	(0.061)
State population	0.007	(0.032)
Lagged State Debt	0.886**	(0.428)
Lagged State Deficit	0.088	(1.558)
Real per-capita Income	0.160	(0.099)
Change in Real per-capita Income	-1.419	(1.256)
Dem legislature, Rep governor	0.146	(0.332)
Unified Republican government	0.238	(0.413)
Rep legislature, Dem governor	-0.962*	(0.525)
No legislative majority, Dem governor	-0.418	(0.632)
Other Government Outcome	0.443	(0.590)
Cubic Spline (1)	-0.279*	(0.167)
Cubic Spline (2)	0.233*	(0.124)
Cubic Spline (3)	-0.056**	(0.025)
Constant	-5.176**	(2.027)

N=224.
Robust standard errors (clustered by state) are reported in parentheses.
* Significantly different from zero at 0.10 level. ** Significantly different from zero at 0.05 level (two-tailed tests).

signature requirement variable is significant. Yet there is strong evidence of an interaction between the presence of the initiative process and voter preferences, demonstrating that the probability of adoption is affected by direct legislation opportunities. States with a higher proportion of religious fundamentalists, as well as states with more conservative identifiers, are significantly more likely to adopt capital punishment.[20] Combined with the lack of significance for these two variables in noninitiative states, these results appear to provide preliminary support for prediction 2: potential voter support is found to matter in initiative states but not in noninitiative states. And given the lack of significance of the initiative indicator and the signature variable, the overall effect increases the probability of adoption in states with the initiative process.

The second hypothesis tested here is prediction 3 regarding the effect of the initiative on policy diffusion. This hypothesis states that policy diffusion occurs between initiative states, but not between other initiative/noninitiative dyads. The first part of the hypothesis receives support: the coefficient for initiative state to initiative state diffusion is significant at the 0.05 level. The fact that it is positive is consistent with my suspicion that the correlation between voters' preferences in neighboring states is positive. Of the other three variables included for diffusion, only one of them is significant (noninitiative state to initiative state diffusion). Thus, the data do not provide full support for prediction 3: while there is significant initiative to initiative state diffusion, the other three diffusion variables are not all insignificant.

So far I have merely reported on the individual significance of variables that affect the probability of adoption in initiative states. Ultimately, however, prediction 2 is a statement about the combined effect of all of these variables. Furthermore, it is easier to assess the political impact of the initiative process by focusing on how likely a state is to adopt specific policies, rather than examining the regression coefficients. To determine whether access to the initiative process significantly increases the probability that a state adopts capital punishment, I performed a series of simulations to assess how simultaneous changes in all the initiative-related variables affect the probability of adoption. To calculate these probabilities, I start by setting each of the initiative-state-specific variables to 0. These variables are: initiative state, signature requirement, religion in initiative states, ideology in initiative states, and initiative to initiative diffusion. The other variables are set at their mean values for initiative states, and the baseline probability of adoption is calculated using the estimated coefficients. I then change the values of the five initiative-related variables to informative combinations and calculate the change in the probability of adoption.[21] Intuitively, this process allows me to determine the effect of the initiative process on the probability of a hypothetical state's adopting Indian gaming or capital punishment for various levels of voter ideology and specific diffusion pressures.

Given the large number of combinations of the five variables, I focus on a few combinations that convey the overall effect. First, the initiative indi-

Table 4.3
Effect of the Initiative on the Probability of Adopting Capital Punishment

	w/Two Neighbors' Adoptions			
	Ideology			
Religion	0	-10	-20	-30
0	-4.96	3.51	23.45*	49.32*
10	-1.11	11.29	35.39**	60.64**
20	4.78	21.59	48.20**	70.48**
30	12.75	33.53*	60.11**	77.95**
40	22.34	45.61**	69.76**	82.95**
	w/Two Neighbors' Adoptions			
	Ideology			
Religion	0	-10	-20	-30
0	3.23	19.61	44.60**	66.01**
10	10.21	30.64**	56.48**	74.50**
20	19.21	42.76**	67.12**	80.83**
30	29.64	54.49**	75.42**	84.96**
40	40.46*	64.53**	81.12**	87.34**

Numbers are percent change in probability of adopting capital punishment.
** Indicates 95% confidence interval does not include zero. * Indicates 90% confidence interval does not include zero. Calculated using Clarify (Tomz, Wittenberg, and King 2001). Other variables set to their mean (continuous) or modal (dichotomous) values in initiative states.

cator is changed from 0 to 1, and the signature variable is changed from 0 to 5, holding the ideology and religion variables at their baseline values of 0. Even though these two variables do not have significant coefficients, it is important to include them to get an accurate estimate of the overall effect. I then change the two voter preference variables by increasing them from 0 to near their maximum values by increments of 10. To include the initiative diffusion effect, I also change the number of neighboring initiative states' adoptions from 0 to 2 in one case, and 0 to 4 in the second case.

The results of these simulations are presented in table 4.3. The results are broken into two panels: the top panel shows the changes when the two neighbors adopt, and the bottom panel shows the results when four adopt. Within each panel, the rows correspond to values of the religious fundamentalism variable, and the columns correspond to values of the ideology variable. Positive entries mean that initiative states with the given combinations of variables are more likely to adopt capital punishment than similar states without the initiative process, holding all the noninitiative-related variables constant. A quick glance at the table demonstrates that for almost all combinations of the variables, the change is in fact positive, as the model predicts. Further support is provided by the fact that the majority of the increases are significantly different from 0.[22]

To understand the simulation results, consider a hypothetical noninitiative state that scores 0 on both the ideology and religious fundamentalism variables. If this state were to suddenly acquire the initiative process, the model predicts that it would be almost 5 percent less likely to adopt capital punishment in a given year. Of course, this scenario does not include the effect of changing voters' preferences, which were the significant components in the event history results. Imagine now that this hypothetical state had 0 religious fundamentalists, but scored -10 on the ideology scale (about the same as Wisconsin and Ohio). Adding the initiative process to such a state would produce a 3.5 percent increase in the probability of adoption. If this state instead scored -20 on the ideology variable (such as South and North Carolina), the increase in the probability would be 23.5 percent and would be significantly different from 0. Now imagine that this state also had 20 percent religious fundamentalists—the increase in the probability of adoption because of the initiative process becomes 48 percent and is significantly different from 0 at 0.05 level.

The bottom portion of the table shows the change in the probability of adoption when the number of neighboring initiative states with capital punishment is four. If a state with a score of -20 on the ideology scale and 0 religious fundamentalists obtained the initiative process, it would be 45 percent more likely to adopt capital punishment. If the same state instead had 20 percent religious fundamentalists, it would be 67 percent more likely to adopt. Both of these results are significantly different from 0 at the 0.05 level.

Overall, the results indicate that the effect of ideology is greater than the effect of religious fundamentalism. When the number of neighboring initiative states with capital punishment is two, the effect of the initiative process is at least 23 percent and is always statistically significantly different from 0 for any state that scores at least -20 or lower on the ideology variable. With four neighboring initiative state adoptions, the effect is at least 30 percent and is significant whenever ideology is less than or equal to -10, with one exception. Overall, then, these simulations provide strong evidence in favor of prediction 2: initiative states are significantly more likely to adopt capital punishment than noninitiative states.

Table 4.4
Event History Analysis of Timing of Indian Gaming Adoptions

	Coeff.	S.E.
Initiative	-0.591	(0.864)
Signature Requirement	-0.153**	(0.066)
Ideology*Initiative	-0.111**	(0.051)
Ideology	0.123**	(0.062)
Initiative to Initiative Diffusion	0.307*	(0.178)
Noninitiative to Initiative Diffusion	0.465	(0.406)
Initiative to Noninitiative Diffusion	0.672**	(0.317)
Noninitiative to Noninitiative Diffusion	0.520	(0.441)
Federally Recognized Indian Tribes	0.081**	(0.021)
Public Law 280	1.173*	(0.709)
Casino Gaming	1.120**	(0.404)
Southern State	1.979**	(0.736)
State population	-0.162**	(0.066)
Lagged State Debt	-0.077	(0.614)
Lagged State Deficit	-0.296	(2.995)
Real per-capita Income	-0.026	(0.101)
Change in Real per-capita Income	-2.211	(4.393)
Dem legislature, Rep governor	1.179*	(0.644)
Unified Republican government	2.031**	(0.942)
Rep legislature, Dem governor	1.275	(0.919)
No legislative majority, Rep governor	2.506**	(0.759)
No legislative majority, Dem governor	2.145**	(0.770)
Other Government Outcome	3.445**	(1.130)
Cubic Spline (1)	-0.206**	(0.056)
Cubic Spline (2)	0.171**	(0.061)
Cubic Spline (3)	-0.102*	(0.059)
Constant	-2.465	(2.140)

N=364.
Robust standard errors (clustered by state) are reported in parentheses.
* Significantly different from zero at 0.10 level. ** Significantly different from zero at 0.05 level (two-tailed tests).

Indian Gaming

The results for the event history analysis of states' adoptions of Indian gaming are presented in table 4.4. The results are similar to those for capital punishment, but focusing on individual coefficients produces some mild differences. Again, the initiative indicator is insignificant. In this case, though, the signature variable is negative, as expected, and is strongly significant. The voter preference variables indicate that while more conservative states are less likely to adopt Indian gaming, this effect is almost eliminated in initiative states, meaning that adding the initiative to a conservative state makes it more likely to adopt.[23]

Examining the diffusion hypothesis leads to a similar conclusion as well. The coefficient for initiative to initiative state diffusion is positive and weakly significant. Of the other three diffusion variables, however, there is again one that is positive and significant, though this time it corresponds to diffusion from initiative states to noninitiative states. Prediction 3 therefore once again receives mixed support: while the initiative state to initiative state diffusion variable has a significant effect, the other three diffusion variables are not all estimated to be 0.

To determine whether the overall effect of the initiative process is positive and significant, I performed another series of simulations similar to those for capital punishment. Since the religious fundamentalism variable was insignificant and excluded, I therefore focus on changes in the ideology and diffusion variables. The results of the simulations are presented in table 4.5.[24]

These results provide support for the model, though not quite as strong as those for capital punishment. Whereas almost three-quarters of the table's entries are positive and two-thirds of those entries are significant, there are also a few negative entries, one of which is significant. All but one of the negative entries occur for states that score 0 on the ideology variable; the significant case occurs when those states have no adoptions by neighboring states. More important, the average ideology score for initiative states is -15, and there are only two states that have scores greater than -6. Thus, the significant and negative prediction applies to only two of twenty-two initiative states in the sample. For the rest of the initiative states, while they may start out with a statistically insignificant change in the probability of adoption, once the number of neighboring initiative states that have adopted starts to increase, the effect of the initiative quickly becomes positive and is larger for states near the average ideology score. Furthermore, once ideology reaches -20, the effect of the initiative is positive and significantly greater than 0 for almost all cases.

The marginal changes for Indian gaming are not quite as great as for capital punishment, but become substantively large once two neighboring initiative states adopt. For an initiative state that scores -20 on the ideology variable and that has one neighboring state with gaming, the effect of the initiative process is almost 5 percent, and it is statistically significantly different from 0. If the number of neighboring states is instead two, the increase is a

Table 4.5
Effect of the Initiative on the Probability of Adopting Indian Gaming

Neighbors' Adoptions	Ideology			
	0	-10	-20	-30
0	-27.64*	-2.27	2.74	2.86*
1	-24.39	0.15	4.60*	4.50**
2	-19.45	4.29	8.02**	7.52**
3	-12.69	10.59	13.65**	12.57**
4	-4.49	18.90	21.61**	19.91**

Numbers are percent change in probability of negotiating a gaming compact with state Indian tribes.
** Indicates 95% confidence interval does not include zero. * Indicates 90% confidence interval does not include zero. Calculated using Clarify (Tomz, Wittenberg, and King 2001). Other variables set to their mean (continuous) or modal (dichotomous) values in initiative states.

little over 8 percent. Once the number of neighboring states reaches four, the effect has jumped up to 21.6 percent and is still significant.[25]

Overall, then, the results for Indian gaming adoptions provide additional evidence for prediction 2. While there are a couple of states for which the initiative process has a negative effect (those that score near 0 on the ideology scale), this effect is only significant when there is no pressure resulting from adoptions in neighboring states. For most initiative states, the effect of the initiative process is positive and usually significant, particularly when diffusion pressures increase.

Conclusion

In this chapter, I have provided evidence for two more of the model's predictions: prediction 2 and prediction 3. The former states that the presence of the initiative process increases the set of circumstances under which states should adopt policies. The latter prediction states that information diffusion should occur only between states with the initiative process. Analysis of states' adoptions of both Indian gaming and capital punishment provides support for both of these predictions.

The diffusion hypothesis is supported by the positive and significant effect on initiative states of the number of neighboring initiative states that have adopted. The other three pairings are generally insignificant, though there is one exception in each of the two different policy areas. Since the exceptions are for two different pairings, it is not clear if they represent some unknown yet systematic diffusion process or are just idiosyncratic to the specific policy areas studied. Given that these findings are inconsistent, whereas the variable that tests initiative to initiative state diffusion is consistently positive and significant, the results provide evidence only of the type of systematic diffusion predicted by the model. Perhaps future work can investigate the idiosyncrasies across a broader array of policy areas.

The adoption hypothesis is more difficult to test because of the many variables in the regressions that involve the initiative process. While the pattern of significance of the coefficients is important, the true test of the model is whether initiative states are more likely to adopt a policy than noninitiative states. To perform this test, I used the regression results to generate a series of predictions for the marginal effect of the initiative process under a variety a circumstances. These probabilities demonstrate that initiative states are almost uniformly more likely to adopt both policies. And while the results are slightly stronger in terms of significance for capital punishment as opposed to Indian gaming, both policy areas provide evidence that under a broad range of circumstances, initiative states are significantly more likely to adopt policies.

The main findings of the chapter are depicted in figure 4.2. This figure is constructed using the same type of simulations, but shows how changes in citizen ideology determine the influence of the initiative process for two different levels of diffusion pressures. Because ideology has the opposite effect in the two policy areas—more liberal states are more likely to adopt Indian gaming and less likely to adopt capital punishment—the effect of the initiative process is greatest in very different states for the two policies. For capital punishment, the effect is largest in very conservative states like Idaho and South Dakota, whereas for Indian gaming it is greatest in more moderate states like Missouri and Arizona.

Furthermore, the effects are politically large, particularly for capital punishment but also for Indian gaming in more conservative states and when diffusion pressures are strong. In most cases, the increase in the probability of adoption resulting from the initiative process is between 20 and 60 percent per year. Of course, many states do not face such strong diffusion pressures for long periods of time, so the typical influence is probably toward the lower end of this range. Yet one should also keep in mind that the increases in the probabilities of adoption are for a single year and will therefore accumulate over time. Thus, even a 5 percent annual increase in the probability of adoption accumulates into a 28 percent increase in the probability of adoption over a five-year period.

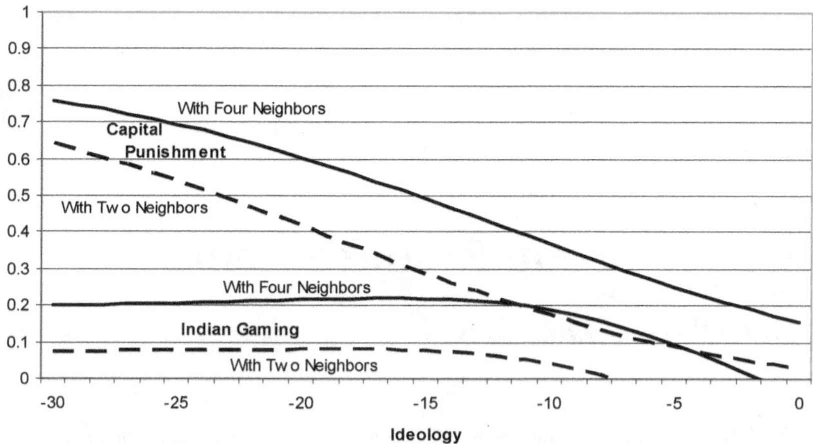

Figure 4.2
Estimated Effect of the Initiative Process on the Probability of Policy Adoption

Besides evidence that the probability of adoption varies, other studies provide indications of how the initiative process may influence the level or extent of adoption. Rather than investigate when states adopt Indian gaming, Boehmke and Witmer (2004) study the number of gaming agreements signed between states and Indian nations. One advantage of this approach is that one can study the direct effect of the initiative process as well as the indirect effect. States such as California and Arizona that pass initiatives see a large increase in the number of subsequent agreements reached. States with the initiative process that do not pass initiatives also see an increase in the number of agreements reached, but it is much smaller and is not quite significant.[26] While not directly testing my model, these results are suggestive that the initiative process does not just influence whether a state adopts, but also influences the extent of adoption. Furthermore, the distinction between the direct and indirect effect of the initiative appears to have some merit.

Combined with the results in the previous chapter, the findings in this chapter establish broad support for two of the model's predictions and two of its implications. Yet so far, all the empirical analyses have utilized aggregate state-level data. To test many of the remaining hypotheses requires data on individual groups' characteristics and lobbying behavior. Therefore, in the next two chapters I turn to individual-level survey data to test the last four of the model's implications and to revisit the representation hypothesis.

5

Interest Group Resources and Lobbying Tactics

> [A]s one reprobates the fanatic who ignores practical considerations and carries his doctrines to extreme lengths, so one should reprobate that type of reasoning that opposes the initiative and referendum on the ground that it will produce every possible absurdity that can be conjured up in the imagination, including the ultimate destruction of representative government.
>
> —Charles A. Beard and Birl E. Schultz (1912), 22–23

The previous two chapters examine the effect of the initiative process on aggregate characteristics of state interest group populations and state policy outcomes. Both of these chapters support my model by showing important differences between initiative and noninitiative states at the aggregate level. While state-level differences are of obvious importance when considering the effect of the initiative process, the model also generates hypotheses about how the incentives offered by the initiative process influence individual groups. Differences at the aggregate level could be caused entirely by initiative mobilizations that add groups, rather than by inducing changes in behavior for groups that would have mobilized anyway. Although my model does not predict that this is the case, studying groups at the individual level helps make the case for both individual and aggregate effects. Thus, to test the remainder of the model's predictions and implications, I analyze data about individual groups' characteristics and lobbying behavior. This chapter, as well as the subsequent chapter, use these data, gathered through a survey of state interest groups, to complete the testing of my model and demonstrate that the initiative process influences organized interests at the level of individual groups.

There are two types of hypotheses left to be tested: those about group resources (implication 3) and lobbying tactics (implication 4) and those about lobbying strategies (implication 5) and legislative responsiveness (implication 6) to those strategies. The first two can be broadly viewed as relating to how the initiative process affects the characteristics of individual groups. Because resources and characteristics help determine how groups lobby, distributional shifts in resources should lead to shifts in which lobbying tactics groups utilize. These two consequences of the initiative process are tested in this chapter by using survey data to compare the average resources and lobbying tactics of groups in initiative states with those of groups in noninitiative states. These differences are important for testing my model, but they also provide an indication and measure of the extent of the effect of the initiative process on state interest group populations.

The second two types of hypotheses concern not just the effect of the initiative on group characteristics, but go further by arguing that even given these characteristics, groups in initiative states behave differently. Thus, interest groups in initiative states should not only look different, but even groups that appear similar behave differently when located in states with the initiative process. After establishing the existence of distributional shifts in this chapter, I test for these differences in behavior in chapter 6.

Separating the effect of the initiative process into its distributional and behavioral components is useful for understanding its overall political impact. Distributional shifts are important because they help determine whose interests are represented in the interest group universe. Behavioral shifts are important because they help determine how those interests are represented. Policymakers must be sensitive to changes in which groups mobilize and must respond to lobbying behavior cognizant of their institutional context.

While the existence of distributional shifts predicted by my model has already been confirmed in chapter 3, this chapter moves from changes in the number and type of groups mobilized to a detailed examination of the characteristics of individual groups. Since groups added by initiative mobilizations are more likely to represent broad-based citizen groups, they should have characteristics that reflect this fact. So not only are there more membership groups in initiative states, but groups in initiative states should have more members. Furthermore, adding traditionally disadvantaged groups should decrease the amount of financial resources and paid staff available to initiative state groups. These differences in resources should also be reflected in their choice of lobbying tactics, with initiative-mobilized groups emphasizing approaches to lobbying that rely on the presence of a broad membership as opposed to those that rely on extensive financial resources.

These distributional shifts in lobbying should be accompanied by behavioral changes as well. Behavioral changes imply that a group with a certain combination of membership and financial resources behaves differently in a state with the initiative process than in a state without it. Direct legislation does not just add new groups to the fold, it alters regular groups' approach to lobbying. For instance, I expect groups in initiative states to place a greater emphasis on outside lobbying strategies as opposed to inside lobbying ones.

Again, these behavioral differences have implications for representation of individuals' interests in and by organized groups. If institutions shape the mix of strategies that groups employ, they may also alter the relative balance of power between different types of groups. A rise in the importance of outside strategies, like protests and mail campaigns, will tend to favor groups that can effectively utilize them (Kollman 1998). If legislators respond to their tactics, then this leads to a different set of policy outcomes that favor different sets of citizens.

The next two chapters provide strong evidence for these differences and support the remaining hypotheses. The results in this chapter provide evidence for the resource hypotheses by demonstrating that groups in initiative states have more members and fewer financial resources, including organizational revenue and staff, than groups in noninitiative states. This finding also provides additional evidence for the representation hypothesis (implication 2) tested initially in chapter 3. The lobbying tactics hypothesis says these differences in resources produce an emphasis on different approaches to lobbying. The tests of this hypothesis indicate that groups in initiative states rely less on certain lobbying tactics, such as contacting legislators and testifying before committees, and more on others, such as using paid advertisements and organizing protests and demonstrations. Since part of my argument is that these differences are caused by experience with and use of the initiative process, I follow up by comparing groups in initiative campaigns with those not involved in initiative campaigns. In chapter 6, I compare lobbying strategies to show that groups in initiative states rely more on outside lobbying strategies and less on inside lobbying strategies, even after controlling for differences in group resources.

Characteristics of Interest Groups

The resource hypothesis (implication 3) states that groups in initiative states tend to have more of the resources that are useful in initiative campaigns, such as a broad-based membership and volunteers and less of the resources that are characteristic of groups that traditionally mobilize in the absence of the initiative process, such as monetary resources and paid staff.

This implication is a result of the incentives that the initiative creates for mobilizations by groups that possess resources that are more useful in initiative campaigns. Based on these differences in resources and the type of campaigns that initiatives produce, implication 4 states that groups in initiative states rely more on lobbying tactics that emphasize these strengths.

To test these implications as well as the remaining two, which are tested in the next chapter, I conducted a survey of state interest groups. To determine the effect of the initiative process on those groups, the survey was designed to include groups in initiative states and groups in noninitiative states. This research design allows me to make direct comparisons of interest group characteristics and lobbying tactics across institutional contexts. This comparison is crucial, since my model generates predictions about how the initiative process influences interest groups. Testing these implications requires a comparison of interest groups operating in states with the initiative process with those operating in states without the initiative process.

The use of surveys to study interest groups has produced a wealth of findings over the past two decades. Although not the first surveys of interest groups, perhaps the two most significant studies are those conducted by Schlozman and Tierney (1986) and Walker (1991). Both of these studies confirmed previous research that argued that the interest group universe is dominated by economic and business interests at the expense of the interests of the typical citizen (e.g., Schattschneider 1960; Salisbury 1984; Olson 1965). These two studies also find that lobbying strategies vary according to group type: citizen groups "tend to rely heavily on political strategies involving public persuasion and mobilization" (Schlozman and Tierney 1986, 198), whereas economic groups do not, focusing more on providing information and working behind the scenes. Further evidence of these differences in lobbying styles is provided by Walker (1991), who conducts factor analysis of group activities and finds two distinct types of strategies revolving around inside and outside lobbying techniques. Regression analysis of the choice of these two strategies indicates that citizen groups and groups with members from the nonprofit sector are more likely to employ outside strategies.

The majority of these studies have, however, focused on the Washington, D.C.-based lobbying community. One exception is a survey conducted by Nownes and Freeman (1998) of groups in California, South Carolina, and Wisconsin. One of their main conclusions is that the inside/outside lobbying distinction made by Walker (1991) is no longer useful, as they find little variation in what groups say they do. Yet this conclusion may be premature, because their study asked groups if they used a tactic at all, rather than asking them how important each tactic was to the overall lobbying effort. Using a finer measure of importance allows me to reevaluate this conclusion and indicates that the distinction still exists, but is more subtle than originally thought. Furthermore, this study did not include questions on groups' involvement with the initiative process. A second state-level survey of interest groups by Gerber (1999) is designed to understand how groups use the initiative process to further their goals; therefore, it necessarily focuses only on groups in initiative states. My survey represents the first state-level examination of the initiative process that compares groups in initiative states with those in noninitiative states.

Survey of State Interest Groups

Survey Sample

To gather the appropriate data for testing my hypotheses, I conducted a survey of state interest groups in the spring of 1999. Taking into account factors besides the presence of the initiative process, such as Gray and Lowery's measures of the diversity and density of group populations (1996), I selected Arizona and Oregon as the two initiative states and New Mexico and Minnesota as the two noninitiative states.[1] The two initiative states were chosen to reflect variation in statewide usage of the process: Arizona is an upper-middle usage state, whereas Oregon is one of the top two users. During the 1990s, there were twenty-two direct initiatives on the ballot in Arizona and only four in 1998, the last election year before the survey was administered. Over the same period, Oregon, one of the highest-use states, had a total of fifty-six direct initiatives on the ballot, with sixteen each in 1994 and 1996. There were only nine in 1998, which was a below-average year. Over the past century, Arizona has had about half as many initiatives per year as Oregon, 1.67 versus 3.13, respectively.[2]

The set of groups to be sampled in each state was obtained by contacting the secretary of state in each case and obtaining the names and addresses of all the groups registered to lobby. Selecting groups based on lobbying registration provides a sample of all groups that can contact the legislature with respect to policy matters. This means that any groups that are systematically excluded are likely to be involved only in the initiative process, so inclusion would only strengthen any results. It also produces data that are comparable to those used in chapter 3 to study the size of state interest group populations.

There were a total of 1,750 registered to lobby in Arizona, 672 in New Mexico, 565 in Oregon, and 1,280 in Minnesota, from which I selected random samples of five hundred groups per state to receive the mail questionnaire.[3] The questionnaire was composed of four sections. The first asked groups about general characteristics such as revenue, group type, or membership levels. The second section asked groups to pick a specific issue—to increase familiarity and avoid what Baumgartner and Leech (1998) term aggregation bias—and answer questions about why they got involved and what lobbying techniques they used.[4] By asking respondents to keep a recent public policy issue in mind when answering questions, these problems are reduced, and the respondents can select an issue that they are knowledgeable about. While for any one group, the issue selected may be atypical, these types of differences should average out over all groups or can be controlled for with more information about the specific issue addressed. The third section, sent only to groups in initiative states, contained questions for groups that indicated they were involved with the initiative process on their current issue.[5] This section contained questions about the extent and nature of this involvement and initiative-related activities the group may have engaged in. The final section asked for details about the respondents, to ensure they were knowledgeable about and had access to information about their respective organizations.[6]

One of the biggest concerns with using surveys to gather data is the problem of response bias.[7] Because it is unlikely that all groups that receive the survey will respond, it is important to consider whether the set of groups that do respond is representative of the original sample or is unusual with respect to the phenomenon being studied. If groups that respond are skewed toward certain types of groups, then the average characteristics of groups that respond may not be an accurate representation of all groups in the state. Since my main task is comparing groups in initiative states with groups in noninitiative states, this problem is only a concern if the factors governing response are different in initiative and noninitiative states, which is unlikely.[8] Furthermore, the problem of representativeness is eliminated by the use of regression analysis, since it controls for the characteristics of groups. However, regression analysis can also be problematic if the groups that respond are atypical in terms of the behavior being studied.[9] Fortunately, these concerns can be alleviated through appropriate statistical techniques and survey design.

To explore the possibility of selection bias and to provide a means to correct for it if any was found, I designed the survey with a dual-sample approach. The primary sample is the two thousand groups selected to receive the mail questionnaire as described above. In addition to these groups, however, I also selected one hundred groups to receive a short telephone survey. These groups were contacted by phone to ensure a high response and to generate a representative sample of groups with which to compare the groups that responded to the mail survey. These groups were asked a small number of questions, including what type of organization they are, how many members they have, and how often they lobby the government. These data can also be used to correct for selection bias in a regression setting using a technique developed in detail elsewhere (Boehmke 2003a).

The dual-sample survey design proved extremely useful in this case. Whereas the response rate for the auxiliary survey conducted via telephone was 78 percent, for the primary mail survey, it was only 17 percent, yielding 306 usable responses. While the latter is low even by the standards of mail surveys of interest groups, which tend to be in the mid- to low twenties, by using the information contained in the auxiliary survey, it is possible to produce results that are more accurate than those obtained with a slightly higher response rate but no additional information.[10] A comparison of these two samples indicates that businesses were extremely less likely to respond to the mail questionnaire than other types of groups: they account for 33 percent of the auxiliary survey but only 10 percent of the mail survey respondents. Thus, the information in the auxiliary sample is used to correct for differential response rates across group types.[11]

The 306 responses indicate the variety of groups and issues in these states and provide sufficient diversity to test my hypotheses. The distribution of different organizations among respondents to the mail survey indicates a diversity of organization types, with 10 percent or more of the responses coming from five different types of groups: trade associations, professional associations, businesses, government associations, and groups in the "other" category. The issues listed by groups also exhibited great variation. Some of the more frequently mentioned subjects include health care, tort reform, taxation, light rail transportation, education, state gaming policies, and election reform. Less frequently mentioned topics include funding to deal with the year 2000 computer bug, allowing beer tastings in grocery stores, and requiring seat belts on school buses. One group in Minnesota even indicated that it was working to establish the initiative and referendum in that state.

Access to the Initiative

Differences in Resources

If the ability to propose initiatives influences the type of groups that mobilize, there should be significant differences between characteristics of the average group in initiative states and the average group in noninitiative states. As implication 3 states, groups in initiative states should have different resources, on average, than groups in noninitiative states. The results obtained in chapter 3 demonstrated that initiative states have significantly more interest groups, especially membership groups. In this chapter, I look more closely at the makeup of these groups.

The first part of the survey asked groups to respond to a series of questions about their characteristics, including membership, financial resources, frequency of government lobbying, and staff size, among others. Each of these questions offered a few categories for answers rather than asking for a specific number. While this reduces the precision of the responses, it should increase the number of responses by making it easier for groups to respond. Neither do they have to spend time determining the exact figure, nor do they have concerns about revealing detailed information. The questions are written so that higher scores on the response scales correspond to higher values of the resource/activity in question.[12] For example, the question on group revenue was phrased as follows: "What was the approximate total (national) revenue for this organization from all financial sources, including grants and contracts, during the last fiscal year?" Categories for this question were coded from 1, for the smallest category, through 6, for the largest category, and similarly for other questions.[13] Thus, the average responses are useful more for comparison than inference about true population values.

To provide a feel for the comparisons about to be made for the different categories, figure 5.1 presents the number of responses in each revenue category for groups in initiative and noninitiative states.[14] The differences across states are striking: the three lowest categories all have more responses from groups in initiative states, whereas the three largest categories all have more responses from groups in noninitiative states. Furthermore, in noninitiative states, the two most common categories are the top revenue values, and in initiative states, the two most common are the lowest and third-lowest revenue categories. These results are precisely those anticipated by my hypothesis about the effect of the initiative process on interest group resources.

Two statistical tests can be performed to confirm the strength of this evidence. The first test just compares the average response in initiative states (3.06) to the average response in noninitiative states (4.08) and calculates a t statistic to determine whether the difference is significant. Not surprisingly, the results for the revenue question indicate that the difference in the average responses is highly significant ($t=2.3$). A second test can be performed to determine whether the distribution of responses across the six categories is different for groups in initiative states. This test can be performed using Pearson's χ^2; for the revenue data, the value of 6.78 is not significant. In general, the results of the t tests are more appropriate for my hypotheses, because they are directional, but the χ^2 tests are more sensitive to subtle differences and are therefore presented also.

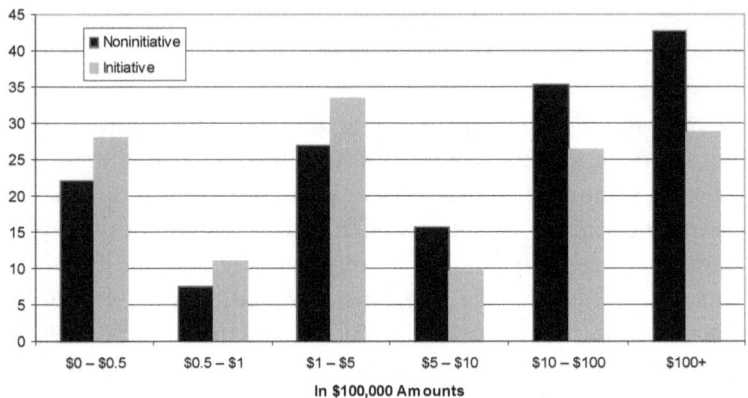

Figure 5.1
Frequency Distribution of Group Revenue by Initiative Possibility

The average responses for the ten measures of group characteristics are presented in table 5.1. The questions about membership, revenue, and paid and volunteer employees are grouped into the resources category; the questions about the group's age, the number of years it has been active on the issue chosen for the survey, and how often it lobbies the government are grouped into the characteristics category; the questions about the number of other groups also active on that issue and the presence and number of other government actors are grouped into the environment category. Note that the questions about years of existence and length of issue involvement did not offer specific categories and are therefore directly interpretable.

Examining the most direct measures of interest group resources provides immediate evidence in favor of my resource hypothesis. Besides the presence of significantly lower levels of financial resources, groups in initiative states have more members and fewer paid employees. The average score on the membership scale (which ranges from 0 to 8) is 2.4, putting them halfway between the 50–100 and 100–250 members categories. Groups in noninitiative states have an average score of 2.0, putting them right at the 50–100 category. The difference is statistically significant using the χ^2 test for the underlying distribution of responses across the different categories, though the *t*-test for difference in means is not quite significant at the 0.10 level with a one-tailed test, because of the relatively large standard errors. In addition to having more members, interest groups in initiative states are significantly more likely to have any members at all: the

Table 5.1
Interest Group Characteristics by Initiative Possibility

	Noninitiative		Initiative				
	Average	S.E.	Average	S.E.	Range	χ^2	*t* statistic
Resources							
Members	1.99	2.81	2.40	2.80	0–8	26.67**	-1.22
Revenue	4.08	1.76	3.60	1.81	1–6	6.78	2.30**
Paid Employees	3.95	2.17	3.61	1.97	1–7	12.30*	1.46†
Volunteer Employees	2.98	2.14	2.99	2.15	1–7	3.17	-0.06
Characteristics							
Group Age	41.53	36.15	35.17	29.39	open		1.65*
Years Active on Issue	13.59	16.36	13.97	19.25	1–7		-0.17
Lobbying Frequency	2.51	1.50	2.33	1.45	1–6	8.98	1.06
Environment							
Other Groups Involved	3.43	1.87	3.39	1.65	open		0.14
Government Actors	0.65	0.48	0.68	0.47	0–1	0.24	-0.48
Number Govt Actors	12.59	52.84	7.12	27.65	open		0.91

Source: Survey of state interest groups (see Appendix C).
Calculated using weights—see Table C.2. Average number of responses in noninitiative states: 141. Average number of responses in initiative states: 120.
** Significantly different from zero at the 0.05 level; * significantly different from zero at the 0.10 level (two-tailed tests); † significantly different from zero at the 0.10 level (one-tailed test). Pearson's χ^2 calculated using response frequencies.

proportion of groups without members is 55 percent in noninitiative states and only 40 percent in initiative states.[15] Thus, the initiative process leads to state interest groups populations that have significantly more members and significantly less revenue, as implication 3 predicts. Additionally, groups in initiative states are significantly more likely to have members at all, which provides additional evidence for the representation hypothesis (implication 2).

While membership and revenue are by far the most relevant characteristics for assessing the effect of the initiative on interest groups, there are other differences as well. Groups in initiative states have significantly fewer paid employees, on average, than groups in noninitiative states. Given the high correlation between revenue and paid staff, this difference is expected. There is not, however, any evidence that groups in initiative states have significantly more volunteer employees. These three differences in resources are crucial, because groups' lobbying strategies are determined in large part by the resources at their disposal. Since groups in initiative states exhibit a different mix of resources, they should emphasize different lobbying techniques.

In addition to the questions about resources, I also asked groups about other aspects of their political activity, including age, amount of government activity, and how conflictual their lobbying environment is. While these questions are not directly related to my prediction about group resources, they help provide a more complete portrait of how the two types of interest group populations compare. They are also linked to the theory of initiative mobilizations. For example, if groups in initiative states encouraged to mobilize by a specific initiative have a more tenuous existence, I would expect that the average group would therefore be younger. The survey included a question to address this possibility by asking groups how long they had been in existence. The results for average group age are consistent with my expectation: groups in initiative states have an average age of thirty-five years compared with forty-two years in noninitiative states. The difference is significant at the 0.10 level with a two-tailed test or at the 0.05 level with a one-tailed test.[16]

None of the other variables have any significant differences. Groups in initiative states indicate slightly higher levels of lobbying activity.[17] Groups in both types of states have been active for about fourteen years on their specific issue. There is about a two-thirds chance that other government actors are also involved on this issue and, if there are any involved, the average number in initiative states is seven, whereas the average number in noninitiative states is almost thirteen. While this latter difference is relatively large, it is not statistically significant. Lastly, groups in initiative states do not appear to be involved in issues that have systematically more or less conflict as measured by the number of other groups involved on that issue.

Overall, then, these results provide support for the resource hypothesis. Specifically, my survey data show that groups in initiative states have significantly less money, fewer paid employees, and more members. Combined with the fact that groups in initiative states are more likely to have members at all, these resource differences also provide support for my representation hypothesis, as it predicts that initiative states have proportionately more membership groups. Further comparisons between groups' basic lobbying environments did not result in many systematic differences, yet this does not imply that groups in initiative states lobby in the same

Table 5.2
Importance of Lobbying Tactics by Initiative Possibility

	Noninitiative		Initiative			
	Average	S.E.	Average	S.E.	χ^2	*t* statistic
Contacting Legislators	4.81	0.54	4.50	0.95	12.90**	3.55**
Policy Research	3.38	1.25	3.41	1.28	3.19	-0.20
Press Releases	2.63	1.33	2.62	1.30	0.55	0.06
Litigation	1.73	1.17	1.86	1.17	9.52**	-0.90
Testifying to Committees	4.09	1.14	3.88	1.32	9.14*	1.47†
Mobilizing Members	3.72	1.35	3.66	1.29	2.11	0.37
Campaign Contributions	2.12	1.42	2.18	1.40	2.88	-0.33
Paid Advertising	1.30	0.77	1.49	0.98	8.19*	-1.81*
Supplying Information	3.74	1.22	3.73	1.16	2.85	0.03
Having Citizens Contact	3.19	1.52	3.20	1.36	6.05	-0.06
Drafting Legislation	3.46	1.46	3.24	1.46	5.44	1.26
Contacting Agencies	3.76	1.40	3.55	1.19	19.06**	1.33†
Public Opinion	2.45	1.34	2.56	1.48	5.36	-0.70
Monitoring Policy	3.48	1.34	3.44	1.34	4.49	0.27
Mail or Phone Campaigns	2.51	1.58	2.59	1.56	1.09	-0.43
Policy Implications	3.01	1.41	3.09	1.49	6.86	-0.45
Electioneering	1.77	1.16	1.97	1.30	4.85	-1.38†
Protests & Demonstrations	1.32	0.78	1.50	0.94	5.22	-1.80*
Seeking Endorsements	2.99	1.53	2.72	1.46	12.18**	1.49†
Building Leg. Coalitions	4.24	0.98	3.78	1.20	13.95**	3.51**

Source: Survey of state interest groups (see Appendix C).
Calculated using weights—see Table C.2. Average number of responses in noninitiative states: 149. Average number of responses in initiative states: 133.
** Significantly different from zero at the 0.05 level; * significantly different from zero at the 0.10 level (two-tailed tests); † significantly different from zero at the 0.10 level (one-tailed test). Pearson's χ^2 calculated using response frequencies.

fashion. In fact, it suggests that if there are differences in lobbying tactics, studied in the following section, they are due to resource differences, as I have argued.

Differences in Lobbying Tactics

Because they have different resources, groups in initiative states tend to emphasize different lobbying tactics (implication 4). Testing this hypothesis requires me to compare the usage of different lobbying tactics for groups in initiative states with those for groups in noninitiative states. The latter should emphasize more traditional, inside lobbying tactics such as contacting legislators and testifying before committees, whereas the former should emphasize outside lobbying tactics like organizing protests and letter-writing campaigns.

To gauge the importance of different lobbying tactics, the survey asked groups to indicate how important each of twenty different lobbying tactics were for them on their specific issue. Groups were asked to respond using a five-point scale, where a 1 corresponded to "not very important" and a 5 corresponded to "very important." Previous studies of state interest groups have found that there is little distinction between inside and outside lobbying tactics (Nownes and Freeman 1998), but this finding may be influenced by the dichotomous nature of the response scale used in their survey, which provides less variation than a five-point scale. So instead of asking groups whether they engaged in a given tactic at all, I asked them to indicate how important each tactic was on a scale of from 1 to 5. This gives a better distinction between tactics that were critical and those that were used but may have been more peripheral.

The average scores for groups in initiative and noninitiative states are presented in table 5.2. Note that there is a wide variation in the importance of different strategies, with paid advertisements and organizing protests and demonstrations receiving scores of 1.3 and contacting legislators receiving a score of 4.8 in noninitiative states. As predicted, there are important differences between groups in initiative states and groups in noninitiative states.

Consider the five tactics on which the *t* statistic for a difference in means indicates that groups in noninitiative states score significantly higher: contacting legislators, contacting agencies, testifying before committees, organizing legislative coalitions, and seeking endorsements from elected officials. They also barely miss scoring significantly higher on drafting legislation. All of these are clearly inside tactics that involve direct contact between interest groups and elected officials. In fact, there are few, if any, essential inside tactics that are not on this list. The results so far are clear: groups in initiative states rely less on inside lobbying, as the logic of initiative mobilizations would suggest.

Do they, however, rely more on outside lobbying tactics, as the model also predicts? Consider the tactics for which groups in initiative states score significantly higher: paid advertisements, electioneering, and organizing protests and demonstrations. These are clearly outside lobbying tactics that do not involve direct interaction between groups and elected officials. There are a few tactics where the difference is as expected, such as organizing letter-writing and telephone campaigns and monitoring public opinion, but is not significant. There is one case where the difference is in the opposite direction, but not near significance: groups in initiative states score lower, on average, on mobilizing members. In the main, though, the results confirm that groups in initiative states emphasize outside lobbying tactics more than groups in noninitiative states. Combined with the results for inside lobbying tactics, the data therefore indicate systematic differences in lobbying behavior in initiative states and provide strong evidence in favor of implication 4.

Motivations for Involvement and Legislative Interaction

Another way to explore how political activity differs between initiative and noninitiative states is to study the reasons that interest groups get involved in specific issues and how they interact with the legislature. While the model developed in chapter 2 makes no direct predictions about these phenomena, the logic of initiative mobilizations has some implications that can be tested. In addition, studying these motivations and choices by interest groups allows me to further document the effect that the initiative process has on interest group populations.

Since initiative politics is high-profile compared with legislative politics—the public is expected to weigh in on any issue that reaches the ballot—groups in initiative states may be more likely to get drawn into issue involvement in response to actions taken by other groups. Furthermore, since the additional groups that mobilize in initiative states are less well-suited to engage in legislative lobbying, they may not be able to organize and implement lobbying campaigns that target the legislature. So when they do become involved in legislative politics, they may do so in a less sophisticated way than better-funded groups that traditionally focus on influencing the legislature.

These differences should manifest themselves in groups' responses to questions about why they are involved in specific issues and what factors influence their interaction with members of the legislature. First, the logic of initiative mobilizations suggests that groups in initiative states should exhibit a more reactive approach to issue involvement. This means that their choices of which issue to lobby on are influenced more by what other groups are doing and less on their own ability to place important issues on the agenda. This problem may be exacerbated by the fact that membership groups have a harder time changing gears and switching issues (Rothenberg 1992), causing their reasons for involvement to be based more on inertia than are those of business groups.

Second, when initiative-mobilized groups do become involved in legislative politics, their choices of which legislators to contact should be influenced by their resources and relative lack of experience. For example, groups with membership resources would tend to contact legislators that can be swayed by public opinion or have large concentrations of members in their district. Examining the responses that groups gave to these two survey questions provides evidence for both of these expectations.

Issue Involvement

To study the effect of the initiative process on issue involvement, the survey asked groups to rate the importance of nine factors in determining their involvement on the specific issue chosen. These factors included measures of issue importance, the actions of other groups, and the desire to indicate support and contribute resources to their side of the conflict. Groups were asked to rate the importance of these factors on a five-point scale. The average responses for groups in initiative and noninitiative states are presented in table 5.3 and confirm my expectation that groups in initiative states are more reactive and less expert.

The biggest difference between motivations for getting involved in their specific issue is the importance of legislative connections. Besides the importance of the issue, this is the highest-scoring reason for groups in noninitiative states to get involved, with an average response of 4.0. In contrast, groups in initiative states give this motivation an average importance of 3.2, and it is only the fourth-most important reason for getting involved. The difference in the scores is highly significant. This result is not surprising given the findings on the type of lobbying tactics that the different groups engage in.

While the importance of the issue to the group is the most important reason for involvement for groups in both types of states, groups in noninitiative states give it a significantly larger importance. Groups in noninitiative states also give more importance to increasing the number of active supporters and to adding resources. The only motivations that groups in initiative states score higher on are responding to opposing groups' actions and gaining information. Only the former difference is significant, however.

The combination of these findings is consistent with my portrayal of initiative mobilizations. Interest groups in states with direct legislation are more reactive in choosing their issues: they cite opposition actions as more

Table 5.3
Reasons for Issue Involvement by Initiative Possibility

	Noninitiative		Initiative			
	Average	S.E.	Average	S.E.	χ^2	*t* statistic
Legislative Connections	3.98	1.33	3.23	1.57	16.31**	4.15**
More Supporters	3.38	1.44	3.08	1.49	4.81	1.63†
Adding Resources	3.27	1.48	2.79	1.35	10.81**	2.63**
Issue's Importance	4.74	0.64	4.50	1.02	16.75**	2.29**
Historical Involvement	3.55	1.31	3.53	1.45	7.39	0.16
Public Duty	3.32	1.45	3.20	1.40	4.34	0.68
Technical Knowledge	3.69	1.23	3.58	1.32	3.17	0.68
Opposition's Actions	2.57	1.61	3.04	1.50	12.63**	-2.38**
Gaining Information	3.07	1.39	3.21	1.44	2.90	-0.80

Source: Survey of state interest groups. Calculated using weights—see Table C.2. Average number of responses in noninitiative states: 143. Average number of responses in initiative states: 114. ** Significantly different from zero at the 0.05 level, (two-tailed test); † significantly different from zero at the 0.10 level (one-tailed test). Pearson's χ^2 calculated using response frequencies.

important and the issue's importance to the group as less important motivations for getting involved. At the same time, they are less likely to cite resource-based motivations, scoring lower on the importance of increasing the number of supporters and increasing the amount of resources available. These findings suggest that initiative-mobilized groups are more likely to get involved not because of what they bring to the battle, such as legislative connections and resources, but because they are drawn in by other groups' activities.

Legislative Interaction

Given that groups in initiative states are less likely to cite contacting legislators as an important lobbying tactic and they are less likely to cite legislative connections as a reason for getting involved, it is reasonable to expect that there might be important differences in which legislators they do contact. Besides allowing me to further elucidate the differences between the behavior of groups in initiative and noninitiative states, any systematic patterns are important for drawing conclusions about the effect of initiative mobilizations on legislative politics. If groups in initiative states tend to contact legislators for different reasons, then we might expect that their ability to successfully influence legislative outcomes also differs. If this is indeed the case, then different lobbying styles and different legislative targets of lobbying may lead to different interests being represented.

The survey questionnaire included an item that asked groups to identify the importance of various characteristics of legislators when deciding whom to contact. Given that the results so far indicate that groups in initiative states have less interaction with the legislature and tend to get involved reactively rather than proactively, I expect that groups in initiative states will cite characteristics of legislators as less important and characteristics of the issue and opposition as more important. Groups that are less involved in legislative politics may not have as many well-established legislative allies to contact when necessary and they may not have as detailed knowledge about how the legislative process works and who the key legislators are. Additionally, groups that have more members and that rely more on outside lobbying tactics may base their lobbying efforts more on a representative's constituency rather than her institutional position, since they may have more success lobbying that way.

The question asked groups to rate the importance, using a five-point scale, of eight different factors in determining which legislators they contacted. These factors include various institutional characteristics such as committee membership, historical issue involvement, and previous interactions, as well as external characteristics such as constituency and activity by other groups. The average importance cited by groups for each of eight different motivations for contacting legislators are listed in table 5.4. There are clear differences in the importance of various factors in determining which legislators groups contact. More important, these differences are consistent with my expectation about the effect of the initiative process. In both types of states, committee membership is the most important reason by a wide margin, but it is more important in noninitiative states, and the difference narrowly misses statistical significance at the 0.10 level with a one-tailed test ($p = 0.11$). Groups in noninitiative states also cite historical issue involvement as more important, but the difference is not near traditional significance levels ($p = 0.18$, one-tailed test).

All of the other motivations received larger average scores from groups in initiative states, and the differences are all statistically significant at the 0.05 level or better, with the exception of previous interaction with a legislator. Two of these again indicate a more reactive lobbying style: initiative state groups contact legislators because other groups have already contacted that legislator or because they are seeking more information on the issue. The

Table 5.4
Reasons for Deciding Which Legislators to Contact by Initiative Possibility

	Noninitiative		Initiative			
	Average	S.E.	Average	S.E.	χ^2	*t* statistic
Committee membership	4.71	0.60	4.60	0.80	2.00	1.21
Historical issue involvement	3.73	1.18	3.58	1.38	6.53	0.92
Previous interaction	3.89	1.00	3.99	1.08	17.53**	-0.76
Constituent characteristics/ concerns	3.27	1.34	3.56	1.25	4.72	-1.69*
Similar policy opinions	3.08	1.25	3.53	1.30	16.19**	-2.72**
Dissimilar policy opinions	2.40	1.19	2.73	1.35	7.61	-1.99**
Other groups already contacted	2.56	1.34	2.92	1.22	7.86*	-2.08**
Request for information	2.79	1.30	3.07	1.27	4.40	-1.69*

Source: Survey of state interest groups.
Calculated using weights—see Table C.2. Average number of responses in noninitiative states: 137. Average number of responses in initiative states: 105.
** Significantly different from zero at the 0.05 level; * significantly different from zero at the 0.10 level (two-tailed tests). Pearson's χ^2 calculated using response frequencies.

other three are directly related to political preferences: groups in initiative states cite constituent characteristics, similar policy opinions, and dissimilar policy opinions as more important reasons for contacting specific legislators.

These results suggest that because of the public nature of initiative campaigns and the requirement of persuading a majority of voters to side with their position, groups in initiative states are more used to gauging public opinion and using that information even when they directly lobby the legislature. This leads them to contact legislators with a large or intense constituency on the issue, since their membership-based lobbying style may help them place pressure on such members. Simultaneously, these findings may be an indication that groups in initiative states have a shallower understanding of the legislative process and are not as well equipped to push their issues in this venue. They rely more on readily observable cues like public opinion, legislative policy preferences, and other groups' actions. This does not imply, of course, that their approach is less effective than that of their counterparts in noninitiative states, just that the presence of the initiative process produces groups that interact with the legislature in a slightly different fashion.

Effect of Initiative Involvement

Most of the predicted differences between groups in initiative states and groups in noninitiative states are based on an understanding of how groups that use the initiative process differ from groups that do not use it. The implications from the model in chapter 2 build on this understanding in a crucial way. While there is ample previous research, reviewed in chapter 3, that suggests that broad-based membership groups benefit from access to the initiative process, and the results in chapter 3 and in this chapter also bolster this expectation, the data from my survey of interest groups provides an excellent opportunity to evaluate these differences in more detail. Most previous research (e.g., Ernst 2001; Donovan, Bowler, McCuan, and Fernandez 1998) utilizes a dichotomous breakdown to conclude that membership groups use the initiative process more than economic groups to implement policy change or compares the number of citizen and economic groups in a state to the frequency of initiative usage (Boehmke 2003b). A more detailed comparison is provided by Gerber (1999), who surveys direct legislation users and non-users.

The three individual-level studies have the common feature that they only include groups whose initiatives actually make it to the ballot. Given that the majority of initiatives that are even submitted to the state for approval before signature gathering begins in earnest do not make the ballot, these studies are not fully capturing the effect of access to the initiative process. Additionally, given the hurdles associated with qualifying an initiative, it is likely that groups whose initiatives make the ballot are not representative of all groups that try to use the initiative process. While it is of obvious importance to understand what types of groups are successful in getting initiatives on the ballot, it is also important to understand what types of groups try to use the initiative process, even though many of them may ultimately fail.[18] Furthermore, as discussed in the presentation of the model in chapter 2, most models of the initiative process predict that besides the direct effect of initiatives on the ballot, there is also an indirect effect of making the legislature more responsive to groups that can threaten to propose an initiative. Consideration only of groups whose initiatives make it to the ballot risks systematically overlooking groups who are successful with indirect influence. If these groups are different from groups that rely on the direct effect, comparisons based solely on groups involved with initiatives on the ballot do not fully reflect the effect of the initiative process on state interest groups.

The survey data collected here thus provide a unique opportunity to compare groups that are attempting to use the initiative process with groups that are not attempting to use the initiative process.[19] A few obvious differences are expected. Groups using the initiative process should have the type of resources that allow them to be more successful in this venue than in direct legislative lobbying. In fact, this is one of the key assumptions underlying my model (assumption 1). Groups that attempt to use the initiative process should have more members and less revenue than groups that are not involved with potential initiatives. Given that these resources also influence groups' overall lobbying style, we would expect to see them reflected in which lobbying tactics are considered important. These differences may not be entirely the same, however, as implication 6 states that using the initiative process may make the legislature more responsive to a group's inside lobbying efforts.

Differences in Resources

If my assumption about which groups attempt to use the initiative process is correct, then these differences should be reflected in the average characteristics of groups currently involved in potential initiative campaigns. Table 5.5 presents the average responses for the survey questions about resources and lobbying environment reported in table 5.1, but compares the average scores only for groups in initiative states, divided into groups involved in potential initiatives and groups not involved in initiatives. Overall, about one-third of the groups indicated involvement in potential initiatives.[20]

As expected, there are notable differences between the two types of groups. Groups involved in potential initiatives have many more members than groups not involved: the average response for the former category is 3.0, whereas the average for the latter is only 2.0. This difference is significant at the 0.05 level even though there is a relatively large amount of variation in responses. Also as anticipated, groups involved in initiatives have less revenue to draw upon, though the difference narrowly misses significance at the 0.10 level ($p = 0.102$, one-tailed test). Another measure of resources is staff size. Here initiative groups have fewer paid staff members, but more volunteers. While the t statistics for differences in means do not indicate a significant difference, the χ^2 statistic for differences in the response frequencies indicate that both variables have significantly different distribution. These four measures of group resources provide strong evidence consistent with assumption 1 and indicate that groups with more members and less revenue are more likely to turn to the initiative process to achieve their goals.

The rest of the variables also produce some interesting results. Groups involved in initiatives tend to lobby more often, are older, and have spent

Table 5.5
Interest Group Characteristics by Initiative Involvement

	Not Involved		Involved				
	Average	S.E.	Average	S.E.	Range	χ^2	*t* statistic
Resources							
Members	1.99	2.55	3.00	3.05	0–8	21.54**	-2.13**
Revenue	3.76	1.84	3.36	1.77	1–6	4.18	1.28
Paid Employees	3.67	2.07	3.51	1.83	1–7	12.32*	0.50
Volunteer Employees	2.81	2.04	3.24	2.29	1–7	14.18**	-1.03
Characteristics							
Group Age	32.29	28.81	39.49	29.98	open		-1.43†
Years Active on Issue	9.69	9.03	18.60	25.49	1–7		-2.44**
Lobbying Frequency	2.46	1.55	2.12	1.26	1–6	4.27	1.39†
Environment							
Other Groups Involved	3.26	1.60	3.54	1.70	open		-0.87
Government Actors	0.68	0.47	0.68	0.47	0–1	0.00	0.01
Number Govt Actors	3.32	11.19	11.79	39.21	open		-1.48†

Source: Survey of state interest groups (see Appendix C).
Calculated using weights—see Table C.2. Average number of responses for uninvolved groups: 81. Average number of responses for involved groups: 49.
** Significantly different from zero at the 0.05 level; * significantly different from zero at the 0.10 level (two-tailed tests); † significantly different from zero at the 0.10 level (one-tailed test). Pearson's χ^2 calculated using response frequencies.

almost twice as long on their current issue. All of these differences are significant. This result suggests that groups may get involved with initiatives on issues for which they have been struggling to achieve success for a long time. Thus, the initiative process may be viewed by better-established groups more as a last resort than as a first approach. Given the high-profile nature of initiative politics and the longer struggles that groups have been through, it is not surprising, then, that there tend to be more other groups involved and more government officials involved, though it is not more likely that any government officials are involved in the first place.[21] Initiative campaigns tend to draw more political actors in, thereby creating a more conflictual environment.

Table 5.6
Importance of Lobbying Tactics by Initiative Involvement

	Not Involved		Involved			
	Average	S.E.	Average	S.E.	χ^2	*t* statistic
Contacting Legislators	4.54	0.93	4.44	0.97	6.95	0.58
Policy Research	3.22	1.32	3.67	1.18	4.74	-2.03**
Press Releases	2.30	1.32	3.07	1.13	18.11**	-3.52**
Litigation	1.94	1.31	1.73	0.94	11.23**	1.00
Testifying to Committees	3.84	1.37	3.94	1.24	10.87**	-0.43
Mobilizing Members	3.53	1.34	3.85	1.20	10.57**	-1.43†
Campaign Contributions	1.96	1.34	2.48	1.44	5.38	-2.11**
Paid Advertising	1.20	0.54	1.89	1.28	19.66**	-4.20**
Supplying Information	3.57	1.24	3.96	0.99	13.46**	-1.93*
Having Citizens Contact	3.17	1.42	3.25	1.29	4.63	-0.32
Drafting Legislation	3.02	1.57	3.55	1.23	9.44*	-2.10**
Contacting Agencies	3.54	1.27	3.57	1.09	4.61	-0.14
Public Opinion	2.05	1.34	3.28	1.39	26.87**	-5.14**
Monitoring Policy	3.33	1.40	3.60	1.25	12.97**	-1.14
Mail or Phone Campaigns	2.16	1.45	3.19	1.52	16.92**	-3.95**
Policy Implications	2.87	1.52	3.42	1.39	5.40	-2.08**
Electioneering	1.71	1.12	2.34	1.46	10.38**	-2.76**
Protests & Demonstrations	1.33	0.72	1.75	1.14	6.86	-2.58**
Seeking Endorsements	2.45	1.51	3.11	1.30	13.42**	-2.60**
Building Leg. Coalitions	3.76	1.24	3.79	1.17	8.78*	-0.11

Source: Survey of state interest groups (See Appendix C).
Calculated using weights—see Table C.2. Average number of responses for uninvolved groups: 84. Average number of responses for involved groups: 50.
** Significantly different from zero at the 0.05 level; * significantly different from zero at the 0.10 level (two-tailed tests); † significantly different from zero at the 0.10 level (one-tailed test). Pearson's χ^2 calculated using response frequencies.

Differences in Lobbying Tactics

The examination of average group characteristics for groups involved in potential initiative campaigns provides support for assumptions about which groups view the initiative as beneficial to achieving their goals. These differences in resources should be reflected in their decisions about which lobbying tactics to emphasize. Clearly, groups involved in initiatives have the resources, the motivation, and often the experience to emphasize outside lobbying tactics. The relationship between initiative involvement and inside lobbying tactics is less obvious. While resource-based arguments would lead one to conclude that these groups should rely less on inside lobbying, the model presented here predicts that use of the initiative process can make the legislature more receptive to the same group's inside lobbying tactics. The net effect on the importance of inside lobbying is therefore not obvious.

The average importance scores for the different lobbying tactics are presented in table 5.6. The results are clear: groups involved in potential initiatives receive much higher scores on almost all of the outside lobbying tactics and score just about the same on most of the inside lobbying tactics. Groups involved in initiatives have average scores that exceed those of groups not involved by at least a full point on two tactics: monitoring public opinion and organizing mail and phone campaigns. They score at least half a point higher on seven tactics: issuing press releases, making campaign contributions, using paid advertisements, drafting legislation, studying implications of proposed policies, electioneering, and seeking endorsements. They also score significantly higher on policy research, mobilizing members, supplying information, and organizing protests and demonstrations. Thus, the data indicate that groups involved in initiatives rely more on outside lobbying tactics as well as tactics relating to elections. The latter finding is potentially related to their experience in previous initiative campaigns and the public nature of their current initiative campaign.

The comparison of the importance of inside lobbying tactics indicates that the resource and threat effects of the initiative process roughly cancel each other out. There are only two tactics that groups involved in initiatives score lower on: litigation and contacting legislators, though neither of these differences is significant. Other tactics with no significant differences include testifying before committees, contacting agencies, building legislative coalitions, and monitoring policies. So while we might expect that groups that are well-suited to use the initiative process are less capable when it comes to inside lobbying (or that groups use the initiative because they have failed at inside lobbying), the data indicate that the threat that a potential initiative poses to the legislature may be enough to make up this ground.

Motivations for Involvement and Legislative Interaction

As in the previous section that examines the differences between initiative and noninitiative state groups, I turn last to a comparison of why interest groups get involved and the reasons they give for which legislators they contact. These two questions help determine what drives involvement in

Table 5.7
Reasons for Issue Involvement by Initiative Involvement

	Not Involved		Involved			
	Average	S.E.	Average	S.E.	χ^2	*t* statistic
Legislative Connections	3.33	1.57	3.11	1.58	6.20	0.74
More Supporters	2.91	1.51	3.28	1.45	3.03	-1.28
Adding Resources	2:80	1.44	2.78	1.25	4.71	0.07
Issue's Importance	4.47	1.17	4.55	0.81	9.88**	-0.38
Historical Involvement	3.46	1.53	3.61	1.36	2.36	-0.55
Public Duty	3.21	1.50	3.19	1.30	3.52	0.05
Technical Knowledge	3.40	1.46	3.80	1.10	10.68**	-1.60†
Opposition's Actions	2.59	1.49	3.57	1.34	16.15**	-3.55**
Gaining Information	3.39	1.39	2.99	1.49	9.05*	1.44†

Source: Survey of state interest groups (see Appendix C).
Calculated using weights—see Table C.2. Average number of responses for uninvolved groups: 68. Average number of responses for involved groups: 46.
** Significantly different from zero at the 0.05 level; * significantly different from zero at the 0.10 level (two-tailed tests); † significantly different from zero at the 0.10 level (one-tailed test). Pearson's χ^2 calculated using response frequencies.

initiative campaigns and how it relates to the factors that determine involvement in more traditional legislative politics. These differences have important consequences for how the initiative process alters the process and level of representation by affecting how and why groups get involved in different issues.

The average importance scores for the nine different reasons for involvement that groups were offered are presented in table 5.7. These results somewhat mirror those for the comparison between initiative and noninitiative state groups. Groups involved in potential initiatives give less importance to factors like legislative connections and gaining information. They give about the same importance to factors like adding resources and public duty. Of these four motivations, only gaining information has a significant difference, however.

The reasons to which they assign greater importance are increasing the number of supporters, importance of the issue, historical issue involvement, technical knowledge about the issue, and opposing groups' actions. These results suggest two things. First, groups get involved in initiatives in response to other group's actions: the differences for responding to opposition is significant. Second, groups involved in initiatives may be better informed: they score significantly higher on technical knowledge and significantly lower on gaining information, which could be caused by their already established knowledge regarding the issue and their longer involvement with that issue, as seen in table 5.5.

Table 5.8 lists the average importance given to different reasons for deciding which legislators to contact. These scores provide further evidence in favor of the reactionary nature of initiative groups. When determining which legislators to contact, groups involved in initiatives rely significantly more on factors such as similar and dissimilar policy opinions and whether other groups have already contacted that legislator. Structural factors such as committee membership are significantly less important as are historical factors such as previous interaction between the group and legislator, though the latter difference is not significant.

The findings here on why groups get involved in initiatives once again suggest that an important component of initiative politics is reaction. Groups get involved with initiatives as opposed to the legislature more in response to what other groups have done rather than focusing on what they wish to accomplish. This may be caused by their inability to successfully influence the legislative agenda, inexperience at effective inside lobbying tactics, or even by the need to put up a fight in order to maintain their membership and stay visible. Even when they do contact legislators, groups involved in potential initiatives focus more on other groups' actions and legislators' policy preferences rather than on institutional characteristics such as committee membership.

Conclusion

The findings in this chapter provide support for my model of the initiative process in two ways. First, comparisons between groups in initiative and noninitiative states provide additional direct evidence about the effect of the initiative process on which groups mobilize and what types of lobbying tactics they emphasize. Groups in initiative states have more members, less revenue, and fewer paid employees, as the resource hypothesis (implication 3) predicts. Additionally, groups in initiative states are significantly more likely to have members, providing individual-level support for the

Table 5.8
Reasons for Deciding Which Legislators to Contact by Initiative Involvement

	Not Involved		Involved			
	Average	S.E.	Average	S.E.	χ^2	*t* statistic
Committee membership	4.71	0.69	4.42	0.93	4.81	1.78*
Historical issue involvement	3.55	1.37	3.63	1.40	0.65	-0.30
Previous interaction	4.08	1.11	3.85	1.03	4.19	1.01
Constituent characteristics/ concerns	3.50	1.29	3.66	1.20	2.21	-0.63
Similar policy opinions	3.34	1.36	3.84	1.16	6.42	-1.91*
Dissimilar policy opinions	2.48	1.25	3.11	1.42	10.03**	-2.20**
Other groups already contacted	2.63	1.23	3.33	1.10	12.74**	-2.88**
Request for information	3.05	1.28	3.10	1.26	0.58	-0.18

Source: Survey of state interest groups (see Appendix C).
Calculated using weights—see Table C.2. Average number of responses for uninvolved groups: 67. Average number of responses for involved groups: 38.
** Significantly different from zero at the 0.05 level; * significantly different from zero at the 0.10 level (two-tailed tests). Pearson's χ^2 calculated using response frequencies.

representation hypothesis in addition to the aggregate-level support found in chapter 3, which showed that there are disproportionately more citizen groups in initiative states.

These differences in resources lead to important differences in which lobbying tactics groups cite as important to their overall objectives. Because groups in initiative states have more members and less revenue, my model predicts that they rely more on lobbying tactics that emphasize these resources. The survey responses given by groups about their choice of lobbying tactics are different in exactly the way expected and provide support for the lobbying tactics hypothesis (implication 4). Groups in initiative states cite outside lobbying tactics such as electioneering and organizing protests and demonstrations as more important and inside tactics such as contacting legislators, agencies, and committees as less important. Ultimately, these differences are likely to have important consequences for initiative-state politics.

The magnitude of some of the important differences is indicated by figure 5.2, which summarizes many of the crucial findings in this chapter. In

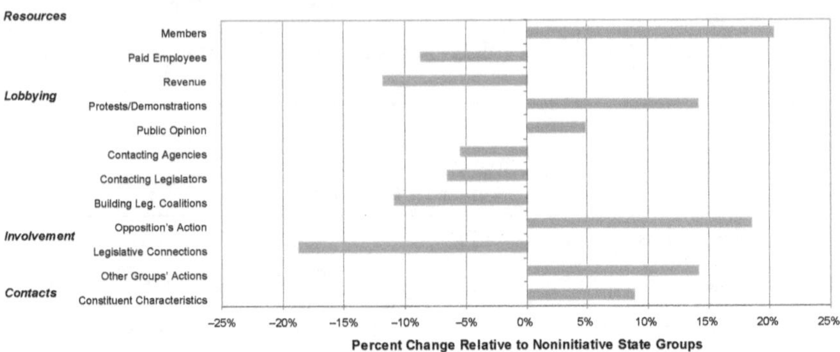

Figure 5.2
Estimated Effect of the Initiative on Interest Group Characteristics and Behavior

terms of the average responses for resources, groups in initiative states score 20 percent higher for members, 12 percent lower for revenue, and 9 percent lower for paid employees. In terms of lobbying tactics, groups in initiative states score 14 percent higher on organizing protests and demonstrations and 5 percent higher on monitoring public opinion. They score lower on contacting agencies (6 percent), contacting legislators (7 percent), and building legislative coalitions (11 percent). For the different reasons for issue involvement, groups in initiative states score 18 percent higher for opposition's actions and 19 percent lower on legislative connections. Finally, for the reasons they cited for contacting specific legislators, they scored 14 percent higher for other groups' actions and 9 percent higher for constituent characteristics.

The second comparison made is within initiative states between groups that are involved in initiative campaigns and groups that are not. This comparison provides additional support for my assumption about which groups use the initiative process. It also mirrors the results of previous research that examines groups that are involved in initiatives that have successfully been placed on the ballot, but does not suffer from the drawback that not all groups that want to put initiatives on the ballot are successful in that regard. Additionally, these studies did not have detailed information on group characteristics and were not able to make direct comparisons between the size of groups' membership and their financial resources. Nor did they have information on legislative lobbying behavior to compare how these resource differentials impact lobbying style. Important for my model, the fact that groups that get involved in favor of initiatives have more members and less revenue provides support for my assumption about which groups benefit from access to the initiative.

Having provided extensive evidence for the fact that groups in initiative states do have different resources and use different lobbying tactics, the last issue to be resolved concerns determining whether these differences in lobbying are caused solely by shifts in groups' resources, or whether they are also caused by choices made by individual groups. That is, having demonstrated that the initiative process influences the distribution of resources among interest groups and hence the distribution of lobbying tactics used by those groups, I must now test whether there is a behavioral difference that alters lobbying strategies above and beyond the shift in resources. In other words, are resource differentials the only reason for a greater reliance on outside lobbying tactics, or does the initiative process more fundamentally alter interest group lobbying choices? This is the question answered in the next chapter.

6

Interest Group Lobbying Strategies

> You can't do anything unless you love it. And I mean I love—absolutely love—this initiative [I-695] and the initiative process. It's fun, the whole thing is fun. The whole idea is fun.
>
> —Tim Eyman, initiative activist (quoted in Ellis 2002, 100)

In the previous chapter, I used survey data from interest groups in initiative and noninitiative states to show that the incentives created by the initiative process lead to distributional shifts in the characteristics of interest groups that mobilize. The average interest group in initiative states has more members and fewer financial resources to draw on. I then showed that these differences in resources lead to differences in the type of lobbying tactics that groups emphasize. Groups in initiative states relied more heavily on outside lobbying activities and less heavily on inside lobbying tactics that involved direct interaction with elected representatives.

These differences are clearly important both for the groups involved in initiatives and for our understanding of how initiative state politics differ from noninitiative state politics. If there are different groups with different resources emphasizing different lobbying tactics, then we might expect that the political process results in different policy outcomes because different groups are more able to get their voices heard. Legislators must be sensitive to the potential for groups to propose initiatives, which increases the relative effectiveness of membership-based groups and groups with public opinion on their side.

The findings in the previous chapter also provide support for three implications of my model of the initiative process. According to my theory of initiative mobilizations, however, ballot access should result in more than just distributional shifts in the composition of state interest group populations. That is, the initiative process induces differences in interest groups' lobbying decisions above and beyond those due merely to shifts in the resources at their disposal. As I argued in chapter 2, because the lobbying tactics that are necessary for successfully waging or threatening an initiative campaign are different from those that are necessary for directly lobbying elected representatives, interest groups in initiative states rely more on these tactics than groups in states without the initiative process. Because initiative campaigns require greater facility with outside lobbying tactics, groups' overall lobbying strategies should reflect a greater reliance on outside lobbying.

The objective of this chapter is to test this prediction, developed from the model as implication 5, as well as to test the effect of the threat of using the initiative process on groups' ability to inside lobby (implication 6). While initiative mobilizations may produce groups that rely more on outside lobbying and less on inside lobbying, the threat of proposing an initiative should lead to an increase in the effectiveness of inside lobbying. Because of these two competing effects, the model makes no clear prediction about the overall effect of the initiative process on inside lobbying. Under the assumption that the legislature perceives the threat as more immediate once a group begins the process of proposing an initiative, stated formally as assumption 5, the model predicts that groups can use this threat as leverage, thereby increasing their ability to successfully lobby the legislature. Thus, groups involved in initiative campaigns should notice an increase in the effectiveness of their inside lobbying tactics. This is the other hypothesis tested in this chapter.

To develop these results, I first explain the difference between lobbying tactics and lobbying strategies. I then use my survey data to construct measures of the different lobbying strategies and interpret the results, following which I compare the average scores of groups in initiative states and groups in noninitiative states. To test my two remaining hypotheses requires controlling for group resources and other factors, so I describe the empirical model I use to test these hypotheses. I then present the results of the empirical models, which provide support for both of the model's implications.

The Effect of the Initiative on Lobbying Strategies

In the previous chapter, I studied the effect of the initiative process on interest group resources and lobbying tactics. Yet an important distinction is made in the interest group literature between lobbying tactics and lobbying strategies. Lobbying tactics are specific actions that an interest group can take to influence policy outcomes. Each of the twenty activities, including mobilizing members, writing press releases, seeking elected officials' endorsements, and the rest in table 5.2, is a different example of a lobbying tactic. Yet groups do not pick willy-nilly from this list of actions when they set out to achieve influence. Most groups combine a few of these lobbying tactics into an overall lobbying strategy. Thus a lobbying strategy is a combination of various tactics that complement each other and provide the best chance for the group to achieve its goals.

This definition parallels that of Walker (1991, 9), who argues that early on in a group's existence, its leaders settle on a strategy that gives it the best chance to maintain and attract members by achieving lobbying success. Many factors determine which lobbying strategy a group decides on: membership composition, sources of funding, resources, and the nature of its lobbying environment. Ultimately, he identifies two different lobbying strategies: inside lobbying and outside lobbying. Groups that use an inside lobbying strategy tend to emphasize lobbying tactics that allow them to work directly with legislators and other elected officials. Groups that use an outside lobbying strategy tend to work through the media and grass roots to put external pressure on political leaders.

These different approaches are reflected among the groups that responded to my survey. An example of an outside lobbying strategy comes from a group in Arizona with few members and small amounts of financial resources. This group's responses to the twenty lobbying activities questions indicate a heavy reliance on outside lobbying. It rated contacting legislators and agencies at 2 on the importance scale and contacting committees and building legislative coalitions at 3, indicating a lower-than-average reliance on core inside lobbying tactics. On the other hand, it reported monitoring public opinion at 3, mobilizing members at 4, and having influential citizens contact policymakers at 5, indicating a heavy reliance on outside lobbying tactics. This type of lobbying approach is clearly different from one that emphasizes close interaction with legislators and other policymakers.

The choice of a lobbying strategy by a group is important for a variety of reasons. Once a group chooses a lobbying strategy, either explicitly or implicitly, this choice guides its decisions about which lobbying tactics to employ. Since government officials may respond differently to inside and outside lobbying, this choice is a crucial decision that shapes a group's ultimate success. This importance is magnified if Walker (1991) is correct in his assertion that groups may have a hard time reversing course once they have begun to emphasize one lobbying strategy over another.[1] This has important implications for interest group populations in initiative states, as the initiative process creates opportunities and incentives to emphasize outside lobbying over inside lobbying. Decisions made during a group's formative years that are shaped by the presence of the initiative process may therefore have long-term implications for how that group's lobbying strategy evolves over time. This may help explain the finding in the previous chapter that interest groups in initiative states tend to be more reactive in terms of their lobbying decisions.

These differences and the potential consequences are based on the predictions of my model. Specifically, the initiative theory of mobilization argues that interest groups that form as a result of the added incentives provided by direct democracy are more likely to depend on outside lobbying strategies because passing an initiative requires a group to mobilize broad support among voters through use of the media and grassroots lobbying. Thus, groups that mobilize in response to the incentives that ballot access creates are more likely to be those that can successfully accomplish these objectives. The evidence in chapters 3 and 5 indicates that these are precisely the groups that are the product of initiative mobilizations. Furthermore, the results from the latter chapter demonstrate that groups in initiative states do emphasize lobbying tactics that are consistent with outside lobbying rather than those that are consistent with inside lobbying.

These differences in lobbying, however, may be entirely due to differences in resources. Yet there are other ways that the initiative process can lead groups to rely more on outside lobbying strategies above and beyond shifts in resources. Two of these involve either learning to outside lobby through previous initiative campaigns or using outside lobbying tactics to signal the willingness and ability to propose an initiative to put pressure on the legislature to act. Groups involved in initiative campaigns obtain greater experience with outside lobbying relatively early in their existence; these groups may then continue to rely on outside strategies disproportionately more than other groups, even when they are trying to achieve their goals through the legislature.

Alternatively, a group may attempt to put pressure on the legislature to act in its favor by signaling support for a potential initiative. The objective of this strategy is to convince the legislature that the group is serious about achieving its goals. Gerber (1999) describes this strategy as indirect modifying: groups do not directly use the initiative process to modify policy, but they use its presence to pressure the legislature to modify policy. The important point is that the initiative process creates incentives for groups to signal support for potential initiatives and that this support is more easily indicated through outside strategies since they correlate with passing initiatives.

These arguments are summarized by my lobbying strategies hypothesis (implication 5) and my threat-of-use hypothesis (implication 6). Implication 5 states that interest groups in initiative states rely more on outside lobbying strategies, even after controlling for resource differentials. Implication 6 states that the threat of initiative proposal makes the legislature more responsive to a group's inside lobbying efforts. If the legislature is unsure about how committed a group is to actually paying the cost of proposing an initiative, if it is not sure that the group can muster the necessary resources, or if it does not believe that the initiative will pass, then by signaling its intentions or demonstrating voter support for its proposal, the group may induce legislative cooperation. While there are many different approaches the group could take to accomplish this, perhaps the most straightforward is to qualify an initiative for the ballot. As the group goes about drafting the initiative, gathering signatures, and campaigning for its passage, the legislature may at some point become convinced that it is in its best interest to work with the group rather than risk an all-or-nothing vote. This is precisely what happened with the charter school reform advocated by Reed Hastings. As described in chapter 4, once Hastings had submitted over a million signatures to place a charter school expansion measure on the ballot, the legislature finally responded with a compromise measure.

To test these two hypotheses requires determining which lobbying strategy groups emphasize, coming up with a measure of groups' use of these lobbying strategies, and then determining the effect of access to the initiative process and involvement with a potential initiative on their use of the different strategies. Ascertaining whether the presence or use of the initiative process alters interest group lobbying strategies above and beyond changes due to resources requires controlling for resources in a regression model. In the rest of this section, I explain the method of determining which strategies groups use, how I construct a measure of each group's reliance on each strategy, and explain the empirical model that I estimate to determine the effect of the initiative on each of them.

An Updated Typology of Lobbying Strategies

Most work on interest group lobbying strategies focuses on the inside/outside lobbying dichotomy described above. This dichotomy is relatively recent, but different types of lobbying strategies have been discussed before. The early focus in the interest group literature was on groups' ability to work within iron triangles where the use of inside strategies was the preferred tactic.[2] There was also some attention to the use of outside lobbying, through which groups try to pressure legislators to act or vote a certain way by demonstrating the existence of broader public support. A real division of lobbying into inside and outside strategies did not emerge, however, until Walker's (1991) study of Washington, D.C.-based interest groups. He conducts factor analysis of groups' responses to their use of eight different lobbying tactics to uncover the underlying dimensionality and nature of lobbying strategies. The results indicate that a group's reliance on the different tactics is best explained by two dimensions: an inside dimension composed of legislative lobbying, administrative lobbying, litigation, and electioneering; and an outside dimension that includes working with the mass media, protests or demonstrations, providing speakers, and sponsoring lay conferences.

Recent work has brought even more attention to this dichotomy and the factors that influence which direction a group will take. Building on Walker's (1991) finding that groups involved in greater levels of conflict are more likely to supplement their inside lobbying activities with outside lobbying, Kollman (1998) conducts in-depth interviews with groups in specific policy areas to better understand the outside lobbying choice. He finds that groups will go outside primarily to expand the conflict arena, particularly at the agenda-setting stage or before prominent votes. These groups generally need certain minimum amounts of favorable public opinion to do this, but there is increasing evidence of false grassroots campaigns—"astroturf" lobbying—conducted by groups to create the false impression in legislators that there is broad support among their constituents when there is, in fact, none.

Both of these studies use data on Washington, D.C.-based groups, so an important question is whether outside lobbying has spread to groups at the state level and how the initiative process influences it. One study that has examined interest group lobbying activity at the state level was conducted by Nownes and Freeman (1998) and concludes that "group politics in the states is now similar to group politics in Washington" (109). Because this implies that traditional inside groups are increasingly using outside techniques and vice-versa, they conclude that "the 'inside/outside' lobbying dichotomy should be rethought: . . . the line between 'inside' and 'outside' is hazy at best" (102).

Part of this conclusion seems valid: professional and business groups are increasingly using outside lobbying to their advantage, "astroturf" or not. On the other hand, it seems premature to conclude that the distinction is of little use. While the rise of mass communication technologies and savvy political marketing makes it easier for groups to stimulate and shape public opinion, legislators' time is still a limited commodity. Whereas groups that have the resources to focus on inside lobbying campaigns can use those resources to attempt to expand their lobbying efforts when necessary, often by hiring public relations firms (Kollman 1998), groups that are used to outside lobbying may have a harder time marshalling the resources necessary to wage a complementary inside lobbying campaign. Furthermore, groups that inside-lobby may do so because they are invited to participate by legislators (Kollman 1997), and invitations may not be extended to all groups. So there are important political reasons to expect that the inside/outside dichotomy still offers a useful distinction for interest group lobbying. One factor that may cause its apparent decline in Nownes and Freeman's data is the coarse measure that they employ: groups are merely asked whether they engaged in a host of activities, rather than being asked to differentiate the importance of each.[3] Studies that allow groups to differentiate between the importance of different tactics consistently find evidence of both inside and outside lobbying (Kollman 1998; Walker 1991).

To generate a measure of different lobbying strategies, I follow Walker's (1991) and Kollman's (1998) lead and construct factor scores from the groups' responses to the importance of the twenty lobbying activities on the survey. Basically, factor analysis assumes that groups' responses for each of the tactics are determined by a smaller number of common factors and tries to estimate the relationship between the different factors and which lobbying tactics a group employs. For example, the choices to contact legislators and contact agencies are probably not distinct, but are rather the consequences of a prior inclination or decision about how to approach a certain issue. Rather than leaving it to the researcher to decide what underlying factors determine lobbying choices, factor analysis has the advantage of estimating the number and type of underlying lobbying strategies.[4]

The lobbying tactics in the survey are designed to elicit information about inside strategies, such as contacting legislators, agencies, or committees, and outside lobbying strategies, such as organizing protests or letter-writing and phone campaigns and should provide sufficient information and variation to estimate what the underlying determinants of groups' lobbying choices are. The responses are made using a five-point scale, where a 1 indicates that the strategy was not considered important and a 5 indicates that the group considered it to be very important. The number of responses varies from 275 for election campaigning to 290 for contacting legislators. The latent dimensions were computed using principle components, and the observations were weighted to reflect the true distribution of groups using the information gained in the auxiliary sample.

The results of this analysis are presented in table 6.1. The numbers represent how each lobbying tactic relates to the two different lobbying strategies.[5] Larger numbers indicate that a tactic is part of that lobbying strategy and smaller numbers indicate that it is not. Tactics that score high on one dimension and low on the other are not complementary, as they are part of distinct lobbying strategies. Overall, the relationship between the two dimensions, or factors, and the lobbying tactics that score high or low on each suggest that the two dimensions correspond to the familiar inside and outside lobbying strategies, though with some differences. The results were easiest to interpret when ordered by the second dimension, which appears

Table 6.1.
Factor Analysis of Lobbying Tactics: Principal Components' Eigenvectors

	Factor 1	Factor 2
Paid Advertising	0.194	0.368
Electioneering	0.171	0.334
Campaign Contributions	0.148	0.329
Protests & Demonstrations	0.155	0.242
Mail or Phone Campaigns	0.294	0.204
Public Opinion	0.259	0.165
Litigation	0.113	0.153
Mobilizing Members	0.285	0.087
Press Releases	0.235	0.081
Policy Implications	0.285	0.023
Seeking Endorsements	0.186	-0.006
Having Citizens Contact	0.200	-0.006
Monitoring Policy	0.266	-0.032
Policy Research	0.264	-0.123
Supplying Information	0.219	-0.176
Drafting Legislation	0.254	-0.184
Contacting Agencies	0.157	-0.202
Building Leg. Coalitions	0.235	-0.295
Testifying to Committees	0.245	-0.316
Contacting Legislators	0.189	-0.412
Proportion	0.271	0.114

Source: survey of state interest groups (see Appendix C).
N=245. Calculated using weights—see Table C.2

to correspond strongly to the traditional outside lobbying strategy. The first dimension loads highly on many of the traditional inside lobbying tactics, but also on some of the outside lobbying tactics as well, suggesting that traditional inside lobbying approaches have been augmented by some outside lobbying tactics as well.

Modern Inside Lobbying

The first dimension has high loadings for all the traditional inside lobbying techniques: contacting legislators, doing policy research, contacting agency officials, testifying before committees, responding to requests for information, having influential citizens contact policymakers, monitoring policy, building support among groups of legislators, and seeking public endorsements. Clearly, these are groups that have strong ties to the legislature and are able to work within it to further their policy goals. As Nownes and Freeman (1998) suggest, though, these groups are also expanding into some outside techniques. Activities that also load high on this dimension include writing press releases, mobilizing members, monitoring public opinion information, and organizing mail and phone campaigns.[6] This finding is consistent with Kollman's analysis, which finds that corporations and trade associations use public relations firms to outside lobby.

There is strong evidence, then, that traditional groups have taken advantage of some aspects of outside lobbying and have incorporated it into their bag of tricks. It is no longer sufficient to stick with the old methods of inside lobbying; groups have been forced, or have decided, to go outside as a regular part of their lobbying strategies. To reflect this apparent evolution of the traditional inside lobbying strategy, I refer to this dimension as modern inside lobbying.

Traditional Outside Lobbying

The second dimension indicates that despite the encroachment of the inside lobbying strategy on outsider tactics, there is still a large set of groups that only utilize traditional outside lobbying tactics. These are groups that may have trouble accessing the legislature and are forced to use their comparative advantages in organizing protests and other tactics to further their goals. This dimension has high loadings for tactics such as campaign contributions, paid advertisements, organizing mail and phone campaigns, election campaigning, and organizing protests. It also has reasonably high loadings for public opinion, mobilizing members, and litigation.

Unlike the inside lobbying dimension, the outside lobbying dimension exhibits many factors with strong negative loadings. As might be expected, they are all inside tactics: contacting legislators, testifying before committees, responding to requests for information, drafting legislation, contacting agency officials, and building support among groups of legislators. These are all activities that loaded high on the first dimension, so the clearest demarcation between these two dimensions is that the second relates to groups that cannot get access for some reason. Groups that are excluded from policy decision makers do their best to utilize a host of outside lobbying techniques. The inside/outside dichotomy is not dead, as Nownes and Freeman (1998) have suggested; it is just that the inside groups have expanded their repertoire while the outside groups have not been able to: going outside may be easier than getting inside.

The Initiative and Lobbying Strategies

Now that I have determined the presence of two lobbying strategies, the next step is to generate a score for each group for each strategy so that I can study how groups' resources, environment, and the initiative process affect the choice of which strategy to use. The inside score is generated by multiplying the importance the group assigned to each tactic by the loading of that tactic for the inside strategy in table 6.1 and then adding them all up. The score on the outside lobbying dimension is generated the same way, but using the loading of each tactic on the outside dimension. Thus, each group has an inside lobbying score and an outside lobbying score. High scores on a dimension indicate that the group used that strategy, whereas low scores indicate the group did not use that strategy.

For example, a group that indicates that contacting agencies and legislators and testifying before committees are important would score high on the inside lobbying dimension but low on the outside lobbying dimension, since these tactics have large and positive loadings for the former and large and negative loadings for the latter. A group that gave low responses for the importance of these strategies would score much lower on the inside lobbying dimension, but higher on the outside lobbying dimension. The previously mentioned Arizona group that employed an outside lobbying strategy had a very low -5.9 score on the inside lobbying strategy and a relatively high value of 1.9 on the outside lobbying strategy.

Figure 6.1 provides histograms of the scores for the two lobbying strategies for groups in initiative states and groups in noninitiative states. The scores range from a low of -6 to a high of 6 and are grouped into seven bins. The outside lobbying scores are in the top two histograms and the inside scores are in the bottom two. One obvious feature is that the scores for inside lobbying are more dispersed over the entire range whereas the outside lobbying scores tend to be concentrated in the middle.

The important comparison is between the two types of states and demonstrates how the initiative process influence lobbying strategies. There are two notable differences for the inside lobbying scores. First, the scores for groups in initiative states are more spread out, with the middle category dropping from 40 to 28 percent. Second, all of this difference is moved to lower scores, with an increase of 12 percent across the three categories below 0 and an increase in each of these individually as well. Not surprisingly, then, the average score in initiative states is less than in noninitiative states. The increase in the variation of inside lobbying scores is also consistent with its multiple effects. While it creates more groups that are ill-suited to inside lobby, it also makes the legislature more responsive to inside lobbying under some circumstances. These two competing

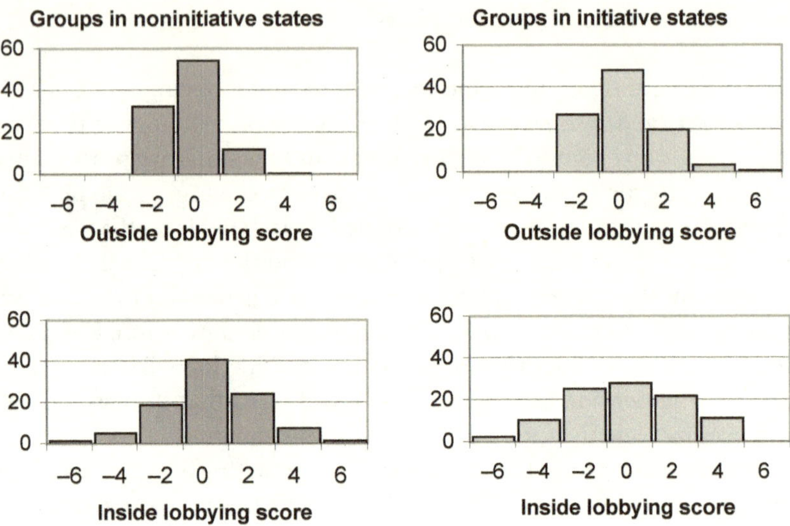

Figure 6.1
Distribution of Inside and Outside Lobbying Scores by Initiative Possibility

influences may produce the increased variation in the reliance upon the inside lobbying strategy.

For outside lobbying, there is also a shift in the lobbying scores. The two lowest categories are both smaller in initiative states, with a total loss of 11 percent of the groups. These groups are shifted to the positive scores, resulting in a larger average outside lobbying score in initiative states than in noninitiative states. To test whether groups in initiative states do rely more on outside lobbying, as predicted by implication 5, the average scores and test statistics are presented in table 6.2. The numbers in the table suggest that this is indeed the case: groups in initiative states have an average score of 0.35 on the outside lobbying strategy, and groups in noninitiative states have an average score of -0.37. This difference is dramatic and highly significant. The results are similar, but not quite as strong for the inside lobbying strategy. Groups in initiative states score lower on this strategy than groups in noninitiative states, though the difference is not significant at standard levels.

While the model makes no clear prediction regarding the overall effect of the initiative on inside lobbying, with the addition of assumption 5—the legislature feels more threatened once a group has already begun the process of proposing an initiative—the model predicts that groups that are

Table 6.2
Average Lobbying Strategy Scores by Initiative Possibility and Involvement

	Modern Inside	Excluded Outside	N
Noninitiative	-0.011	-0.365	158
Initiative	-0.237	0.346	147
t statistic	0.840	-4.380**	
Not Involved	-0.827	-0.026	100
Involved	0.790	0.995	47
t statistic	-3.880**	-3.710**	
Noninitiative	-0.011	-0.365	158
Involved	0.790	0.995	47
t statistic	-2.200*	-5.940**	
Noninitiative	-0.011	-0.365	158
Not Involved	-0.827	-0.026	100
t statistic	2.74**	-2.17**	

Source: survey of state interest groups (see Appendix C).
Calculated using weights—see Table C.2
** Significantly different from zero at the 0.05 level; * significantly different from zero at the 0.10 level (two-tailed tests). Two-tailed test, null hypothesis is equal means, assuming equal variances. Due to missing data, results are based on multiple imputation using Amelia (Windows version). See King, Honaker, Joseph, Scheve, and Singh (2001) for more information.

involved in potential initiatives see an increase in their ability to inside lobby. Given this perceived increase, I would expect groups involved in initiatives to report a greater reliance on inside lobbying strategies. Table 6.2 provides evidence consistent with this hypothesis: groups in initiative states that are involved in initiatives score significantly higher on the inside lobbying strategy than groups not involved in initiatives. Furthermore, they also score significantly higher on this strategy than groups in noninitiative states. This latter comparison is particularly important, since the average importance of inside lobbying in noninitiative states can be viewed as a baseline against which to compare the effect of initiative proposal on groups' ability to inside-lobby in initiative states.

While the model makes no specific prediction about the net effect of access to the initiative on inside lobbying, it does suggest that there are two competing effects. The first occurs through initiative mobilizations and learning through initiative campaigns and leads to a decrease in inside lobbying. The second occurs through the legislature's response to the threat that an initiative poses and increases the ability of groups to inside-lobby. The results appear to indicate that the former effect dominates the latter, though the difference between the use of inside lobbying in initiative states and in noninitiative states is not significant at conventional levels. Lastly, the results in the table indicate, not surprisingly, that groups involved in initiatives rely much more heavily on outside lobbying strategies than groups not involved in initiatives. Even groups not involved in initiative campaigns score higher on outside lobbying than groups in noninitiative states, though the results of this comparison are only weakly significant.

Even though the type of groups involved in initiatives is different from those not involved in initiatives, the results for a comparison of groups involved in initiatives and those in noninitiative states provide evidence for my theory of initiative mobilizations. Groups involved in initiatives score significantly higher on the inside lobbying dimension than groups in noninitiative states, whereas groups not involved in initiatives score significantly lower. The same comparisons for outside lobbying demonstrate that groups in initiative states all score significantly higher on the outside lobbying dimension, though the difference is greater for groups involved in potential initiatives.

These results provide preliminary evidence consistent with my model's predictions that the initiative process increases the use of outside lobbying tactics (implication 4) and the threat of initiative proposal increases the ability to inside-lobby (implication 6). A better test of the latter implication, as well as a test of implication 5, which states that these differences are caused by changes in behavior and not just by distributional shifts in groups' resources, requires controlling for resources when determining how the initiative process influences their choice of lobbying strategy. That is the subject of the following section.

Determinants of Lobbying Strategies

While the comparisons between the average importance of lobbying strategies for interest groups in initiative states and noninitiative states, as well as between users and non-users in initiative states, provide evidence that is consistent with implications 5 and 6, the test of these two hypotheses is not yet complete. Both of them make statements about the initiative process's influence on interest groups' choices of lobbying strategies above and beyond its influence through group resources. Since the average importance scores presented in the previous section do not control for resource shifts due to the initiative, they do not provide a direct test of these two implications. To estimate the behavioral effect of initiative access and involvement requires that I control for resources and other factors that influence the choice of lobbying strategies by estimating a regression model that includes measures of all these factors.

To perform this test, I estimate separate linear regression models for groups' scores on each of the two distinct lobbying strategies. Implication 5 asserts that groups in initiative states rely more on outside lobbying, so to test it I include an indicator variable for whether the group is in an initiative state. The coefficient for this variable in the outside lobbying model should be positive. While the model makes no clear prediction about the net effect of the initiative on inside lobbying, I also estimate the same model with the group's inside lobbying score as the dependent variable.

Implication 6 is about the effect of the potential use of the initiative process on a group's ability to inside-lobby. It therefore requires me to include a variable for whether a group is currently involved in an initiative campaign. If the prediction is correct, the coefficient on this variable is positive for the inside lobbying strategy. Again, there is no clear prediction about how involvement affects outside lobbying, but given my argument that successfully passing an initiative requires a campaign that involves many outside lobbying tactics intended to garner majority support, I would expect an increase in the outside lobbying strategy.[7] Furthermore, if groups are not proposing initiatives with the intent of passing them, but rather with the intent of pressuring the legislature into passing legislation, the group would still want to demonstrate that there is enough support for its cause to warrant legislative response. This too would require using outside lobbying tactics to evince evidence of public support. Thus, both arguments lead me to conclude that the coefficient for initiative involvement is positive for the outside lobbying strategy.

Because the two hypotheses I test using these regressions are intertwined, I estimate two separate regressions for each lobbying strategy. The first regression tests whether groups in initiative states employ different lobbying strategies than groups in noninitiative states but does not consider the effect of initiative involvement. This allows me to test whether groups in initiative states rely more on outside lobbying, as predicted by implication 5. The second regression includes this variable and adds variables for whether a group was involved with a potential initiative, either in support of or in opposition to it.[8] This analysis allows me to separate the effect of the initiative into three components: the effect on groups not involved in initiatives, the effect on groups supporting initiatives, and the effect on groups opposing initiatives. Estimating only this model would not, however, indicate the average effect of the initiative process on all groups.

There are other factors to control for besides the presence of and involvement with the initiative process. Most important, testing my two hypotheses requires me to account for group resources. I accomplish this by including variables for groups' survey responses for membership and revenue. These are generally considered to be the two most important resources in determining which type of lobbying strategy a group pursues. Groups with more members should rely more on outside lobbying strategies, whereas groups with greater revenue should emphasize inside lobbying strategies.

Besides revenue and group membership, Walker (1991) argues that it is important to control for resources more broadly by including measures of organizational characteristics and political environment. Organizational resources are measured by including indicator variables for different organizational types: professional and trade associations, labor unions, government associations, and a category for "other" groups that combines foundations, charities, nonprofit research groups, social organizations, and groups that responded "other" to the organizational type question.[9] Political environment is captured by including a measure of conflict: the number of other groups currently involved in the same issue. Groups facing more conflict are more likely to increase their level of inside lobbying, but also to supplement it with outside lobbying. As Kollman (1998) and Nownes and Freeman (1998) have found, traditional inside groups have been forced to expand their political repertoire through the use of an outside lobbying strategy to pressure legislators at key moments in the policy-making process.

I also attempt to control for the group's experience by including group characteristics such as the age of the group, the number of years it has been involved in its specific issue, and the frequency with which it is involved in lobbying efforts. Older groups may be more likely to have achieved access to legislators and have built up political capital and know-how over time, leading them to rely more on inside lobbying than outside lobbying. The number of years that a group has been involved with a particular issue should produce a similar effect as groups accumulate knowledge about a particular issue area and are more likely to be viewed as permanent players by elected officials.[10] Finally, groups that lobby on a more regular basis may have established connections that they can use during their current efforts, suggesting an increase in inside lobbying. While these groups may have established better connections and therefore need less outside lobbying, they may also have a better understanding of how to mount a successful lobbying campaign and may therefore know precisely when to engage in some outside lobbying.

These variables are entered in the regression model to predict a group's score on each of the inside and outside lobbying dimensions. Implication 5 predicts that the coefficient for the initiative state variable in the first regression is positive for outside lobbying; implication 6 predicts that the coefficient for the initiative support variable in the second regression is also positive. Before estimating these models, however, I briefly discuss how I deal with the problem of selection bias in the regression context.

Controlling for Selection Bias

As discussed earlier, selection bias is a problem in a regression setting whenever any unexplained factors that influence whether a group responds to the survey are related to the unexplained factors in the regression model being estimated. If they are related, the coefficients produced by the model are incorrect, and any inference based on them is suspect.[11] In the context of my analysis of interest groups' lobbying scores, selection would be a problem if the unknown reasons that influence whether a group responds to my survey are related to the unknown factors that determine groups' reliance on inside or outside lobbying strategies. If this were the case, it would be difficult to assess the impact of known factors, such as group resources and institutional context, on the choice of these strategies.[12] Fortunately, the problem can be alleviated by incorporating the selection process into the empirical model. When the dependent variable of interest is continuous, as is the case for my lobbying scores, the standard correction is to use the model developed by Heckman (1979).

This correction cannot be applied in my data, however, since it requires data on nonrespondents, which I do not have. While there are models that are designed to account for selection when no data are available for nonrespondents, they are often difficult to estimate and may produce unreliable estimates.[13] Because of these difficulties, I adapt a method developed by Boehmke (2003a) for models with a binary dependent variable to the continuous variable case.

The method involves using the data I obtained through the auxiliary survey to estimate the selection process and then account for this process when estimating the model for lobbying scores. Using this method allows me to control for the selection process and obtain more accurate estimates of the coefficients of interest. As discussed in the previous chapter, the data from the auxiliary survey indicate that business groups were extremely unlikely to respond to the survey (66 percent less likely than other groups). The concern is that the businesses that did respond are not representative of the businesses that did not respond. The selection model therefore controls for whether the group is a business or not. Further, I expect that the groups that did respond might be more open about their lobbying efforts, which would suggest a positive correlation between unobserved factors in the outside lobbying model and a negative relationship in the inside lobbying model. That is, the process of deciding whether to share information by answering my survey might be related to the decision to share information with the public in an outside lobbying campaign. Controls for resources might not fully capture this aspect of the group's responses, which are potentially related more to characteristics of the particular issue being addressed.

The Influence of the Initiative on Lobbying Strategies

Going Outside

The results for the regressions that estimate the effect of the initiative process on the two lobbying strategies are contained in table 6.3.[14] Implication 5 predicts that interest groups in initiative states rely more on outside lobbying than groups in noninitiative states. The results of the regression support this prediction: the coefficient for the initiative state variable is positive and significant at the 0.05 level. Even after controlling for group resources and lobbying environment, initiative state groups score higher on the outside lobbying dimension.

While the model makes a clear prediction about the effect of the initiative process on interest groups' use of outside lobbying, it makes no clear prediction about its net effect on inside lobbying. The coefficient for initiative states in the inside lobbying model is negative, but it is not quite significant ($p = 0.13$). Thus, the results indicate that initiative states have groups that rely less on inside lobbying and that the implicit threat of proposing an initiative does not make up for this decrease.

Turning to the rest of the results demonstrates that both interest group resources, experience, and lobbying environment affect the choice of lobbying strategies. The amount of conflict a group faces determines the use of both inside and outside lobbying: the coefficients for the number of other groups involved are both positive and significant. When faced with more competition, groups respond by increasing their lobbying activity on both dimensions. Interest group resources have a less consistent effect. The coefficients for organizational revenue are both negative, though neither approach statistical significance. Group membership has a positive impact on both strategies, though it is only significant in the inside lobbying model.

The measures of interest group characteristics also matter. Groups that lobby less often rely less on inside lobbying and more on outside lobbying, though the latter effect narrowly misses statistical significance ($p = 0.101$).[15] Groups' experiences as measured by organizational age do not

Table 6.3
Determinants of Lobbying Strategies: Group Factors and Initiative Possibility

	Inside Lobbying		Outside Lobbying	
	Coefficient	S.E.	Coefficient	S.E.
Initiative State	-0.429	(0.287)	0.428**	(0.215)
Lobbying Frequency	-0.541**	(0.089)	0.099	(0.061)
Revenue	-0.111	(0.114)	-0.028	(0.051)
Number of Groups Involved	1.208*	(0.642)	0.550*	(0.307)
Members	0.095*	(0.057)	0.041	(0.033)
Group's Age	-0.757	(0.815)	0.532	(0.588)
Years on Issue	1.481**	(0.730)	-0.296	(0.347)
Trade/Professional Group	-0.837	(0.956)	1.046	(1.172)
Labor Union	-1.053	(1.199)	1.259**	(0.472)
Government Association	-0.295	(0.973)	0.858	(1.289)
Other Groups	-1.042	(0.946)	0.956	(1.206)
constant	3.39	(2.367)	-4.051	(3.234)
Rho	-0.522	(0.521)	1.311**	(1.497)
Sigma	0.846**	(0.196)	0.615**	(0.395)
Selection Equation				
Business/Corporation	-0.886**	(0.144)	-0.886**	(0.144)
constant	-0.778**	(0.071)	-0.778**	(0.071)

Source: survey of state interest groups (see Appendix C).
N=306.
** Significantly different from zero at the 0.05 level; * significantly different from zero at the 0.10 level (two-tailed tests). Due to missing data, results are based on multiple imputation using Amelia (Windows version). See Honaker, Joseph, King, Scheve, and Singh (2001) for more information.

have an effect on lobbying, though group experience on the specific issue does: the longer a group has been working on its current issues, the higher it scores on the inside lobbying dimension.

How to Get Back Inside

While the results of the analysis in the previous section provide support for the effect of the initiative process on interest group lobbying strategies, the test of implication 6 requires me to control for involvement in potential initiative campaigns. Once a group begins the process of proposing an initiative, the legislature may become more responsive to its inside lobbying efforts. The test of this implication requires me to control for whether groups are involved in potential initiative campaigns.

The results of this model are presented in table 6.4 and provide support for this hypothesis. Groups that are involved in potential initiative campaigns score significantly higher than groups not involved in initiatives on the inside lobbying dimension, whether they are in support of or opposed to the potential initiative. The rest of the groups in initiative states that are not involved in potential initiatives score significantly lower on the inside lobbying dimension.[16] These results therefore demonstrate that although groups in initiative states rely less on inside lobbying, when they get involved in potential initiative campaigns they can leverage this involvement to significantly increase their ability to effectively utilize inside lobbying.

While the model makes no specific prediction about the effect of the initiative involvement on outside lobbying, one would expect that groups involved in initiatives would rely more on outside lobbying strategies. While groups in initiative states score higher on the outside lobbying dimension regardless of whether they are involved in initiatives, only groups involved against specific initiatives score significantly higher on the outside lobbying dimension. Combining the effect of the initiative process with the effect of supporting or opposing a specific initiative also indicates that groups in these two categories score significantly higher on the outside lobbying strategy than groups in noninitiative states, though the evidence is stronger for groups opposing initiatives.

The rest of the results remain similar to those from the previous model, with a couple of small changes. Lobbying frequency is now significant at the 0.10 level for the outside lobbying dimension, while the effect of membership on inside lobbying now slips below the 0.10 significance level.

Conclusion

In this chapter, I used groups' responses to questions about lobbying tactics to determine their overall lobbying strategies. The results of this analysis reveal two basic lobbying strategies, which fall along the well-known inside and outside lobbying dimensions. One difference relative to previous studies is that while inside lobbying appears to have expanded to include some outside lobbying tactics, there are still many groups that only utilize an outside lobbying strategy. I then use these results to generate lobbying scores on each of these two dimensions to test the model's final two implications.

The results indicate that groups in states with the initiative process score

Table 6.4
Determinants of Lobbying Strategies: Initiative Possibility and Involvement

	Inside Lobbying		Outside Lobbying	
	Coefficient	S.E.	Coefficient	S.E.
For Initiative	0.972**	(0.487)	0.294	(0.269)
Against Initiative	1.430*	(0.796)	2.451**	(0.494)
Initiative State	-0.765**	(0.326)	0.236	(0.185)
Lobbying Frequency	-0.520**	(0.088)	0.100*	(0.057)
Revenue	-0.086	(0.118)	-0.028	(0.055)
Number of Groups Involved	1.108*	(0.651)	0.493*	(0.286)
Members	0.081	(0.057)	0.033	(0.030)
Group's Age	-0.830	(0.807)	0.529	(0.504)
Years on Issue	1.572**	(0.696)	-0.149	(0.351)
Trade/Professional Group	-0.725	(1.006)	1.071	(0.858)
Labor Union	-1.332	(1.279)	1.678**	(0.842)
Government Association	-0.181	(1.028)	0.952	(0.903)
Other Groups	-0.992	(0.982)	1.006	(0.853)
constant	3.252	(2.441)	-4.275**	(2.145)
Rho	-0.523	(0.541)	1.431	(0.993)
Sigma	0.832**	(0.201)	0.604*	(0.309)
Selection Equation				
Business/Corporation	-0.886**	(0.144)	-0.886**	(0.144)
constant	-0.778**	(0.071)	-0.778**	(0.071)

Source: survey of state interest groups. N=306. ** Significantly different from zero at the 0.05 level; * significantly different from zero at the 0.10 level (two-tailed tests). Due to missing data, results are based on multiple imputation using Amelia (Windows version). See King, Honaker, Joseph, Scheve, and Singh (2000) for more information.

higher on the outside lobbying dimension, even after controlling for group resources. This result provides support for implication 5. Considering groups that are involved in potential initiatives demonstrates that they score significantly higher on the inside lobbying dimension, providing support for implication 6 by demonstrating that when made tangible, the threat of initiative proposal increases the legislature's responsiveness to a group's inside lobbying efforts.

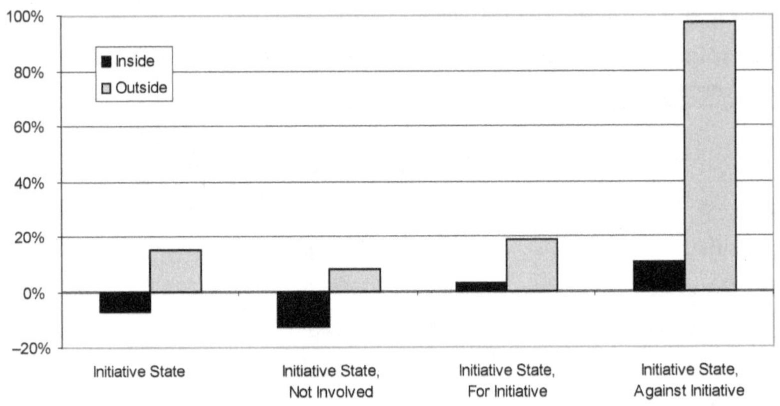

Figure 6.2
Estimated Effect of Initiative Possibility and Involvement on Interest Group Lobbying Strategies Relative to Noninitiative State Groups

The empirical models also indicate other ways that the initiative process affects interest group lobbying. Groups in initiative states rely less on outside lobbying, especially when they are not able to leverage initiative involvement. On the other hand, groups involved against specific initiatives score much higher on outside lobbying. This is not surprising, as the best way to discourage a potential initiative is to attempt to mobilize broad opposition to it. Studies of initiatives on the ballot demonstrate that opposition expenditures on media campaigns can have a great effect on whether the initiative passes (Gerber 1999; Banducci 1998).

The main results of this chapter are summarized in figure 6.2, which displays the percentage increase in the use of the two lobbying strategies resulting from the presence or use of the initiative process.[17] The first category shows that groups in initiative states score 16 percent higher on outside lobbying and 7 percent lower on inside lobbying than groups in noninitiative states. The second pair of effects shows that groups in initiative states that are not involved in specific initiatives score 12 percent lower on inside lobbying and 8 percent higher on outside lobbying. The last two pair of results show that groups involved in initiatives score higher on both lobbying strategies, particularly the outside lobbying strategy. The increase in outside lobbying for groups supporting an initiative is 19 percent and almost 100 percent for groups opposing an initiative.

The consequences of these results for initiative state politics are many. Most important, the increased reliance and importance of outside lobbying strategies can lead to different groups achieving influence. Because the legislature is concerned about initiative proposals, not only does it have to pay heed to group's outside lobbying efforts as a signal of potential initiative support, but it also becomes more responsive to their inside lobbying efforts. Thus, groups that may have a harder time successfully lobbying the legislature in noninitiative states find themselves more able to get their voices heard.

7

Interest Groups and the Initiative Process

> A government can no more make laws through its voters than it can make laws through its newspapers. . . . What I mean to say is that popular initiative is an inconceivable thing.
>
> —Woodrow Wilson, quoted in James Boyle, *The Initiative and Referendum: Its Follies, Falacies and Failure* (1912), 5

In the introduction of the book, I told the story of Californians for Medical Rights, which mobilized to push for policy reform in one state. After successfully passing its policy through the initiative process, this group took its case to other states and helped to start other interest groups to achieve the same policy change. Given the importance of the initiative process for achieving these successes, I asked whether this is a widespread phenomenon that significantly impacts interest group politics in initiative states. Based on the theory and the empirical analyses I have conducted in this book, it would appear that the answer is yes: there are important and systematic differences in interest group mobilizations, characteristics, and lobbying behavior across institutional contexts.

My argument for why these differences appear is straightforward and developed in detail in chapter 2. It concludes that access to the initiative process alters the incentives for interest groups to mobilize and for how they lobby and that the change is more consequential for broad-based membership groups. The empirical tests of the predictions of the model provide a myriad of ways in which these incentives are manifested. First, initiative states have more interest groups than states without the initiative process, and they also have a higher proportion of traditionally underrepresented citizen groups. These consequences are demonstrated in chapters 3 and 5, which study aggregate and individual-level data. Second, the presence of these initiative-mobilized groups leads to important differences in the way that groups lobby. Chapters 5 and 6 show that groups in initiative states rely more on outside lobbying tactics and strategies when trying to influence policy outcomes. Lastly, chapter 6 shows that the effect of the initiative leads to changes in behavior for groups that would have mobilized anyway by demonstrating that there are differences in lobbying style above and beyond those caused by shifts in resources.

Besides these effects on state interest group populations, I also show that the efforts of these interest groups have a substantial impact on state policy adoption. In addition to examples such as medicinal marijuana and term limits, where the initiative process has almost certainly played a crucial role, chapter 4 shows that even in less obvious policy areas such as Indian gaming and capital punishment, the initiative process has had an impact on when states adopt, with initiative states adopting earlier, on average, than noninitiative states. These results demonstrate that the effect of the initiative process on interest groups has immediate consequences for state politics beyond shifts in interest group mobilization, resources, and lobbying behavior.

In this chapter, I provide a broad overview of the salient points of my theory of the initiative process and its hypotheses regarding interest groups and state politics in general. I then provide a brief summary of the main results, focusing on the magnitude of the political impact of the various indirect effects I studied. Following this, I discuss some of the ways that my work differs from and builds on previous work on interest groups as well as the initiative process. I then offer a discussion of research questions that extend or are suggested by my results. In the final section, I discuss some of the broader implications that these findings have for our understanding of interest groups, the initiative process and elite evaluations, and proposed reforms of direct legislation.

Review of my Argument and Findings

The Theory of Initiative Mobilizations

My theory of interest group behavior focuses on the incentives that political institutions offer interest groups and how groups respond to these incentives. Other studies have clearly demonstrated the ways that interest groups can utilize the initiative process to further their goals; my model allows me to understand the reciprocal effect of this ability on the groups themselves. Groups do not operate in an institutional vacuum, so it is reasonable to develop theories that describe how they respond to variations in their institutional context.

My theory argues that access to direct legislation benefits groups that are seeking policy change in a variety of ways, which can be traced over the course of their evolution. Groups, whether latent or already mobilized, that desire policy change realize that their chances of success are greater in states with the initiative process. This is true for two reasons. First, if they fail to persuade the legislature to enact policy change, they have another option through which to accomplish it. Second, the presence of the initiative process makes it easier to achieve success through the legislature. This can be attributed to the legislature's response to the ability of the group to propose an initiative when the legislature does not satisfy it: the legislature is willing to move policy for a smaller contribution. Both of these facts mean that interest groups' resources are more effective in initiative states.

This conclusion has both immediate and less immediate consequences for how groups respond to the initiative process. Since groups can accomplish more with their resources, the most direct result is that they are more likely to mobilize or become active in a specific policy area. This leads to the prediction that initiative states have more interest groups. Additionally, since the magnitude of the change in effectiveness due to the initiative process varies across groups, the initiative's presence matters more for broad-based citizen groups rather than for narrow, economic groups. This generates an additional prediction that while both types of groups mobilize in greater numbers in initiative states, the increase is proportionately greater for citizen groups.

These interest group mobilizations engendered by the initiative process, which I refer to as initiative mobilizations, lead to a variety of additional differences between interest group populations. Foremost, my model argues that there is a shift in the distribution of resources across the interest group system. Groups in initiative states have more members and less financial resources, on average. These differences in resources then lead to differences in average lobbying behavior as well.

Besides influencing which groups mobilize and what resources they have, my model also argues that groups in initiative states adopt different lobbying styles. Groups that are the result of initiative mobilizations are likely to learn about specific types of lobbying from their experience in initiative campaigns. Since these campaigns involve garnering broad, public support for a measure, initiative campaign experience is most likely to hone outside lobbying skills rather than inside lobbying skills. Once groups have invested in learning these skills and have become more facile with them, they are likely to continue to emphasize them in the future. Thus, groups in initiative states tend to rely more on an outside lobbying strategy relative to groups in noninitiative states.

The legislature's response to potential initiative proposals may also influence interest groups' lobbying choices. Because the legislature is concerned about the potential consequences of initiative proposals, groups may wish to create the impression, whether real or illusory, of broad public support for their measure to increase pressure on the legislature to respond. This creates an incentive for groups in initiative states to emphasize outside lobbying even more, as it may have a greater impact on their ability to work with the legislature relative to the effect of public support in noninitiative states. If the legislature does respond to this show of support, groups may see an increase in the effectiveness of their inside lobbying efforts as well.

Lastly, my model makes specific predictions about the impact of the initiative process on state policy adoption and diffusion. Because the initiative process makes it relatively easier for groups to achieve policy influence, states with the initiative process are likely to experience policy adoption under a wider range of conditions than noninitiative states. This is a consequence not just of an increase in the relative effectiveness of interest group lobbying, but is also caused by the mobilization of groups that would have otherwise remained latent.

The fact that policy adoption in initiative states is influenced by voters' preferences also implies that the initiative process should play a unique role in policy diffusion. Learning that voters in other states support a policy can be useful for decision makers trying to figure out whether their own voters also want the policy. Because political elites, including representatives and interest group leaders, are unsure about the exact level of support for a policy in their state, they can use information from states where voters have similar preferences to become more sure about what their own citizens want. In my model, information is conveyed when similar states adopt the policy in question. But because this information is only useful in initiative states and must be drawn from other initiative states, it leads to a specific form of diffusion only between states with the initiative process.

Gathering the Evidence

After the development of the theory, the remainder of the book is spent testing its predictions. In each instance, the empirical tests provide support for the model's predictions. Even more important is the fact that the predictions of the model are supported across a variety of data sets measured at different levels. This broad pattern of support bolsters the overall confidence in the model's predictions and demonstrates its usefulness for providing insight into the effect of the initiative process on interest group and state politics. In this section, I review and interpret my main findings.

Because the primary objective of this book is to study the indirect effect of institutions such as the initiative process on interest groups, I summarize the results by focusing on the many different ways that it does so. Rather than repeat the conclusions for the various empirical tests I performed, I focus on the political relevance of the effects by discussing the magnitude of key differences between initiative states and noninitiative states. In this spirit, each of the empirical chapters concluded with a figure that depicts how the initiative process influences interest group and state politics. Combined, these figures indicate that the indirect effect of the initiative process is substantial across a host of different areas. Consider the following differences:

Initiative states have 28 percent more interest groups.

Initiative states have 45 percent more citizen interest groups, compared with 23 percent more economic groups, making them more representative.

Initiative states have 33 percent more membership groups.

The average initiative state is 9 percent more likely to adopt Indian gaming and almost 30 percent more likely to adopt capital punishment each year when two neighboring initiative states have already adopted.

When an initiative state adopts a policy, neighboring initiative states are 5 to 10 percent more likely to adopt that same policy each year.

Groups in initiative states score 20 percent higher on my survey's membership question and 12 percent lower on the revenue question.

Groups in initiative states indicated that contacting legislators and agencies are about 6 percent less important and that organizing protests and demonstrations is 14 percent more important.

Groups in initiative states indicated that legislative connections are 19 percent less important and that opposition groups' actions are 18 percent more important in determining which issues they are active on.

Groups in initiative states score 26 percent higher for outside lobbying and 4 percent lower for inside lobbying.

Groups involved with potential initiatives score 13 percent higher on inside lobbying and 50 percent higher on outside lobbying than groups in noninitiative states.

Among groups in initiative states, groups involved with initiatives score 30 percent higher on both inside and outside lobbying than groups not involved with initiatives.

Clearly, the initiative process produces a multitude of changes in the political environment in a state. Some of these changes even extend to other, neighboring states, suggesting the possibility of a second-order indirect effect of the initiative process. Many of these changes are politically large in their own right, but taken together the combined effect is even greater.

The magnitude of these findings should be compared with the direct effect of the initiative process that follows from initiatives that pass and influence public policy. Over the past one hundred years, less than one initiative per year has been successful in the average initiative state. And while the cumulative effects of one additional statute or constitutional change per year may be substantial, it is certainly possible that the sum total of the indirect effects outweighs the direct effects. I return to this comparison in detail shortly. For the moment, however, the important point is that the scope and magnitude of the indirect effects provide strong evidence for my theory and indicate that they must be accounted for when evaluating the initiative process.

Distinguishing Features of This Study

Other studies of interest groups and the initiative process are discussed throughout this book. In some cases, I rely on their findings in important ways. Yet the questions adopted and approaches taken in this study are distinct in several key ways that I wish to highlight.

First, this study explicitly compares interest group populations across institutional contexts. By comparing the mobilization and lobbying behavior of groups in states with and without the initiative process, I am able to reach conclusions about how institutions impact the decisions of organized interests. Specifically, the direct initiative process influences interest group mobilizations, resources, lobbying tactics, and lobbying strategies. Other studies that attempt to determine the effect of institutions on the behavior of organized interests rarely take this approach, either across states or over time at the federal level.

Second, while almost all studies of the initiative process focus only on activities in initiative states, I utilize information from noninitiative states for comparison. This allows me to more fully understand how the presence of the initiative process impacts interest group behavior. Furthermore, the studies that do include initiative and noninitiative states generally focus either on policy outcomes or voter turnout. Thus, this research expands upon these latter studies by examining a different part of the political process that is shaped by the initiative process and in a less direct fashion.

Third, I use a formal model to generate predictions about the indirect effect of the initiative process on state politics. Formal models are useful for explicitly stating assumptions and ensuring that the theoretical perspective is internally consistent. By testing or verifying assumptions, as I have done for some of the key ones I made, one can increase confidence in the accuracy of the model and its predictions. In addition, formal models also offer the opportunity to discover relationships between variables that might not have been linked otherwise. In this case, for example, no one has previously investigated how the initiative process influences interest group mobilizations, lobbying behavior, or policy diffusion. This benefit has been particularly important in this instance, as the model guided me to more than one hypothesis that I would otherwise not have considered.

My model of the initiative process differs from previous models in important ways. These differences are motivated mostly by differences in the focus of my study, particularly my interest in modeling a greater variety of interest group activities. Specifically, my model explicitly incorporates lobbying between the interest group and the legislature, albeit in a simplified fashion. Another important difference is that my model conceives of policy change as a binary phenomenon, whereas other formal models (Gerber 1996; Matsusaka and McCarty 2001) use a continuous policy space. My decision was motivated primarily by a desire to increase the ease of presentation, but also by a desire to generate as tight a link as possible between the model's predictions and empirical tests.

In addition, I have attempted to take care in distinguishing direct predictions of the model from implications that follow closely from the model but require some additional assumptions. Distinguishing between these two types of hypotheses is important because it allows the reader to understand precisely how the model is used to generate empirically testable statements. Yet just because some predictions are not derived directly from the model does not mean that they are neither interesting nor useful for evaluating the model. Many of the additional implications that I derive could have been generated directly from a more complex version of the model, yet doing so would have complicated the model and made it more difficult to determine the link between specific assumptions and hypotheses. Thus little theoretical insight would have been gained solely for the purpose of upgrading an implication to a prediction.

Lastly, the model I start with allows me to generate a specific process that describes policy diffusion. Most studies of policy diffusion do not discuss different forms of diffusion and do not explicitly model them. By looking at the role that the initiative process plays in conveying information about voters' preferences, my model offers one perspective on how to unpack the black box of policy diffusion. Additionally, the importance of the dynamics of diffusion leads me to utilize a dynamic model of policy adoption, which, while becoming more common in general, has less frequently been applied to the study of the effect of the initiative process on policy adoption.

Future Work

There are naturally many questions that this study has left unanswered, as well as a few that it may have raised. In an attempt to preserve simplicity and clarity of presentation, I made a conscious decision to simplify my game-theoretic model as much as possible while still generating testable predictions about interest groups and politics. Clearly, there are many assumptions that could be relaxed or extensions that could be made.

One of the more profitable in my estimation would be to incorporate a more explicit model of lobbying into the interest group–legislature interaction. The current model relies on a simple monetary contribution from the interest group to capture lobbying. But lobbying comes in many different flavors. At the very least, one could incorporate inside and outside lobbying into the model as separate choices by the group. Alternatively, one could extend informational models of lobbying (Ainsworth 1993; Austen-Smith 1987, 1993; Austen-Smith and Wright 1994; Kollman 1998; Lohmann 1993) by adding the initiative process to determine whether access to or use of the initiative increases the credibility of groups' signals under certain conditions.

There is also empirical work that needs to be done. One of the implications of the initiative theory of mobilization is that interest groups spawned by the initiative process are less likely to survive than groups that would have mobilized anyway. If this theory is correct, then it has certain implications for how state interest group populations evolve over time as well as for the mortality and morbidity of specific groups. So the next step in testing the theory is to trace the history and growth of initiative-mobilized groups over time. My argument is that while initiative-mobilized groups rely more heavily on outside lobbying strategies due to their comparative resource advantage combined with their previous experience with the initiative process, the groups that do survive are more likely to partially incorporate themselves into traditional approaches to lobbying.

The data in this study are consistent with this expectation, but the argument concerns the evolution of individual groups. To test the process of the incorporation of initiative-mobilized groups into state politics therefore requires multiple observations on the same groups over time. These data could be obtained through a panel survey of state interest groups and should include questions similar to those used in this survey, possibly along with questions regarding a group's previous experience with the initiative process or more detailed information on a variety of issues that saw actual or potential initiatives. This would allow for a more detailed profile of a group's initiative history and how it relates to current and future lobbying activities in general.

Lastly, one might want to study the effect of the initiative process on other aspects of state politics. For example, my model predicts that campaign contributions to elected officials are affected by the presence of the initiative. Previous research has already shown that individuals in initiative states may make a greater number of PAC contributions (Tolbert, McNeal, and Smith 2003). While the direction of my model's predicted effect on the amount of contributions is not clear—sponsoring initiatives may preclude contributions that would be made otherwise, while the potential to propose initiatives may engender new contributions—some assumptions could be made that generate a clearer prediction. For example, one could argue that since there are relatively few initiatives on the ballot each year, this might suggest that the latter effect dominates the former. Furthermore, one could examine states with the initiative process, but with few initiatives on the ballot.

These results for individual participation and my findings for the number of groups in initiative states can be further investigated at the individual level. If there are more groups to join and those groups have more members, then it seems apparent that there must be a greater rate of individual participation in initiative states. This could occur in two different ways. Individuals who are politically active may merely join more groups, thereby duplicating previously existing representation. This would still increase the influence of individuals vis-à-vis business interests, but it would not increase the set of individuals who are represented in the interest group system. Alternatively, the increase in citizen groups could engender political participation by a greater number of individuals, which would both increase the influence of individuals and broaden the set of interests that are represented. In this way then, the initiative process may still be fulfilling the original intent of its founders to increase the role of the common citizen in the political process.

Implications of This Study

The arguments and findings contained in this book have important implications for understanding interest group and state politics. Most important, they demonstrate the crucial role that institutions play in the mobilization and representation of citizens' interests in the political process. Choices about the institutional forms incorporated into governance structures matter in many ways besides the policy changes that may arise directly from them. The initiative process is just one such institution, but the investigation in this book indicates many ways that it affects state politics beyond the few initiatives that reach the ballot. These findings have important implications not just for our understanding of interest groups, but also for the politics of the initiative process, recent discussions about direct legislation reforms, and the process of policy innovation and diffusion. In this section, I treat each of these in turn.

Interest Groups and Institutions

This book primarily adds to our understanding of interest group mobilization by studying the relationship between institutions and groups' decisions about mobilization and lobbying strategies. As Walker (1991) observed, interest group systems are indeed a product of their institutional environment. I have found extensive evidence that the influence of institutions is both systematic and politically significant. When considering interest group lobbying choices, then, future studies should take into account variation in the institutional environment they face along with variation in resources, lobbying environment, and issues.

Because the institutional environment that groups face varies relatively little when studying Washington, D.C., groups, this study also provides a motivation for studying state interest group populations in further detail. Because of the variation in the size and demographic makeup of the states, they have already provided the opportunity to advance our understanding of the factors that influence interest group populations (Boehmke 2002; Gray and Lowery 1996; and Lowery, Gray, Fellowes, and Anderson 2004). Besides the presence of direct legislation, the states have great variety in the rules governing interest group involvement in politics, including campaign finance laws, the presence of term limits, legislative professionalism, and electoral laws. Groups' responses to these other features may have additional consequences for the structure of interest group politics.

By turning to the states to answer questions about interest group populations, one can obtain a better understanding of how variation in institutions and other political and economic factors relates to variation in the number and type of groups that mobilize and how they behave. One of the central findings and concerns resulting from the study of the Washington, D.C., lobbying community is the strong bias in representation toward narrow, economic interests. Yet studying this same community of groups offers little information about what factors help reduce this bias. The expense and resulting paucity of studies of the national interest group system limits the ability of researchers to obtain variation in key measures. This makes it difficult to assess how changes in institutions and regulations influence interest group systems. A better understanding of representation requires more information on how it differs across political, economic, and institutional environments.

Ultimately, the effects of institutions such as direct legislation on the mobilization and behavior of organized interests is of particular concern because of the crucial role that these groups play in representing citizens' interests. Since initiative states have more citizen groups than noninitiative states, these groups are likely to raise and get involved with different issues than the groups that would have mobilized anyway. Furthermore, the initiative process can help all groups raise issues that they otherwise might not have viewed as fruitful pursuits. This is obviously the case with some of the issues discussed in this book, such as term limits and medicinal marijuana reforms, but there are undoubtedly other areas where this occurs as well.

A shift in the efforts and issue concerns of interest groups leads to different policy outcomes in some cases, which means that citizens' interests are translated into public policy in a different fashion. Yet there are other ways in which citizens' interests may be represented differently besides by the issues raised. First, individuals have the opportunity for a greater variety of political participation. With more groups to join, particularly more broad-based membership groups, individuals have more options if they choose to be politically active. Additionally, the presence of more groups working on different issues may spur more individuals to become active. There is, in fact, some evidence to this effect already: citizens in initiative states are more likely to vote (Smith 2001; Tolbert, Grummel, and Smith 2001; Tolbert, McNeal and Smith 2003), are more likely to make PAC contributions to interest groups, have greater political knowledge (Tolbert, McNeal, and Smith 2003), and have greater feelings of efficacy (Bowler and Donovan 2002). Furthermore, Boehmke and Alvarez (2004b) show that signature gathering campaigns for initiatives can influence turnout in the subsequent election, as well as roll-off (i.e., the proportion of people who cast a ballot but skip a specific item) and vote choice on the corresponding ballot measure.

Given the ability of different groups to get involved and the potential for citizens to become involved in issues that would not have been raised otherwise, the presence of the initiative process ought to result in a focus on different issues in initiative and noninitiative states. Although they do not provide a definitive answer, the questions asked in my survey do allow some preliminary insight into this issue. Besides asking questions about resources and lobbying, I also asked groups to rate fourteen different issue areas in terms of their importance. Specifically, groups were asked to respond to the following question: "The diversity of interests varies across groups. For each of the following policy areas, please indicate how active your group is." They were asked to rate the issue areas on a five-point scale, where 1 indicated that they were not active and 5 indicated they were very active. The issue areas included agriculture, civil rights, crime, health policy, government operations, and social welfare, among others.

Table 7.1
Importance of Interest Groups' Issue Concerns by Initiative Possibility

	Initiative	Noninitiative	Difference
Health policy	2.57	2.17	-0.40**
Transportation	2.44	2.04	-0.40**
Government operations	2.70	2.45	-0.25†
State economy	3.15	2.94	-0.22
Civil rights and civil liberties	2.00	1.81	-0.19
Agriculture	1.50	1.41	-0.09
Social welfare	1.96	1.93	-0.03
Education	2.65	2.65	0.00
Technology	1.80	1.86	0.06
Energy and natural resources	2.06	2.15	0.09
Environmental policy	2.28	2.40	0.12
Crime and law enforcement	1.94	2.12	0.17
Sports, Entertainment & Recreation	1.44	1.65	0.21†
Other	4.16	4.58	0.42†

Source: survey of state interest groups (see Appendix C).
N=306.
** Significantly different from zero at the 0.05 level (two-tailed test); † significantly different from zero at the 0.10 level (one-tailed test).

While there are some areas, such as government operations, where one might expect more attention in initiative states, in many others it is less obvious what differences might exist. The full list of issue areas and the average activity of groups by institutional context are presented in table 7.1. The issues are sorted by the size of the average difference in importance indicated by groups in initiative states. At the top of the list are health policy, transportation, government operations, state economy, and civil rights/civil liberties. The first two exhibit significant differences, and the last three exhibit near-significant differences. At the bottom of the list, groups in initiative states are less active in the areas of environmental policy; crime and law enforcement; sports, entertainment, and recreation; and "other" issues.[1] Only the last two categories resulted in near-significant differences. Thus, there is clearly evidence that groups in initiative states have different issue concerns than those in noninitiative states.

These differences suggest another way that the initiative process indirectly influences state politics. Because there are more citizen groups and fewer economic groups, one would expect different issues to emerge as important. They do. And because initiative state groups are more representative, one might conclude that the issues raised are also more important to citizens as well. While the findings here are only suggestive—a more precise test would require asking citizens to rate issues as well—they are consistent with a link between institutions, groups, and representation.

Lastly, it is important to note that these findings have implications for interest group populations beyond those in initiative states. Because groups are mobile and issues can be raised in many different venues, changes in interest group populations and issue preferences in twenty-four states are likely to spill over and have effects in the rest of the states. When groups mobilize and lobby in initiative states, they create organizational capital that can be transferred to similar efforts in other states with or without the initiative process. This possibility may make it easier to raise new issues in noninitiative states, since they can draw on other organizations' experiences and potentially even their organizational or membership structures. As is the case with Americans for Medical Reform, initiative-mobilized groups can serve as important patrons to help new groups form all across the country.[2]

In addition to the potential for spillover effects generated by initiative mobilizations, interest groups can use the initiative process to shape the national agenda in other ways. Policy changes that might be seen as too extreme or sudden at the national level might fit quite well in specific states with a more favorable disposition. Adoption and perhaps even consideration of the policy in these states might increase the visibility and palatability of a policy, thereby allowing the group to eventually move on to more moderate states. Thus, groups can gain credibility for their cause by focusing their efforts and resources on one state. Not only does this process increase the chance of ultimate success, particularly if the early states are chosen carefully, but success in those cases may provide evidence and motivation for people and groups in other states to get involved once they have observed a prior success in the group's past.

Besides medicinal marijuana, advocates of other issues have attempted to use the initiative process to provide credibility. Physician-assisted suicide has seen very little success across the nation, but some progress has been made through the initiative process in Oregon. While legislators and voters in other states have resisted the issue, Oregon voters passed Measure 16 in 1994. After years of legal battles and a failed legislative referendum in 1997 that would have overturned Measure 16, it is clear that supporters would have made even less progress on such a controversial issue without the initiative process. Whether the initiative process has helped propel another issue into the mainstream remains to be seen, but the potential has been demonstrated.

Along with these indirect effects, of course, groups that are successful in initiative states can just go ahead and move to other states as well, leading to a similar spillover process. While casual observation suggests that often these groups turn first to other initiative states, as did AMR with medicinal marijuana and Ward Connerley's American Civil Rights Institute in the wake of California's anti–affirmative action initiative, Proposition 209. If this is in fact a systematic phenomenon, then the initiative process has important consequences for state politics everywhere. One way to study this issue would be to study the history of initiative-mobilized groups over time—when they mobilize, what initiatives they were involved in, what legislative issues they were involved with, and when they stopped being active—perhaps by studying lobbying registrations in the states to look for spillover effects.

Initiative State Politics

The findings in this book raise some interesting questions for the study of initiative state politics. Specifically, how do differences in the type of groups that mobilize and the type of lobbying strategies that groups use influence the overall tenor of initiative state politics? Previous studies have already investigated the existence of policy differences between initiative and noninitiative states (Boehmke and Witmer 2004; Gerber 1999; Lascher, Hagen, and Rochlin 1996; Matsusaka 1995, 2004; Schildkraut 2001), as well as the effect of the initiative on voter turnout (Boehmke and Alvarez 2004b; Everson 1981; Smith 2001; Tolbert, Grummel, and Smith 2001; Tolbert, McNeal, and Smith 2003), PAC contributions and voter knowledge (Tolbert, McNeal, and Smith 2003), and political efficacy (Bowler and Donovan 2002). Important differences have been found in each of these areas at least part of the time.

My findings provide evidence that interest group politics in initiative states is also significantly different from interest group politics in noninitiative states. This suggests that there are potentially important differences in terms of which interests in society are represented by the political process, some evidence for which is presented in the previous section. The fact that there are, at least part of the time, important policy differences engendered by the initiative process provides additional evidence of its consequences for representation. I suspect that policy consequences are driven not just by the direct and indirect threat of using the initiative process, but also by the process of initiative mobilizations that add new interest groups to the mix. These groups then go on to lobby for their issues and may have success in shaping which policy changes pass and the ultimate form that they take. Because my evidence indicates that groups that arise from initiative mobilizations appear not to merely reinforce the existing interest group system, but come from a traditionally underrepresented segment, this difference in their origin should be reflected in the issues they get involved in, as evidenced in table 7.1. This implies that the policy effects of the initiative process, both direct and indirect, are not uniformly distributed across all policies, but may be greater in certain areas.

Yet when determining whether the effect of the initiative process varies across policy areas, one must distinguish between groups' interests and their effectiveness. This is important in light of my finding that interest groups in initiative states appear to be more reactive in their policy activities. They consistently indicated that their political activities were shaped more by the actions of other groups and less by personal preferences and strategic allocation of their resources. Additionally, groups in initiative states indicated a greater concern with simple cues when choosing whom to lobby in the legislature. These findings suggest that while groups in initiative states may prefer to raise new issues, they often find themselves responding to issues that have already been raised rather than forging ahead and being effective on their own issues.

Given that these groups are attempting to influence not just the presence of a policy, but also the form that it takes, many of these differences may be found in the specifics of a given policy rather than merely being a force for earlier adoption. For example, the results for Indian gaming adoptions in chapter 4 show that initiative states tend to adopt such proposals earlier than noninitiative states. Yet states may negotiate separate gaming agreements with each tribe, the number and content of which may also be affected by the initiative process. Studies of the number of gaming agreements indicate that initiative states may negotiate more gaming compacts than noninitiative states (Boehmke and Witmer 2004) and that they also negotiate more amendments to existing compacts than noninitiative states. Similar results are obtained by Matsusaka (1995, 2004), who shows that at the end of the twentieth century, initiative states spent less money per capita, relied more on fees rather than taxes to raise money, and spent more at the local level rather than at the state level. Combined, these results indicate that initiative states do not just adopt some policies earlier, but also have different forms of those policies once adopted. The initiative process may serve as an important bargaining chip that allows groups to influence the content of legislation even when they cannot influence the timing of adoption.

Another issue that this raises is how the political process in the legislature is affected by initiative-mobilized groups. Politics is, as Schattschneider (1960) noted, about the subversion of conflict. The addition of more interest groups, representing a different segment of society, must increase the amount of conflict in initiative states in many different policy areas. How well the legislature and political parties contain this conflict is an important consideration when evaluating how initiative state politics differs from noninitiative state politics. If elites are successful in mediating these differences, then the initiative process may lead to more voices being heard in any given policy debate. On the other hand, the increased conflict may slow down the political process, render decision making more protracted, and may ultimately lead to less effective government as a consequence (Olson 1982).

Direct Legislation Reforms

The recent history and prevalence of attempts to reform the initiative process, almost always to make it more restrictive and harder to use, can best be illustrated with an example. In 1998, there were five states that did not ban cockfighting: Missouri, Arizona, Oklahoma, New Mexico, and Louisiana. That year, voters in the first two states passed ballot measures that finally outlawed it. In the other initiative states in this list, an ongoing battle was raging between opponents of the sport and the industry and its friends in the legislature. Citizens and groups in Oklahoma, led by the Oklahoma Coalition against Cockfighting, were in the process of gathering enough signatures—about one hundred thousand—to qualify a ban for the ballot. By the fall of 1999, their efforts produced State Question 687, which would have made cockfighting a felony offense.

The industry and game fowl breeders attempted to stop State Question 687 in its tracks by arguing that the initiative petition was illegal. At the same time, they were using their influence in the legislature to ensure that future proposals would be more difficult to qualify. In 2002, the legislature complied by placing State Question 698 on the ballot. This proposal would have raised the number of signatures required to qualify animal rights initiatives from 8 to 15 percent of total turnout in the previous general election. The industry was hoping that if this measure passed and their legal challenge to State Question 687 succeeded, proponents would be unable to qualify another measure.

Ultimately, both prongs of this strategy failed. The Oklahoma State Supreme Court ruled that the initiative was valid in time for it to appear on the 2002 ballot, along with State Question 698. Voters proceeded to support the ban on cockfighting, with 56 percent voting in favor; they also rejected the increased signature threshold, with only 46 percent voting in favor. The industry immediately filed injunctions to stop the ban. Legislators also introduced proposals to undermine the ban. One proposal, Senate Bill 829 in 2003, would have declared a state of emergency and suspended the cockfighting ban for a period of 180 days and allowed counties that voted against it to hold special elections to permanently overturn State Question 687 within their boundaries. The bill was referred to committee but no further action has yet been taken.[3]

These activities in Oklahoma are part of a wider trend of attempts by state legislators to inhibit the initiative process. Voters in Utah approved a legislative referendum in 1998 that would require a supermajority of two-thirds of voters to enact new laws regulating the taking of wildlife. Other states have recently added or increased their distribution requirements. In 2002, voters in Montana approved a pair of legislative referendums that increased the number of counties in which the signature threshold for statutory and constitutional measures must be met from two-fifths to one-half. Voters in Wyoming also approved a constitutional amendment in 1998 that increased the distribution requirement from one signature in two-thirds of the counties to 15 percent of eligible voters in two-thirds of the counties. In 2002, Utah increased its distribution requirement from 10 percent in each of fifteen of its twenty-nine counties to 10 percent in each of twenty counties.

The proposed changes have met with resistance from initiative proponents, who have challenged their constitutionality. The Utah reform was struck down by the state Supreme Court. The logic was similar to that used by a U.S. District Court that struck down Idaho's distribution requirement in 2001: voters in sparsely populated counties would have more influence than voters in heavily populated counties. In Utah, the legislature is now considering requiring 10 percent in each of twenty-six out of twenty-nine state senate districts (*Salt Lake Tribune,* 2003).

These increased restrictions on ballot access matter. Increasing the number of signatures required makes it more expensive to qualify measures. Introducing or increasing distribution requirements also makes it harder, as proponents must expend more resources to gather signatures in more sparsely populated counties than in more densely populated areas. In a study of eight initiative petitions in California, Boehmke and Alvarez (2004a) find strong evidence that more signatures were gathered in densely populated counties, even after controlling for population. Their evidence also indicates an equitable geographic distribution of signatures relative to population and suggests that a moderate distribution requirement would not have invalidated these petitions, despite the fact that California does not have one. Yet in Idaho, proponents of the more stringent distribution requirement argued that it was necessary to keep the number of initiatives low, despite the fact that only twenty-five measures have appeared on its ballot since 1912.

Had the Idaho and Utah reforms held, they would likely have decreased the number of proposals even further. In a study of the effect of regulations, social factors, and interest group populations on initiative use in all states from 1976 to 2000, Boehmke (2003b) finds that states with distribution requirements have about two fewer initiatives per two-year election cycle. Along with signature requirements and the circulation period for gathering the signatures, distribution requirements are one of the most important regulations governing ballot access. Increasing these requirements decreases groups' access to the ballot and their ability to influence policy directly or indirectly. The consequences are evident in chapter 4, which shows that larger signature requirements made it less likely that a state adopted Indian gaming.

If reforms along these lines continue, the initiative process will become more difficult to use.[4] With their ability to influence policy through the ballot reduced, many of the indirect effects of the initiative process on interest groups will evaporate. All of the consequences of the initiative process predicted by my model are predicated on groups' ability to propose or to credibly threaten to propose a ballot measure. As their ability to do this decreases, so too does the indirect effect of the initiative process. Fewer groups mobilize, and the state's interest group population would look increasingly like those in noninitiative states.

It is likely that these trends of tightening ballot access will continue. In 2002, the National Conference of State Legislatures released a report condemning the initiative process. It concluded that states without the initiative process should not even consider adopting it and states that currently have it should make it harder to utilize:

> The task force does not recommend that states that currently do not have an initiative process adopt one. The task force believes that representative democracy is more desirable than the initiative. The disadvantages of the initiative as a tool for policymaking are many, and the opportunities for abuse of the process outweigh its advantages. (National Conference of State Legislatures 2002, ix)

These conclusions certainly make sense given elected officials' general disdain of the process and frustration over having their monopoly on the ability to legislate broken. It also makes sense in light of recent research by journalists (Schrag 1998; Broder 2000) and academics (Smith 1998; Ellis 2002) that implies that the initiative process has been taken over by self-interested groups and is no longer a tool for grassroots movements.

In light of these conclusions and findings, where does the evidence in this book leave us? While certainly not demonstrating that they are all inaccurate—the initiative does take policymaking out of the legislature's hands, and it is used by organized interest groups—it leads me to believe that at the very least these critics and reformers have not considered the full extent to which the initiative process influences state politics. Rather, they have focused on the effect of specific initiatives that reach the ballot. Yet the theoretical and empirical results in this book show that the indirect effect is both pervasive and substantial. Furthermore, the indirect effect operates to reduce bias in interest group representation by empowering citizen interest groups vis-à-vis economic groups. State institutions that increase representation for the common citizen should be seen as beneficial and a potential counter to some of the perceived drawbacks of the initiative process as currently practiced.

The question remains, then, whether the theory and evidence contained in this book outweigh some of the perceived problems with the initiative process. Although I do not claim to have a definitive answer, a few comments are in order. First, the number of initiatives that make the ballot is relatively small and has actually been decreasing from its high-water mark in the mid-1990s. Since its inception, the average number of direct and indirect initiatives that appear on statewide ballots every year is one. The average number that actually pass is less than one-half. Even in the two highest-use states, California and Oregon, the average number that pass every year is still only one. And even during the period of the 1990s, these two states saw only two successful initiatives per year. In the greater scheme of things, then, use of the initiative pales in comparison with what happens in the legislature every year.[5] Certainly, this does not invalidate the argument that initiatives can occasionally have far-reaching consequences and that those consequences may be worse than those resulting from legislative statutes, but it is a healthy reminder for maintaining perspective on the nature and extent of the potential problem.

Second, it is almost inconceivable that the initiative process today could exist and not be used by organized interests. The way that ordinary citizens are represented before government has changed radically over the past century. Interest groups now represent a much more diverse array of citizens, and a large part of political representation has shifted from the individual level to the group level.[6] This makes it exceedingly unlikely that an issue could reach the ballot that does not stir the passions of an already organized collection of individuals. So while the original intent of the founders of the initiative and referendum may have been to break the influence of powerful economic interests by returning power to the common citizen, perhaps in today's environment this goal is better accomplished by fostering the mobilization and participation of a broader array of organized interests. In fact, similar logic has been applied to the role of government as a patron of typically underrepresented interest groups (Walker 1991) and the relationship between PAC regulations and which groups form PACs (Gais 1996).

These increases in mobilization and representation are only one part of the indirect effect of the initiative process. While the criticisms of the direct effect focus mainly on specific proposals and voters' ability to decide them, the indirect effect permeates state politics on a day-to-day basis. These new groups are constantly advocating for their interests, and not just at the ballot box, but also in the legislature. And the legislature is forced to pay attention to their positions because of the threat that the group could propose an initiative. This allows groups to leverage their resources in different ways and shifts the balance of power, if only a little, from groups with predominantly financial resources to groups with a membership base.

Although the evidence in this book focuses on the characteristics and behavior of these groups, the cumulative indirect effect also includes the consequences of their existence and activities. These consequences are manifested in their ability to set or shift the agenda, their ability to advocate for or against new bills, their ability to provide evidence to bureaucrats, and their ability to influence voters and elections. While it may be difficult to isolate specific cases of these consequences, when taken together, they are likely to have significant political ramifications for initiative state politics.

Whether one concludes that the initiative process does, on balance, benefit citizens depends on how heavily one weights the increase in representation against its potential to subvert representative democracy. While there is still mixed evidence on the part of academic studies of the policy effects of the initiative process, the results of this study and those that look at other aspects of state politics such as voter turnout, knowledge, or efficacy (Boehmke and Alvarez 2004b; Bowler and Donovan 2002; Smith 2001; Smith and Tolbert 2004; Tolbert, McNeal, and Smith 2003) almost uniformly show an increase in either political activity or the diversity of those involved in these other areas. Given the overall concern regarding decreased participation in American politics, the increase in activity in initiative states is one way to help overcome it.

On balance, then, even if the concerns of critics of the process are valid, the countervailing effects should also be taken into account. Before advocating the abolition of the process, one should attempt to more fully appreciate the broader effect of institutions such as the initiative process on interest groups and state politics in general.

Appendices

Appendix A: Rules and Regulations for Initiatives and Referendums

Table A.1
Initiative and Popular Referendum Provisions by State

State	Provisions	State	Provisions
AL		MT	S,C,PR
AK	S,PR	NE	S,C,PR
AZ	S,C,PR	NV	IS,C,PR
AR	S,C,PR	NH	
CA	S,C,PR	NJ	
CO	S,C,PR	NM	PR
CT		NY	
DE		NC	
FL	C	ND	S,C,PR
GA		OH	IS,C,PR
HI		OK	S,C,PR
ID	S,PR	OR	S,C,PR
IL	C	PA	
IN		RI	
IA		SC	
KS		SD	S,C,PR
KY	PR	TN	
LA		TX	
ME	IS,PR	UT	S,IS,PR
MD	PR	VT	
MA	IS,IC,PR	VA	
MI	C,IS,PR	WA	S,IS,PR
MN		WV	
MS	IC	WI	
MO	S,C,PR	WY	S,PR

Source: Gerber (1999), Zimmerman (2001), National Conference of State Legislatures (2002).
S = Direct Statutory, C = Direct Constitutional, IS = Indirect Statutory, IC = Indirect Constitutional, PR = Popular Referendum.

Table A.2
Years of Initial Initiative or Popular Referendum Adoption

State	Year Adopted	State	Year Adopted
SD	1898	NE	1912
UT	1900	OH	1912
OR	1902	WA	1912
ND	1905	MI	1913
MT	1906	NV	1914
OK	1907	KY	1915
ME	1908	MD	1915
MO	1908	MA	1918
AZ	1910	AK	1956
CO	1910	FL	1968
AR	1911	WY	1968
CA	1911	IL	1970
NM	1911	MS	1992
ID	1912		

Sources: Matsusaka (2004), state documents, Initiative and Referendum Institute.

Table A.3
Signature Requirements for Initiative Provisions (%)

	Direct		Indirect			Direct		Indirect	
State	Stat.	Const.	Stat.	Const.	State	Stat.	Const.	Stat.	Const.
AL					MT	5	10		
AK	10				NE	7	10		
AZ	10	15			NV		10	10	
AR	8	10			NH				
CA	5	8			NJ				
CO	5	5			NM				
CT					NY				
DE					NC				
FL		8			ND	2	4		
GA					OH		10	3+3	
HI					OK	8	15		
ID	6				OR	6	8		
IL		8			PA				
IN					RI				
IA					SC				
KS					SD	5	10		
KY					TN				
LA					TX				
ME			10		UT	10		10	
MD					VT				
MA			3+0.5	3	VA				
MI		10	8		WA	8		8	
MN					WV				
MS			12		WI				
MO	5	8			WY	15			

Source: Gerber (1999), Zimmerman (2001).
Note: In Massachusetts and Ohio the first number is the signature requirement for putting an indirect statutory initiative before the legislature. If it is not adopted the second number indicates the extra signatures needed to qualify it for the ballot. Stat. = statutory, Const. = constitutional

Appendix B: Derivation of Formal Results

Assume a binary policy space with elements 0 and 1. Let the status quo be at 0.[1] Assume the legislature and the interest group have opposite ideal points: the legislature's ideal point is 0, and the interest group's is 1. Denote the probability that an initiative passes in state *i* as λ_i, and the cost of a proposal as *c*. The utilities to the two actors of the possible outcomes are as follows:

$$u_L(0) = 0,$$
$$u_L(1) = -\beta,$$
$$u_G(0) = -1,$$
$$u_G(1) = 0.$$

Assume $\beta > 0$ and $0 \leq c \leq 1$. If $c > 1$ the interest group will never propose an initiative and the results will be equivalent to those in states without the initiative process. The sequence of moves is as follows. The interest group can offer the legislature contributions in exchange for the legislature's moving policy from 0 to 1. The legislature can agree or disagree with this proposal. If it agrees, the two actors enter a Nash bargaining game to determine the exact amount of money that will change hands. If it disagrees, or if the group does not offer contributions, the group then has the option of proposing an initiative to move policy to 1. If it does propose, the initiative passes and policy moves to 1 with probability λ_i, after which the game ends. If it does not propose an initiative, policy stays at 0 and the game ends.

Proposition 1: *The subgame perfect equilibrium in the game depends on* β. *When* $\beta \leq 1$, *the legislature and the interest group successfully bargain to move policy. When* $\beta > 1$ *the outcome depends on the value of* λ_i.

1. $\lambda_i < \lambda_i^*$ *The group does not propose an initiative and cannot bargain with the legislature.*
2. $\lambda_i^* \leq \lambda_i < \lambda_i^B$ *The group proposes an initiative.*
3. $\lambda_i^B \leq \lambda_i$ *The interest group and the legislature successfully bargain to move policy.*

Proof. The legislature has to decide, based on β and the probability of an initiative's passing, whether to agree to bargain. If it does, it accepts the group's contribution (determined by applying the Nash bargaining solution) and moves policy. Otherwise, the group is left to potentially propose an initiative.

The group has to decide if it wants to propose an initiative, which will depend on the cost c and the probability of passage λ_i and then, given this information, it determines if convincing the legislature to move policy by making contributions is more cost-effective. The interest group is willing to use the initiative when it has an expected utility greater than or equal to -1. This happens when

$$\lambda_i u_G(1) + (1-\lambda_i)u_G(0) - c \geq -1,$$
$$(1-\lambda_i)(-1) - c \geq -1,$$
$$\lambda_i \geq c.$$

Call the value of λ_i that meets this condition with equality λ_i^*. For values greater than this, the initiative will have expected utility greater than or equal to the status quo.[2] Now I derive the Nash bargaining solution for the contributions subgame.

Denote the transfer t and let u^b_i be the utility to $i \in \{L,G\}$ of bargaining and u^r_i be the reservation utility of not bargaining. First I look at the case where $\lambda_i < \lambda_i^*$.

$$u_L^b = -\beta + t,$$
$$u_L^r = 0,$$
$$u_G^b = -t,$$
$$u_G^r = -1.$$

The two actors will only agree to the contributions arrangement if it offers greater utility than leaving policy where it is. This implies

$$u_L^b > u_L^r,$$
$$-\beta + t > 0,$$

and

$$u_G^b > u_G^r,$$
$$-t > -1.$$

This bounds the possible set of transfers:

$$\beta < t < 1.$$

One of the features of the Nash bargaining solution is that if the two bargainers have the same utility function (up to a scale factor), they will split the surplus generated by the bargain, which in this case is $1-\beta$.[3] The Nash

Bargaining Solution therefore dictates that the equilibrium transfer is

$$t^* = \frac{1+\beta}{2}. \qquad (1)$$

In the other case, when $\lambda_i \geq \lambda_i^*$ only the reservation utilities change:

$$u_L^r = -\beta\lambda_i,$$
$$u_G^r = -1 + \lambda_i - c.$$

This alters the bounds on the possible transfers:

$$-\beta\lambda_i < t < 1 - \lambda_i + c.$$

Splitting the difference again,

$$t^* = \frac{c + (1+\beta)(1-\lambda_i)}{2}. \qquad (2)$$

There are two cases to consider in determining when the group will choose to propose an initiative rather than bargain with the legislature. In the first case ($\beta \leq 1$), the group can always persuade the legislature to move policy for contributions. In the second case ($\beta > 1$), the group cannot compensate the legislature for its utility loss unless it has a high probability of success at the ballot.

These two cases are outlined in figures 2.1 and 2.2.

Case 1: $\beta \leq 1$

The group and the legislature always bargain. The interest group prefers to bargain when

$$-t^* \geq -1 + \lambda_i - c, \qquad (3)$$

$$-\frac{c + (1+\beta)(1-\lambda_i)}{2} \geq -1 + \lambda_i - c, \qquad (4)$$

$$\beta(1-\lambda_i) \leq 1 - \lambda_i + c \qquad (5)$$

$$\lambda_i(1-\beta) \leq 1 - \beta + c. \qquad (6)$$

When $\beta = 1$ this condition is always met, since $c \geq 0$. When $\beta < 1$, one additional step shows that the inequality in 6 is always met:

$$\lambda_i \leq \frac{1-\beta+c}{1-\beta}. \qquad (7)$$

Call the value of λ_i that meets this at equality λ_i^B. Taking the same steps for the legislature indicates that it bargains under the same conditions. Since it is obvious that $\lambda_i^B \geq 1$ (since $c \geq 0$ bargaining will always occur in this case.

Case 2: $\beta > 1$

In this case, the group is not able to fully compensate the legislature for its utility loss associated with moving policy when the probability of an initiative's passing is low. As the probability increases, however, the legislature may become willing to bargain. The difference occurs because the inequality in 7 switches directions when $1-\beta<0$. The group and the legislature bargain whenever $\lambda_i \geq \lambda_i^B$, and the group proposes an initiative whenever $\lambda_i < \lambda_i^B$.

In this case, bargaining is always a possibility, since $\lambda_i^B \leq 1$. Initiatives are not always a possibility, however, since $\lambda_i^B \leq \lambda_i^*$ for some combinations of β and c. This gives the equilibrium outcome as outlined in the proposition 1. QED

Proposition 2: *The presence of the initiative process makes the proposing interest group weakly better off in expectation.*

Proof. If the interest group proposes an initiative, it must provide higher expected utility than the status quo, which is at the legislature's ideal point by proposition 1.

All that is needed is to show that it also does better in the bargaining game. The interest group's utility of bargaining is $u^b_G = -t^*$. If there is no expected utility gain from the initiative ($\lambda_i < \lambda_i^*$) the transfer is the same, so the possibility of proposing an initiative has no effect on the group's utility.

When $\lambda_i \geq \lambda_i^*$, the ability to propose an initiative can make the group better off. This can be shown by comparing the transfers made with and without the initiative process (equations 1 and 2):

$$\frac{c+(1+\beta)(1-\lambda_i)}{2} \leq \frac{1+\beta}{2} \qquad (8)$$

$$c+(1+\beta)(1-\lambda_i)-(1+\beta) \leq 0 \qquad (9)$$

$$c \leq \lambda_i(1+\beta). \qquad (10)$$

I now substitute $\lambda_i^* = c$ into 10 and use the fact that the transfer is only reduced by access to the initiative when $\lambda_i \geq \lambda_i^*$.

$$\lambda_i^* \leq \lambda_i(1+\beta) \qquad (11)$$

$$\frac{\lambda_i^*}{\lambda_i} \leq 1+\beta \qquad (12)$$

Since $\beta>0$ the last inequality always holds. When there exists a utility-increasing initiative for the interest group, either it makes the reduced equilibrium transfer to the legislature, or it proposes an initiative. Because the group would only decline contributions in favor of an initiative if the initiative offered greater expected utility, it is always weakly better off with the initiative.

Proposition 3: *If voters' preferences are positively correlated, neighbors' adoptions increase policy adoptions in initiative states, but not in noninitiative states, and only if the neighboring state is also an initiative state.*

Proof. Given that λ_i is drawn according to some distribution at the start of the game, the actors' best guess is just the mean of this distribution, $E[\lambda_i]$. When there is correlation between the two states' draws, $\rho=\text{Corr}(\lambda_i,\lambda_j)$, then the outcome in state j is useful for estimating λ_i, which can be written as $\text{E}[\lambda_i|\lambda_j,\rho]$. When ρ is positive, $\text{E}[\lambda_i|\lambda_j,\rho>0]\geq E[\lambda_i|\lambda_j,\rho=0]$; when ρ is negative, the opposite relationship holds.

Actors do not directly observe their neighbor's realization of λ_j, however—just whether the policy was adopted or not. This information can be used to update their beliefs about the realization of λ_j, though, since the players in state i know that initiative states will only adopt for certain values of this variable.[4]

Appendix C: Survey Instrument

Selection of Sample

I set out to survey groups in four states, two with the initiative and two without. A pretest was also conducted, which added a fifth state. In choosing the states, I tried to generate variation in the characteristics of their interest group populations, location, and use of the initiative process. Drawing on Gray and Lowery's (1996) state-level interest group population characteristics from 1990, I compiled the set of states shown in table C.1.

Table C.1
Rankings of Selected States' Interest Group Populations

	Initiative	Total Groups	Density	Diversity
Arizona	Yes	17	30	49
Minnesota	No	7	32	32
New Mexico	No	26	44	28
Oregon	Yes	16	36	25
South Dakota	Yes	37	45	27

Source: Gray and Lowery (1996)
Numbers are for 1990.

Data Sources and Procedures

After adjusting the survey instrument using the results of a pretest of 50 groups in Minnesota and South Dakota (which had a response rate of 28 percent), I obtained lists of groups registered to lobby in the four main survey states (Arizona, Minnesota, New Mexico, and Oregon) from the secretary of state for each state. I then randomly selected five hundred groups in each state, as many as finances would allow, to receive a copy of the mail survey and assigned each group a unique identification code to ensure anonymity. Groups in initiative states received an extra section requesting information about their involvement with the initiative process. After the surveys were sent, I waited ten days and sent a postcard reminding them to return the survey and including information about how to get another if they had misplaced the first. A final reminder card was sent in another ten days. Of the 2,000 surveys mailed, about 200 were returned to me by the post office as "addressee not found," and of the remaining 1,800, 292 were returned at least partially completed by the

Table C.2
Response Frequencies and Survey Weights

	Mail Survey	Phone Survey	Weight
Trade associations	0.16	0.13	0.85
Professional associations	0.18	0.08	0.44
Labor unions	0.04	0.07	1.72
Business firm or corporation	0.10	0.33	3.42
Government association	0.10	0.08	0.82
Social organization	0.04	0.00	0.25
Charity	0.03	0.00	0.25
Non-profit research group	0.01	0.00	0.25
Foundation	0.00	0.04	0.00
Other	0.34	0.27	0.77
Number of Groups Sampled	2000	100	
Number of Responses	292	73	

The categories with zero cells in the phone survey were assigned weights of 0.25 since they have non-zero frequencies in the mail survey. Since there were no foundations in the mail survey responses, they received a weight of zero, though it does not matter.

groups for a response rate of 16 percent. Because of the relatively low response rate in the main survey, I added the responses from the pretest (adjusting the responses to account for slight differences in wording and response categories). These responses comprise the data set for the analysis in chapters 5 and 6.

The sample for the telephone portion of the survey, used to construct the sampling weights, was drawn randomly from the set of groups not selected to receive the mail survey. Fifty groups in each state were drawn. Phone calls were then placed to groups in Oregon and New Mexico, who were asked four identical questions. Of the one hundred numbers drawn, about seven groups were not found at their listed number or any other number, though efforts were made to track down groups through the phone book or on the Internet. Responses were given by seventy-three groups for a response rate of 78 percent.[1] Their responses on these questions were used, along with the frequencies of responses in the mail survey, to compute the weights used in the analysis, as outlined in table C.2.

Survey Instrument

Following is a copy of the survey questionnaire mailed to two thousand groups in the winter of 1999. Copies of this survey were sent to groups in Arizona, Minnesota, New Mexico, and Oregon. A pretest version of this survey was sent to fifty groups in Minnesota and South Dakota. Minor modifications were made to the wording of questions and the response categories based on the pretest results; otherwise the content was quite similar. Note that this is a copy of the survey used in initiative states. The version for groups in noninitiative states omitted references to the initiative process and did not include questions 23–31.

State-Level Survey of Group Activities

The purpose of this survey is to learn more about how groups such as yours are represented at the state level. Your response is very important to us in accomplishing this goal.

To help us understand the different ways in which organizations make themselves heard, it is important that we get information from all types of groups, including those that may not view government and policy-related activities as an important part of their overall functions. This will help us get a more accurate view of what the typical group does.

In the following survey you will be asked questions about the general characteristics of your group as well as questions relating to different types of activities that organizations engage in at the state level. Your response will be kept **completely confidential,** and the results of this survey will only be reported in statistical formats that will prevent individual organizations from being identified.

. . . .

Please answer all questions as well as you can. If you do not know the answer, or do not have access to the relevant information for a particular question, please move on and answer as many of the others as you can. When asked to choose from a set of responses, please mark the one that best describes your answer. If there are no boxes available for your response, please check the one that best applies and indicate your answer in the margin.

Your organization has been contacted due to its activities in the state of Oregon. Please answer all questions with respect to your resources or activities in that state only.

Background Information

The following series of questions is to provide background information on your organization and its activities.

1. Which best describes your organization? Please check one.
   Trade association ❑
   Professional association ❑
   Labor union ❑
   Business firm or corporation ❑
   Government association ❑
   Social organization ❑
   Charity ❑
   Nonprofit research group ❑
   Foundation ❑
   Other (Please indicate)________________

2. How many years has your organization been active in Oregon?

   ____

3. What was the approximate total (national) revenue for this organization from all financial sources, including grants and contracts, during the last fiscal year?

Less than $50,000	❑	$500,001–$1,000,000	❑
$50,001–$100,000	❑	$1,000,001–$10,000,000	❑
$100,001–$500,000	❑	$10,000,001 or more	❑

4. Does your organization have an affiliated political action committee?
   Yes ❑ No ❑
   If yes, what is the name of that PAC, and how much money did it contribute to candidates' last election cycle?

   Name________________________________
   $________________

5. Does your organization accept individuals as members?
   Yes ❑ No ❑
   If you answered yes, please indicate how many individual members your organization has, otherwise please skip to the next question.

0–50	❑	501–1,000	❑
51–100	❑	1,001–5,000	❑
101–250	❑	5,001–10,000	❑
251–500	❑	More than 10,000	❑

6. How many full time equivalent employees does your organization have? How many full-time equivalent volunteers does it have in Oregon?

Paid staff		Volunteers	
None	❑	None	❑
1	❑	1	❑
2–5	❑	2–5	❑
6–20	❑	6–20	❑
21–50	❑	21–50	❑
51–100	❑	51–100	❑
More than 100	❑	More than 100	❑

7. How often is your group active in government relations, including monitoring government activities, preparing reports or comments about proposed policies, mobilizing citizens regarding proposed policies, or contacting government officials?

Daily	❑	Several times a year	❑
Weekly	❑	Once a year or less	❑
Monthly	❑	Never	❑

8. The diversity of interests varies across groups. For each of the following policy areas, please indicate how active your group is. A 1 indicates that you are not active in that policy area (no resources expended on it in the last two years), while a 5 indicates that you are very active in that area.

	Not active in this area				Very active in this area
Agriculture	1	2	3	4	5
Civil rights and civil liberties	1	2	3	4	5
Crime and law enforcement	1	2	3	4	5
State economy (money supply, taxation, and regulations affecting business, insurance, labor, or banking)	1	2	3	4	5
Education	1	2	3	4	5
Energy and natural resources	1	2	3	4	5
Environmental policy	1	2	3	4	5
Health policy	1	2	3	4	5
Government operations (including state personnel policy, administrative organization, and elections)	1	2	3	4	5
Social welfare	1	2	3	4	5
Sports, entertainment, and recreation	1	2	3	4	5
Technology (e.g., space, science, or communications policy)	1	2	3	4	5
Transportation	1	2	3	4	5
Other (please specify) ______________________	1	2	3	4	5

9. Please answer the following questions with respect to legislative bills in Oregon from the last year.

   To how many did you considered devoting any resources?

   ____

   Of those, to how many did you actually devote some resources (staff time, money, etc.)?____________________

   Of those, to how many did you devote a large amount of resources?____________________

10. From the previous question, when choosing from the bills that you considered devoting some resources to, how important were the following in determining which you devoted a large amount of resources to?

	Not very				Very
Total resources available	1	2	3	4	5
Importance of policy	1	2	3	4	5
Member support	1	2	3	4	5
Public support	1	2	3	4	5
Legislative activities on that issue	1	2	3	4	5
Lack of other groups' activity	1	2	3	4	5
Lack of opposition	1	2	3	4	5

Particular Issue

One method that organizations have at their disposal to change public policy in Oregon is the direct initiative process, whereby groups can place legislation directly on the ballot for voters to decide on. If your organization was involved with an initiative or a potential initiative within the last two years, please use the issue that it concerned in answering the following questions. It is not necessary that your involvement ended with an initiative on the ballot, or that if it did, your group was still involved in the effort. If you were involved in a campaign against an initiative, please use that issue.

If you were not involved with any initiatives within the last two years, please choose the most recent public policy issue (including state rulemaking procedures) in which this organization has been involved and with which you are familiar. It is not necessary for the issue to be directly tied to a particular bill or regulation. If your organization stays in contact with government officials to advise them about the general problems facing members of your organization or your industry, you may use that as your issue.

11. What was that issue? Please note general policy area and specific details if possible.

12. Was this organization for or against changes on this issue?

13. For how many years has this organization been involved in this issue in Oregon?
_______________ years

14. Does this organization plan to register to lobby next year (1999–2000)?
Yes ❑ No ❑

15. Besides this organization, about how many organizations were active on this issue?

None	❑	16–25	❑
1–5	❑	26–50	❑
6–10	❑	51 or more	❑
11–15	❑		

16. If you answered none in the previous question, please skip to the next question; otherwise, please indicate approximately how many of those groups fall into the following categories.

About how many of those were in agreement with you? _________________

Of the groups that were in agreement with you, how many did you interact directly with? ______

Of those groups that you interacted directly with, how many did you share information with? ______

Of those groups that you shared information with, how many did you coordinate activities with? ______

17. In general, organizations often engage in the following activities in their attempts to make their voices heard. Different groups, however, use different methods. For each of the following activities, please indicate how important it was for your group in this instance.

	Not very				Very
Contacting legislators or staff	1	2	3	4	5
Policy research	1	2	3	4	5
Press releases	1	2	3	4	5
Litigation	1	2	3	4	5
Testifying before committees	1	2	3	4	5
Mobilizing members	1	2	3	4	5
Making campaign contributions	1	2	3	4	5
Paid advertisements	1	2	3	4	5
Responding to requests for information	1	2	3	4	5
Asking influential citizens to contact legislators	1	2	3	4	5
Drafting legislation	1	2	3	4	5
Contacting agency officials	1	2	3	4	5
Public opinion information	1	2	3	4	5
Monitoring policy	1	2	3	4	5
Organizing mail/phone campaigns	1	2	3	4	5
Pointing out other policy implications	1	2	3	4	5
Election campaigning	1	2	3	4	5
Public demonstrations or protests	1	2	3	4	5
Seeking elected officials' endorsements	1	2	3	4	5
Building support among groups of legislators	1	2	3	4	5

18. Organizations often express their views directly to legislators when trying to influence public policy. If you contacted any regarding this particular issue, please indicate the importance of the following in determining whom you contacted. Otherwise, please skip this question.

	Not very				Very
Committee membership	1	2	3	4	5
Historical issue involvement	1	2	3	4	5
Previous interaction	1	2	3	4	5
Constituent characteristics/concerns	1	2	3	4	5
Similar policy opinions	1	2	3	4	5
Dissimilar policy opinions	1	2	3	4	5
Other groups already contacted	1	2	3	4	5
Request for information	1	2	3	4	5

19. How important were the following factors in motivating your involvement on this issue?

	Not very				Very
Legislative connections	1	2	3	4	5
Increasing number of supporters	1	2	3	4	5
Increasing total resources available	1	2	3	4	5
Importance of issue to group	1	2	3	4	5
Historical involvement	1	2	3	4	5
Public duty	1	2	3	4	5
Detailed technical knowledge	1	2	3	4	5
Opposition groups' actions	1	2	3	4	5
Need for current information on policy	1	2	3	4	5

20. Were any other types of governmental actors, such as courts, the state governor, state or local governments, etc., active in this issue?
Yes ❑ No ❑

About how many?

Please list them.

21. Relative to your most desired outcome, when your group got involved on this issue where did you expect government policy to be when it was resolved, compared to where it was then?

Much closer	❑	A little farther	❑
A little closer	❑	Much farther	❑
No change	❑	Don't know	❑

22. At the present moment, how has government policy moved on this issue, relative to your most desired outcome, compared to where it was when your group became involved?

Much closer	❑	A little farther	❑
A little closer	❑	Much farther	❑
No change	❑	Don't know	❑

If you were not involved in an initiative on this issue, please skip to the concluding section on page eleven. If you were involved in an initiative, please continue with question twenty-three.

23. With respect to this initiative or initiative attempt, please check all of the following activities in which your group was directly involved.

Drafting the initiative	❑
Doing technical research about implications	❑
Paid advertisements	❑
Preparing press releases	❑
Gathering signatures	❑
Legal research/advice	❑
Mobilizing members	❑
Gauging public opinion	❑

Providing funds to supporting groups ❑
Providing funds to opposing groups ❑
Public endorsement ❑
Testifying before committees ❑
Testifying before agencies ❑
Seeking elected officials' or candidates'endorsements ❑
Other (Please indicate): ________________ ❑

24. If your group was involved in the drive for a potential initiative, what forces led you to consider its use?

Check here if not involved ❑
Public support ❑
Legislative unresponsiveness ❑
Organized opposition ❑
Focus election on this issue ❑
Increase voter turnout ❑
Opposition's lobbying power ❑
Another initiative ❑
Other (Please indicate): ________________ ❑

25. Before the initiative was drafted, did you engage in any of the following activities on this issue? Please check all that apply.

Contacting legislators ❑
Research/Providing information ❑
Litigation ❑
Media campaign ❑
Gauging public opinion ❑
PAC contributions ❑
Testifying before committees ❑
Working with other groups ❑
Other (Please indicate): ________________ ❑

26. Besides those that you sought out, did any other politicians take a public stand:
Opposing your position on this issue? Yes ❑ No ❑
Supporting your position on this issue? Yes ❑ No ❑

27. If you responded that politicians took a stand supporting your position on this issue in the previous question, please indicate whether you publicized their support, otherwise please skip to the next question.

Publicized ❑ Did not publicize ❑

28. If you began to gather signatures for qualification, what percentage of volunteer signature gatherers did you use?
If no signature gathering started, check here

Zero percent	❑	26–50 percent	❑
One to ten percent	❑	51–75 percent	❑
11–25 percent	❑	76–100 percent	❑

29. Did the initiative reach the ballot?

    Yes ❑ No ❑

    If not, please check all reasons that apply. Otherwise, please skip to the next question.

    Monetary ❑
    Lack of public support ❑
    Legislative action ❑
    Organized opposition ❑
    Not enough signatures ❑
    Not reflective of your policy desires ❑
    Legal concerns ❑
    Other (Please indicate): ____________ ❑

30. What were your group's total expenditures on the initiative campaign?

    $ _______

31. Were any bills drafted and introduced in the legislature on this issue? If so, please indicate when the first action occurred.

    Check here if no bills introduced or drafted
    Before signature collection began ❑
    During signature collection ❑
    After ballot qualification ❑
    After placed on ballot ❑
    After election ❑

Concluding Section

To help us in our analysis, the final few questions concern you, the person who completed this survey.

Who completed this survey?

Director of this organization ❑
Director of government relations ❑
Public relations director ❑
Public relations staff member ❑
Government relations staff member ❑
Other (Please indicate)____________ ❑

33. How long have you been with this organization? ______________________

34. Are there any topics not treated in this questionnaire that you feel are important for understanding how organizations like this one are represented? Are there any comments that you would like to make about this study? Please give us any reactions you may have. Use the back of this questionnaire or attach additional sheets if necessary.

We would welcome other information that you think might help us

understand your organization or the policy issue that you discussed above. Examples of things you might enclose when returning the survey include this organization's annual statement, organizational newsletters, or recent press releases.

May we have permission to contact you by phone, if necessary, to learn more about your organization or clarify an answer? If you are willing to be contacted by phone, please list your name and telephone number below.

Name ____________ Phone ____________

Thank you for your help and cooperation in completing this survey.

If your organization would like to request a copy of the survey results in statistical form only, please include a phone number and a mailing address for this to be sent to.

Notes

Chapter 1

1. The initiatives in Colorado and the District of Columbia were nullified for procedural reasons, however. The Colorado ballot measure was nullified as a result of a judge's ruling that the initiative had not mustered enough signatures. Initially, it was unclear whether the District of Columbia measure had passed, because the results were held up by the U.S. Congress in light of previous legislation that prohibited federal funds to be used on any district initiative that would legalize drugs (Shinkman 1998).

2. A significant amount of financial contributions for these and other medicinal marijuana initiatives came from George Soros, including $400,000 for Washington's I-685 and I-692 (some of which also came from Lewis and Sperling) (George 1998), as well as over $1 million combined for Proposition 215 and in Arizona (Miller 1996).

3. For examples, see Schmidt's (1989) list of ten common criticisms leveled against the initiative process.

4. Gerber, Hajnal, and Louch 2002 perform an extensive test of whether ethnic minorities find themselves on the wrong side of initiatives and conclude that this is the case in only a very small number of initiatives. See also Gamble (1997) and Bowler and Donovan (1998).

5. Though see chapter 15 in Gerber, Lupia, McCubbins, and Kiewiet (2001) for evidence that the effects of Proposition 13 have been overstated.

6. For a counterargument to the existence of an initiative golden age in the early 1900s, see Ellis (2002) or Smith and Lubinski (2002).

7. A systematic discussion of the variation in initiative provisions and regulations across states is contained in the next chapter and in Appendix A.

8. See Smith and Tolbert (2004) for an extended study and review of findings regarding the effect of the initiative process on citizen participation.

Chapter 2

1. Quoted from the Initiative and Referendum Institute's Web site: http://www.landrinstitute.com/New%201R%20Webwite%201Info

/drop%20Down%20Boxes/Quick%20Facts/Almanac%20-%20I&R% Quotes%20Regarding%20the%20I&R%20Process.pdf, taken from a letter to M. Dane Waters, president of the Initiative and Referendum Institute, 1999.

2. Ibid.

3. Both Alaska and Wyoming have forms of the direct initiative that are similar to the indirect initiative, since they require that proposals cannot be placed on the ballot until the legislature has met and had an opportunity to act. Because the measures are not formally submitted to the legislature, I list these as direct forms of the initiative process.

4. See table A.1 in appendix A for complete listings.

5. Furthermore, there are only two states with popular referendums that do not have some form of initiative, which would make it difficult to distinguish its effect.

6. Eight states added provisions in 1834 that prevented their constitutions from being amended without voters' approval, and after 1857 Congress required all new states to submit their constitutions to a popular vote (Initiative and Referendum Institute).

7. See Cain and Miller (2001) for a discussion of the different goals of Populists and Progressives.

8. See table A.2 in Appendix A for a complete list of years of adoption.

9. Although Mississippi originally adopted the initiative and referendum in 1914, its state Supreme Court overturned the process in 1922 (Matsusaka 2004).

10. These bans were overturned when the Supreme Court ruled in *Meyer v. Grant* [486 U.S. 414 (1988)] that they violate the First Amendment and that there is not a sufficient state interest in regulating the process to reduce fraud to warrant such an infringement (Ellis 2003; Lowenstein and Stern 1989; Tolbert, Lowenstein, and Donovan 1998). See Lowenstein and Stern (1989) for an extended discussion of this decision.

11. Minnesota has actually had a majority of votes cast for the initiative and referendum three times during the twentieth century, but each time the measure failed to garner the required majority of all voters who voted on any item on the ballot (Schmidt 1989).

12. George Pataki, Governor of the State of New York, in a March 12, 2002, press release announcing his support for an initiative and referendum constitutional amendment. Quoted on the Initiative and Referendum Institute's Web site: http://www.iandrinstitute.com/New%20IRI%20Website%20Info/Drop%20Down%20Boxes/Quick%20Facts/Almanac%20-%20I&R20Quotes%20Regarding%20the%20I&R%20Process.pdf, January 9, 2005.

13. Initiative usage data taken from the Initiative and Referendum's Web site: http://www.iandrinstitute.com/New%20IRI%20Website%20Info/Drop%2

0Down%20Boxes/Historical/Statewide%20Initiatives%201904–2000.pdf, January 9, 2005. See Banducci (1998), Matsusaka and McCarty (2001), and Boehmke (2003b) for studies that seek to explain variation in statewide initiative use across states and over time.

14. At various times, some of these examples were, in fact, controversial. When daylight saving time first appeared on California's ballot in 1930, it was the most voted-on measure and was defeated with 76 percent voting against it. After five attempts in the legislature, the issue reappeared on the ballot ten years later and was again defeated with opposition coming from movie theaters, labor organization, agricultural interests, religious interests, and women's groups. Only nine years later, however, with opposition in decline, the issue passed with 55 percent of the vote. See Allswang (2000) for more information on this issue in California. Similar turnarounds on this issue occurred in Colorado and Washington.

15. See table A.3 in appendix A for more details on signature requirements. Boehmke and Alvarez (2004a) study how demographic and economic factors influence the number of signatures gathered across California counties for eight different petitions.

16. A fact that it turns out the sponsors were probably aware of long before election day.

17. See Gerber, Lupia, McCubbins, and Kiewiet (2001) for a broad study of initiative implementation; see Bali (2003) for a study of countywide variation in the implementation of California's antibilingual education Proposition 227.

18. For introductions to the use of game theory in political science, see Morrow (1994) or Ordeshook (1992). This approach is not without its critics, however. See Green and Shapiro (1994) for one critique.

19. This assumption is made in many studies of interest groups. See, for example, Schlozman and Tierney (1986), Walker (1991), or Gerber (1999).

20. One could easily add a governor with veto power to the model, but it would not substantively change the effect of the initiative process on interest groups; it would just make it more difficult to achieve success through the legislature.

21. These models are variations on those developed by Romer and Rosenthal (1978, 1979) to study the effect of referendums on budgetary and expenditure issues; these models also assume a monopoly setter.

22. If the interest group and the legislature are in agreement about whether to adopt a policy, the initiative process has no effect on the outcome, since the legislature will adopt and the group will concur. By configuring the preferences of the actors in the model to be in opposition, I focus on the case where the initiative influences the outcome. As long as there is one policy or (potential) interest group that satisfies this condition, the predictions of the model all hold. I attempt to control for these preferences in the empirical tests whenever possible.

23. I assume that $\beta > 0$.
24. See Baumgartner and Leech (1998) for a discussion of the various findings.
25. See, for example, Grenzke (1989), Wright (1990, 1996), and Austen-Smith and Wright (1994).
26. Of course, the magnitude of this effect will depend on the allocation. If the group gets to keep the entire surplus, then it has less to gain from proposing initiatives; if the legislature gets to keep it all, the group has much to gain from the initiative.
27. This solution is often used in game theoretic models and is known as the Nash Bargaining Solution. It is characterized by the fact that none of the surplus is wasted and that if the bargainers have linear utility functions, as they do in this case, they divide the surplus in half. For more on Nash Bargaining, see Morrow (1994).
28. The equilibrium transfer is $t^* = (1 + \beta)/2$.
29. But see Lupia (1992), Bowler and Donovan (1998), and Boehmke and Patty (2003) for common types of information that rationally uninformed voters can use to make better decisions in initiative campaigns.
30. This uncertainty marks one of the important differences between my model and that of Gerber (1999), which assumes a continuous policy space and perfect information about which initiatives will pass. The combination of uncertainty and a continuous policy space is studied in Matsusaka and McCarty (2001). I treat the binary case for the reasons outlined previously, but also because the addition of bargaining can create difficulties in a continuous model: the interest group will almost always wish to make a proposal even after it successfully negotiates with the legislature, making any agreements tenuous at best. The current framework is more appropriate for my objectives, as it allows me to make specific predictions about the effect of the initiative process on interest group lobbying.
31. Briefly, applying the Nash Bargaining Solution with the initiative process leads to an equilibrium transfer amount $t^* = [c + (1 + \beta) \times (1 - \lambda)]/2$, which is less than $(1+\beta)/2$.
32. It follows that $\lambda^B > \lambda^*$, because the definition of λ^B requires $\lambda > \lambda^*$.
33. An interesting implication of this result is that neither high nor low probability initiatives actually reach the ballot.
34. Note that the group may be worse off in the end if it proposes an initiative and it fails. However, this loss is compensated on average by the fact that the initiative passes often enough to make proposing it worthwhile.
35. It would not be difficult to show, however, that the model predicts more initiatives will be proposed when campaign contribution limits are small. In effect, contribution limits make some of the potential Nash Bargaining outcomes impossible to implement, leading groups to end up at the ballot when they would prefer to bargain.
36. By better off, I mean that policy outcomes are closer to the median voter's

ideal point, not that all voters or even the average voter is better off.

37. A similar outcome obtains in the model with uncertainty developed by Matsusaka and McCarty (2001), who find that the initiative process can make voters worse off in the presence of an extreme interest group and a legislature that worries about its own interests more than its duty to represent voters.

38. I use the term *hypothesis* to encompass both implications and predictions.

39. This is not intended to create the impression that I make only these assumptions. There are, of course, many assumptions made in the model. I highlight these additional assumptions to underline the link between the model's mathematical predictions and what I feel are its broader implications for interest group politics.

40. Even if the group successfully lobbies the legislature, the size of the contribution is the same as without the initiative process, since both actors know the group will not propose an initiative if the legislature ignores it.

41. To the extent that implication 1 is true, however, it may not be the case that the cost of mobilization is the same in initiative states. If there are additional groups that have formed in response to the initiative process, then it may be more costly to form an additional group. Potential members may already be tapped out in terms of making either monetary or temporal contributions to other groups, making it more costly to attract and retain members. Additionally, groups may find it more difficult to access the legislature, especially when they wish to mobilize around issues that have existing interest group activity and representation. These additional costs are only incurred after extra interest groups have mobilized as a result of the initiative process, however, so they should be interpreted as merely limiting the number of additional mobilizations, just as they do in noninitiative states.

42. See Chavez (1998) for a detailed discussion of the individuals, parties, and groups involved in Proposition 209.

43. Neither the model nor the empirical tests assume that the correlation is positive, but since it is probably more reasonable than the alternative, I use this language for the purpose of explication.

44. But see Glick and Hays (1991), Hays (1996), and Boehmke and Witmer (2004) for studies that focus on how diffusion changes over time.

45. Studies that focus on social learning include Walker (1969), Glick and Hays (1991), Mooney (2001), and Mooney and Lee (1995). Examples of studies that focus on economic competition include Berry and Berry (1990) and Eadington (1999). Boehmke and Witmer (2004) attempts to distinguish between the two and find that both influence the extent of states' adoption of Indian gaming.

46. Investigated first by Schattschneider (1960), the first broad empirical studies were performed by Schlozman (1984) and Schlozman and Tierney (1986), and their findings have been repeated by Walker (1991), Heinz, Laumann, Nelson, and Salisbury (1993), and Baumgartner and Leech (2001) in the Washington, D.C., lobbying community and by Gray and Lowery (1996) at the state level.

47. While Walker (1983, 1991) examines the effect of patrons, including the government, on interest group mobilization, a more closely related study by Gais (1996) shows how government regulations influence PAC formation. In addition, Berry and Arons (2003) provide a detailed study of the consequences of tax-exempt [501(c)(3)] status for interest groups.

48. Furthermore, there is evidence that citizens in initiative states are more politically active, providing groups a broader base from which to draw potential members (M. Smith 2001; Tolbert, McNeal, and D. Smith 2003).

49. This type of signaling would parallel that in Kollman (1998): instead of using outside lobbying to signal salience, groups would be attempting to demonstrate how much the policy is worth to them or whether they could raise enough money to sponsor (or pass) an initiative.

50. Of course, whether the legislature should believe these signals is another question. A model of asymmetric information would be required to precisely lay out the role that signaling could play.

51. Note that this is different from campaign contributions, because although contributions not made appear to be 0 (despite the fact that the group would have liked to have made them), passed-up opportunities for inside lobbying would be perceived by the group as an indication of infinite unresponsiveness on the part of the legislature. This is why the prediction is worded in terms of the group's perception rather than the observed level of lobbying.

Chapter 3

1. The analysis in this chapter builds on previous work that examines the effect of the direct initiative process on state interest group populations (Boehmke 2002).

2. Investigated first by Schattschneider (1960), the first broad empirical studies were performed by Schlozman (1984) and Schlozman and Tierney (1986), and their findings have been repeated by Walker (1991), Heinz, Laumann, Nelson, and Salisbury (1993), and Baumgartner and Leech (2001), among others, at the federal level and by Gray and Lowery (1996) at the state level.

3. For example, Chong (1991) argues that interest groups attempt to structure the interest group's success as hanging on an all-or-nothing situation to increase the incentives to cooperate—if all potential members must join to achieve success, there is no incentive to free ride.

4. See McAdam (1988) for the role that interpersonal relationships can play in increasing the chances that individuals join a political activity.

5. In fact, if registration is more costly in initiative states, it just increases the hurdle that groups must overcome and makes any findings of greater mobilization that much more persuasive. Given that many of the reforms adopted in conjunction with direct legislation were good-government reforms, if any-

thing, one might suspect that the costs of lobbying would be greater in initiative states.

6. The economic category is formed by combining the groups in agriculture, mining, construction, finance, trade, service, transportation, and manufacturing, while social and government groups are combined into the citizen category.

7. Gray and Lowery (1996) also combine the social and government categories into what they call the not-for-profit category, asserting that "it is this balance . . . that motivates much of the debate in the literature over the diversity of interest organization populations" (101).

8. Because of missing data, there are six states for which these numbers are not available in 1975 and 1980 (Alabama, Hawaii, Nevada, Rhode Island, Utah, and West Virginia).

9. For example, 71.1 percent of the groups with Washington, D.C., representation in Schlozman's study (1984) are domestic or foreign corporations or trade associations; an additional 6.9 percent are professional associations. Seventy-five percent of the groups in Schlozman and Tierney's study (1986) are businesses, trade, or professional associations. Sixty-three percent of organizations in Washington, D.C., in 1995; 62 percent of lobbying firm clients in 1996; and 72 percent of lobbyists in 1996 represent groups that fall into these categories (see table 1 in Baumgartner and Leech [2001]).

10. While the hypothesis being tested is that there are more groups in initiative states, I report the results for two-tailed tests to maintain consistency throughout the book. In addition, however, I also indicate when differences are significant with a one-tailed test at the 0.10 level (since significance at the 0.10 level with a two-tailed test is equivalent to significance at the 0.05 level with the appropriate one-tailed test).

11. See Opheim (1991) for a study that measures the stringency of lobbying regulations. Gray and Lowery (1998) find almost no evidence that regulations influence registrations overall and in six different issue areas, with one exception in the case of agricultural registrations.

12. The data on government expenditures are taken from the *Statistical Abstract of the States* (U.S. Bureau of the Census, various years) and represent nominal state and local general expenditures. The data on gross state product are taken from the State Politics and Policy Quarterly Data Resource Web site (http://www.unl.edu/sppq, accessed August 26, 2001) and are then deflated to 1983 dollars. CPI and divided government variables also are taken from the *Statistical Abstract of the States.*

13. This measure is constructed from data in the *Statistical Abstract of the States* (U.S. Bureau of the Census, various years).

14. I use the Erikson, Wright, and MacIver (1993) measure of the difference between the percentages of state liberal identifiers and state conservative identifiers. Including this variable leads to the loss of observations on Alaska

and Hawaii, though Hawaii is already missing in 1975 and 1980. I also tried to control for regional effects by including an indicator variable for the South in an alternative specification, but it did not have a significant effect and does not influence the interpretations of the other variables.

15. Common models for count data include the Poisson, negative binomial, and generalized event count regression models. The latter two relax the Poisson assumption that the variance equals the mean. I estimate my models using the negative binomial with mean overdispersion, though the results were similar to those obtained using a linear regression model or a Box-Cox specification. See King (1988, 1989a, 1989b), Long (1997), and Cameron and Trivedi (1998) for more information on count models.

16. There are two other specifications that I am not able to estimate. First, while I have panel data, I cannot estimate a fixed-effects model, which would allow for state-specific variation. This model is not identified because of the inclusion of the initiative indicator, which is constant for each state over the time period studied.

17. The costs of proposal were measured in the usual fashion, using the signature requirement to obtain ballot access. For states that allow multiple forms of the initiative (direct statutory or constitutional and indirect statutory or constitutional), I used the minimum of the different requirements.

18. An alternative approach would involve using only the cost variable. Yet this approach is incorrect, since it forces the effect of the initiative process to be 0 if the signature requirement is 0. This could lead to a positive coefficient on the signature variable, because it picks up both the costs of proposal and the fact that any proposals are allowed at all.

19. For discussions of the role and importance of assumption tests in political science, see Dion (1997) or Morton (1999).

20. The average passage rate for initiatives may vary for different types of interests, depending on whether there is systematic differences in key parameters of the model for these interests, such as β and λ. If, on average, citizen groups tend to be involved in issues with higher average values of λ^*, then their initiatives will have a higher overall passage rate. Boehmke and Patty (2003) provide a theoretical perspective on initiative passage rates in the context of voter cue-taking.

21. See appendix C for more details on the survey, which will be discussed in chapter 5.

22. The paper incorrectly reports the opposite finding for the lobbying frequency variable—the reported estimates are correct; but for the lobbying frequency variable, larger values correspond to less frequent lobbying.

23. I only report results for the model with the Florida in 1990 variable, but the conclusions from the model without it are the same. The main difference is that excluding it increases the estimated effect of the initiative process.

24. These data are taken from table 5.5 in Gray and Lowery (1996, 105).

25. See Gray and Lowery (1996, 104). This may reduce the effect because it is less clear what role the initiative will play in the tendency of existing groups to join together as a group, such as with peak associations.

Chapter 4

1. I focus on studies of discrete policy adoption, since they relate most directly to my prediction and empirical tests, but other approaches exist. Matsusaka (1995, 2004) studies state expenditures and revenues and finds that initiative states spend less than noninitiative states in the latter half of the twentieth century. Similar results obtain in Swiss cantons that require voter approval of new government spending (2003).

2. This approach is used by Gerber (1999) and Lascher, Hagen, and Rochlin (1996). One problem is that the results ultimately depend upon which year is chosen to make the comparison, particularly if initiative states adopt faster. Even if all initiative states adopt before any noninitiative states, the estimated impact of the initiative will vary if different years are used. The effect of the initiative will be 0 in the first and last years of adoption, because all states have either not adopted or adopted at those two points in time. As the number of initiative states that adopt increases, the estimated effect of the initiative process on adoption will also increase, reaching a maximum once all initiative states have adopted and before noninitiative states begin to adopt. Then as the number of noninitiative states adopting increases, the estimated effect of the initiative will decrease until it reaches 0 when they have all adopted.

3. There are other ways to overturn the results of an initiative, however, including the courts and through the legislature. Smith (2001) examines cases where the legislature voted on statutes that had previously passed via the initiative process.

4. See Box-Steffensmeier and Jones (1997, 2004) and Allison (1984) for a discussion of the event history approach.

5. These variables are created by adding up the number of contiguous states that have adopted the policy in question prior to the current year, using only states of the appropriate dyad type. The contiguity coding is taken from Berry and Berry (1990).

6. Inclusion of the continuous preference variable means that the initiative indicator need not be positive since it merely serves as an intercept for when preferences and the other variables are 0.

7. Specifically, the model predicts that $\delta \text{Pr}\ (adopt_{i,t}) / \delta\ \text{Initiative}_{i,t,} > 0$. As the model predicts that initiative states are more likely to adopt these policies than noninitiative states, I do not have the problems outlined by Matsusaka (2000). He correctly observes that while most empirical tests of the effect of the initiative process on policy attempt to demonstrate that actual policy is

closer to the median voter's preferred policy, this is generally impossible to verify unless policy outcomes and preferences are measured on identical scales.

8. The impact is so great that including other variables does not improve on the predictive power of a simple cross-sectional model that predicts adoption based solely on the presence of the initiative (Tolbert 1998).

9. See Sears and Citrin (1982) or Smith (1998) for a discussion of the tax revolt.

10. The basic change that states made was to separate the assessment of guilt and the punishment imposition phases of the trial. In its 1976 decision in *Gregg v. Georgia,* the Court ruled that the death penalty was not unconstitutional per se and upheld the current format.

11. IGRA defined Class I, Class II, and Class III gaming. Only Class III gaming requires state approval through compacts. See Getches, Wilkinson, and Williams (1998), chap. 9, for an overview of the provisions of and legal challenges to the Indian Gaming Regulatory Act.

12. Mason (2000) provides a good study of Native American gaming; Pierce and Miller (2004) study the politics of legalized gambling in general.

13. See Boehmke and Witmer (2002) for a study of senators' Native American gaming campaign contribution receipts; Boehmke and Witmer (2003) for a study of Native American nations' expenditures on hard money, soft money, and federal lobbying; and Skopek, Engstrom, and Hansen (2004) for a study of Native American campaign contributions in Texas.

14. Proposition 5 was ruled unconstitutional because it was only a statutory initiative and gaming was outlawed by the state constitution. The tribes and the state eventually agreed to modified terms that resulted in Proposition 1A being put on the ballot by the legislature in March 2000 to modify the constitution accordingly. Proposition 1A passed with 64.5 percent of the vote (California Secretary of State's Web page: http://www.ss.ca.gov, accessed October 25, 2001). Although this is an example of tribal use of the initiative process, it is important to note that the first compact with California was signed in 1990.

15. The analysis uses only the 48 contiguous states, and Mississippi did not adopt the initiative process until 1992.

16. Twenty initiative states have tribes, and the average initiative state has 11.8 tribes. Fourteen noninitiative states have at least one tribe, and the average number is only 2.7.

17. I also estimated a cubic spline to control for changes in the probability of adoption over time (Beck, Katz, and Tucker 1998). Data sources are state income, budget deficit, long-term debt, and partisan control of government measures taken from the *Statistical Abstract of the States* (U.S. Bureau of the Census, various years).

18. Public Law 280 states were granted criminal and civil jurisdiction over Native American nations by the federal government in 1953 (Goldberg 1975).

These six states may have a greater history of interaction with these nations and may be able to reach agreements more quickly. Data on the number of federally recognized Native American nations in a state are taken from the Bureau of Indian Affairs current listing (December 1998). Murder rates per capita are taken from the *Statistical Abstract of the States* (U.S. Bureau of the Census, various years).

19. Note that I do not, and should not, exclude states with no federally recognized Native American tribes. An important feature of the compacting process is that Native American nations can negotiate with any state in which they have land in trust, whether or not they presently have reservation lands in that state. Even for states in which no tribe holds land in trust, IGRA provides guidelines for tribes to purchase land and place it in trust in a relatively short amount of time (McCulloch 1994; Getches, Wilkinson, and Williams 1998). A recent example is the state of New York's agreement to allow the Seneca nation to obtain trust land in downtown Niagara Falls and Buffalo for the purpose of building tribal casinos.

20. Recall that the ideology variable measures the difference between the percentage of liberal and the percentage of conservative identifiers and is negative in all states.

21. The simulations were done using Clarify (King, Tomz, and Wittenberg 2000), which accounts for estimation uncertainty by calculating the mean and standard deviation of the change in probability by taking multiple draws of the estimated coefficient vector.

22. Significance is assessed by whether the appropriate level confidence interval includes 0, rather than using a *z*-score. I use this approach because nonlinearities in the model's functional form result in asymmetric confidence intervals.

23. Because of this finding, I present the results with the uninteracted ideology variable to facilitate evaluation of the effect of the initiative process relative to other states. I omitted the religion variable because it had no effect and correlation with the ideology variable ($\rho = -0.7$) reduced the latter's significance. Otherwise, the results are substantively the same.

24. Because the effect of ideology is significant in noninitiative states in these results (unlike the capital punishment results), I first change its value for all states for each simulation before assessing the impact of the initiative process, as the effect of the initiative process is calculated relative to a hypothetical state that is identical in all ways except that it does not have the initiative process.

25. The changes in probabilities do not successively increase with ideology for a given number of neighbors' adoptions because the probability of adoption for the state before adding the initiative process is increasing because of the changes in the overall effect of ideology.

26. To be precise, their second model produces a positive coefficient for initia-

tive states that is significant with a one-tailed test at the 0.107 level (Boehmke and Witmer 2004).

Chapter 5

1. The selection of states was also limited somewhat by the availability of lobbying registration information from the states. See table C.1 in appendix C for characteristics of the states chosen.

2. Initiative totals taken from the Initiative and Referendum Institute's Web page: http://www.iandrinstitute.org/usage/byyear.html.

3. See Appendix C for the questions that were included in the questionnaire.

4. Aggregation bias occurs when groups give responses that are averages across all their issue involvements. This can be problematic when attempting to make inferences, since the variables may be measured at different levels of aggregation. For example, the relationship between the level of conflict and strategic choices by the group may not be the same averaged across all issue involvements as it is in each particular one.

5. Groups were encouraged to discuss recent issues that featured potential initiatives to ensure sufficient observations in this category to make meaningful comparisons with groups not involved in initiatives.

6. Before the full survey was conducted, a pretest was carried out by sending questionnaires to twenty-five groups in both South Dakota and New Mexico, resulting in fourteen responses. Since only minor revisions were subsequently made, I include these fourteen responses in the analyses to follow.

7. For an introduction to issues of response and selection bias in political science, see Achen (1986) or Brehm (1993).

8. The data suggest this is not a concern, as the response rates are almost the same for the initiative and noninitiative states.

9. Specifically, in a regression setting, response bias is a problem if the unmeasured factors that induce response are related to the unmeasured factors that determine the phenomenon being studied.

10. For comparison, Gerber's (1999) survey of state interest groups achieved a response rate of 26 percent and Nownes and Freeman's (1998) a response rate of 41 percent, which they note is unusually high compared with previous studies of state interest groups. The low response rate I obtained was particularly surprising given that the fifty-group pretest I conducted yielded a 28 percent response rate.

11. Table C.2 in appendix C contains detailed information about the response frequencies for different types of groups in the two surveys and how these data were used to correct the analyses that follow. In short, I used the frequency of responses by different types of groups in the two samples to construct weights for each type of group. These weights are then used when analyzing the mail

survey data to make the averages representative of the population being studied.

12. The one exception is the lobbying frequency question, for which larger values correspond to less frequent lobbying.

13. The categories generally have a rough correspondence to a logarithmic scale.

14. Although a total of 306 surveys were returned, the number of valid responses for each question varies somewhat. For the revenue question there are 290 responses; the other resource measures typically have more than 300 responses.

15. These results are not shown, but a *t* test of the null hypothesis that the probability of having members is the same for these two types of states produces a test statistic of 5, which is significant well beyond conventional levels.

16. Since this was an open-ended question rather than one that provided specific response categories, there is no χ^2 statistic to present. This is the case for all variables that do not have a χ^2 value listed. I list both one- and two-tailed results for consistency and discuss both in the text as applicable. For most variables, the predicted direction of the differences is obvious, but for some it is not. Rather than differentiate these cases, I instead report the two-tailed results and also indicate which variables are significant with the appropriate one-tailed test at the 0.10 level.

17. Recall that for this question alone, higher responses indicate less frequent lobbying.

18. One measure of this failure is the fact that in California from 1912 to 1998 only 26 percent of initiatives that are titled actually qualify for the ballot (Donovan, Bowler, and McCuan 2001; Shelley 2002). Obviously, there are many more potential initiatives that do not even get titled.

19. This approach may also overlook groups relying on the indirect effect, but only if they do not need to signal their intention to use the ballot to pressure the legislature. While this is entirely consistent with models of the initiative process, most of the researchers expect that groups may have to take steps to make the threat credible, such as beginning the process of proposing an initiative. Even if some groups are able to exert this extreme form of indirect influence—essentially being able to whisper to the legislature that they could propose an initiative if they do not get what they want—the set of groups studied here still includes a broader range of groups than previous studies.

20. This number is probably an overestimate of the true incidence of initiative involvement given that groups were encouraged to choose a recent issue that involved a potential initiative, though a recent survey by Alexander and Nownes (2004) finds that although 65 percent of groups in California and Michigan have publicly supported or opposed a ballot initiative, only 23 percent have ever attempted to draft an initiative.

21. Recall that the average number of government officials is the average given that at least one is involved.

Chapter 6

1. Kollman (1998) finds evidence that groups tend to lock in to certain strategies and consistently return to them.

2. One of the original studies of iron triangles, also referred to as issue subsystems is by Griffith (1939). This approach lost its popularity over time and was supplanted by the study of broader issue networks (Heclo 1978). See Browne (1990, 1995) for studies of the agricultural issue network and Baumgartner and Leech (1998, esp. 120–25) for an extended discussion.

3. In their survey of Washington, D.C., interest groups, one of the features of the responses that Schlozman and Tierney (1986) note is how many different lobbying tactics groups report using. Asking groups if they do something at all may therefore gloss over important differences in how important each of those activities is. Thus, the approach taken in my survey of asking groups to rate the importance of each tactic on a five-point scale may find continued evidence of more than one lobbying strategy.

4. See Kim and Mueller (1978) for more information on factor analysis.

5. I allowed for more than two dimensions when I did the analysis. I found some evidence of a third dimension, which appeared to correspond to what I term an "issue entrepreneur" strategy that loaded heavily on purely inside tactics like contacting legislators, testifying before committees, and building legislative coalitions, but unlike the modern inside dimension, loaded negatively on tactics like monitoring public opinion, pointing out other policy implications, and mobilizing members. I interpret this as relating to the rise of single-issue groups, nonlegislative government actors, or issue entrepreneurs such as Ron Unz, Ward Connerly, Reed Hastings, or George Soros. Since the model makes no clear predictions about how the initiative might influence this strategy, I omit it from the rest of the discussion.

6. Note that Walker (1991) also finds that working with the mass media loads relatively highly on both of his dimensions as well.

7. This is distinct from the argument that groups that use the initiative have resources consistent with outside lobbying strategies, as I am already controlling for those resources.

8. I separate groups that were for the initiative proposal from those that were opposed to it, since very different lobbying approaches may be involved and since implication 6 is specifically concerned with the effect of proposing initiatives on the ability to inside-lobby. Groups that are opposing initiatives should not see this benefit and in fact may be good at inside lobbying because they probably helped defeat the initiative's supporters in the legislature. While groups were encouraged to use an issue involving a potential initiative whether they were in favor of or opposed to it, four times as many groups indicated they supported an initiative than indicated they opposed one. This discrepancy is likely due to the fact that I asked about potential initiatives,

many of which may have not have reached the point of attracting opposition from other groups.

9. The omitted baseline category is therefore businesses and corporations.

10. This mirrors Hansen's argument (1991) that groups must demonstrate not only the existence of public support, but also that the issue is likely to recur.

11. See Heckman (1979) for a discussion of this problem in general and Achen (1986) or Brehm (1993) for a discussion of selection bias in political science.

12. A common misperception with regard to selection bias is that it is present whenever the sample of respondents is not representative of the population being studied. This is false. As long as a regression analysis includes variables that control for the differences between the sample and the population being studied, the regression estimates are accurate (unbiased and consistent). Selection bias occurs when omitted factors influence both whether a group is observed and its use of lobbying strategies. Thus, the fact that there are fewer businesses in my primary survey responses than in my telephone survey responses is not necessarily evidence of the potential for selection bias.

13. These are known as models with stochastic truncation and are discussed by Bloom and Killingsworth (1985), Maddala (1983), and Brehm (1999). Boehmke (2003a) contains a discussion of the difficulty of estimating these models when the dependent variable is dichotomous rather than continuous and Brehm (1999) reports failure to converge in about 10 percent of his cases.

14. The regression results reported are calculated using multiple imputation to account for item nonresponse on the part of groups. The multiple imputation was implemented in Amelia (Honaker, Joseph, King, Scheve, and Singh 2000) after calculating the factor scores for groups on which data are available and then imputing those that could not be directly calculated (due to missing observations for at least one of the twenty activities) since it is recommended that all transformations should be carried out before imputation (King, Honaker, Joseph, and Scheve 2001).

15. Recall that larger values for the lobbying frequency variable correspond to less frequent lobbying.

16. The effect of initiative involvement is relative to the effect of being in an initiative state, meaning that initiative involvement significantly increases groups' scores relative to all groups in initiative states. The effect relative to groups in noninitiative states is the combination of these two effects. While the combined effect is positive, it is not significant.

17. These effects are calculated using the regression coefficients in tables 6.3 and 6.4. The effects for involvement represent the combined effects of the possibility and use of the initiative process. To obtain to the percentage increases, I normalized both lobbying strategies so that the smallest value was 0.

Chapter 7

1. I discount the differences in the "other" category, because only groups that were active in this category gave a response and it is difficult to interpret what greater activity in other areas means.

2. See Walker (1983, 1991) for an in-depth study of the role of patrons in interest group mobilization and maintenance.

3. Information taken from the Oklahoma Coalition against Cockfighting's Web page (http://www.bancockfighting.org/index.htm), the Oklahoma legislature's Web page (http://www.lsb.state.ok.us), the Humane Society's Web site (http://www.hsus.org/ace/14670), the Oklahoma State Election Board (http://www.state.ok.us/~elections/02result.html), and an article on the American Veterinary Medical Association's Web site, http://www.avma.org/onlnews/javma/apr03/030415e.asp (Kuehn 2003).

4. This is not to imply that the process could not benefit from some types of reform, particularly those that increase the transparency of sponsorship and funding. See Gerber (2001) for a discussion of various proposed reforms.

5. As a comparison, Gray and Lowery (1996) report an average of 4,194 bills introduced in each state during 1990 and 1991 combined, with a total of 876 passing. Note that these data exclude resolutions.

6. See Walker (1991) and Baumgartner and Leech (1998) for a discussion of changes in the composition of the Washington, D.C., lobbying community, particularly during the 1960s and 1970s. Berry (1999) also discusses the rise of postmaterial concerns and the rise of groups representing these concerns at the national level over the same period.

Appendix B

1. I could allow the status quo to be either 1 or 0 and then give the legislature the option to move it, but the results would not change. Given the equilibrium in the rest of the game, the legislature would always choose to move policy to 0 initially.

2. The group may prefer to propose an initiative at indifference, since it may give the legislature an incentive to bargain and make the group strictly better off.

3. For a discussion of Nash bargaining, see Morrow (1994, 112–16).

4. To utilize this information, they need to know and the legislature's utility loss of adoption, or at least have prior distributions over them.

Appendix C

1. For two groups that refused to respond, I filled in answers using information from their Web site.

Works Cited

Achen, Christopher H. 1986. *The Statistical Analysis of Quasi-Experiments.* Berkeley: University of California Press.

Ainsworth, Scott. 1993. "Regulating Lobbyists and Interest Group Influence." *Journal of Politics* 55(1): 41–56.

Alexander, Robert, and Anthony Nownes. 2004. "Organized Interests and Direct Democracy in the States." Paper presented at the Fourth Annual Conference on State Politics and Policy Section of the American Political Science Association, Kent State University, Kent, OH.

Allison, Paul D. 1984. *Event History Analysis: Regression for Longitudinal Event Data.* Sage University Paper Series on Quantitative Applications in the Social Sciences, no. 07–046. Beverly Hills, CA: Sage Publications.

Allswang, John M. 2000. *The Initiative and Referendum in California, 1898–1998.* Stanford, CA: Stanford University Press.

Americans for Medical Rights. 1996. "Repeal of New Ohio Medical Marijuana Law Could Lead to Ballot Initiative in 1998." Press release, December 3.

Associated Press. 2002. "Class-size Amendment Worries Jeb Bush: Governor Says Fla. Doesn't Have Enough Money for Plan." November 7. From CNN's Web site, http://www.cnn.com/2002/EDUCATION/11/07/election.class.size.ap.

Austen-Smith, David. 1987. "Interest Groups, Campaign Contributions, and Probabilistic Voting." *Public Choice* 54: 123–39.

———. 1993. "Information and Influence: Lobbying for Agendas and Votes." *American Journal of Political Science* 37: 799–833.

———, and John R. Wright. 1994. "Counteractive Lobbying." *American Journal of Political Science* 38: 25–44.

Bali, Valentina A. 2003. "Implementing Popular Initiatives: What Matters for Compliance?" *Journal of Politics* 65(4): 1130–46.

Banducci, Susan A. 1998. "Direct Legislation: When Is It Used and When Does It Pass?" In *Citizens as Legislators: Direct Democracy in the United States,* edited by Shaun Bowler, Todd Donovan, and Caroline J. Tolbert, 132–48. Columbus: Ohio State University Press.

Baumgartner, Frank R., and Beth L. Leech. 1998. *Basic Interest: The Importance of Groups in Politics and Political Science.* Princeton, NJ: Princeton University Press.

———. 2001. "Issue Niches and Policy Bandwagons: Patterns of Interest Group Involvement in National Politics." *Journal of Politics* 63: 1191–1213.

Beard, Charles A., and Birl E. Schultz. 1912. *Documents on the State-Wide Initiative, Referendum and Recall.* New York: MacMillan.

Beck, Nathaniel, Jonathan N. Katz, and Richard Tucker. 1998. "Taking Time Seriously: Time-Series-Cross-Section Analysis with a Binary Dependent Variable." *American Journal of Political Science* 42: 1260–88.

Berry, Frances Stokes, and William D. Berry. 1990. "State Lottery Adoptions as Policy Innovations: An Event History Analysis." *American Political Science Review* 84: 395–415.

Berry, Jeffrey M. 1999. *The New Liberalism: The Rising Power of Citizen Groups.* Washington, DC: Brookings Institution Press.

———, and David F. Arons. 2003. *A Voice for the Nonprofits.* Washington, DC: Brookings Institution Press.

Billingsley, K. Lloyd. 1998. "Silicon Valley Pushes California into School-Reform Action." Editorial, *Washington Times,* May 3.

Black, Duncan. 1958. *The Theory of Committees and Elections.* Cambridge: Cambridge University Press.

Bloom, David E., and Mark R. Killingsworth. 1985. "Correcting for Truncation Bias Caused by a Latent Truncation Variable." *Journal of Econometrics* 27: 131–35.

Boehmke, Frederick J. 2002. "The Effect of Direct Democracy on the Size and Diversity of State Interest Group Populations." *Journal of Politics* 3: 827–44.

———. 2003a. "Using Auxiliary Data to Estimate Selection Bias Models, with an Application to Interest Groups' Use of the Direct Initiative Process." *Political Analysis* 11: 234–54.

———. 2003b. "Sources of Variation in Statewide Use of the Initiative Process: The Role of Interest Group Populations." Paper presented at the 2003 meetings of the American Political Science Association, Philadelphia, PA.

———, and R. Michael Alvarez. 2004a. "Where the Good Signatures Are: Variation in the Number and Validity of Initiative Petition Signatures across California Counties." Typescript, University of Iowa.

———. 2004b. "The Influence of Signature Gathering Campaigns on Political Participation." Typescript, University of Iowa.

———, and John W. Patty. 2003. "Size Matters: Information and Inference in the Initiative Process." Working paper, University of Iowa.

———, and Richard C. Witmer. 2002. "Resource Growth and Indian Lobbying: Gaming Revenue and the Empowerment of Native Americans." Paper presented at the annual meeting of the American Political Science Association, Boston, MA.

———. 2003. "Hard Money, Soft Money, or Direct Lobbying Expenditures? The Emergence and Growth of American Indian Lobbying." Paper presented at the annual meeting of the Midwest Political Science Association, Chicago, IL.

———. 2004. "Disentangling Diffusion: The Effect of Social Learning and

Economic Competition on State Policy Innovation and Expansion." *Political Research Quarterly* 57: 39–52.

Bowler, Shaun, and Todd Donovan. 1998. "Direct Democracy and Minority Rights: An Extension." *American Journal of Political Science* 42: 1020–24.

———. 2002. "Democracy, Institutions, and Attitudes about Citizen Influence on Government." *British Journal of Political Science* 32: 371–90.

Box-Steffensmeier, Janet M., and Bradford D. Jones. 1997. "Time Is of the Essence: Event History Models in Political Science." *American Journal of Political Science* 41: 1414–61.

———. 2004. *Event History Modeling: A Guide for Social Sciences.* Cambridge: Cambridge University Press.

Boyle, James. 1912. *The Initiative and Referendum: Its Follies, Fallacies and Failure.* Columbus, OH: A. J. Smythe.

Brasher, Holly, David Lowery, and Virginia Gray. 1999. "State Lobby Registration Data: The Anomalous Case of Florida (and Minnesota Too!)." *Legislative Studies Quarterly* 24: 303–14.

Brehm, John. 1993. *The Phantom Respondents: Opinion Surveys and Political Representation.* Ann Arbor: University of Michigan Press.

———. 1999. "Alternative Corrections for Sample Truncation: Applications to the 1988, 1990, and 1992 Senate Election Studies." *Political Analysis* 8: 147–65.

Broder, David S. 2000. *Democracy Derailed: Initiative Campaigns and the Power of Money.* New York: Harcourt Brace.

Browne, William P. 1990. "Organized Interests and Their Issues Niches: A Search for Pluralism in a Policy Domain." *Journal of Politics* 52: 477–509.

———. 1995. *Cultivating Congress: Constituents, Issues, and Interests in Agricultural Policymaking.* Lawrence: University of Kansas Press.

Cain, Bruce E., and Kenneth P. Miller. 2001. "The Populist Legacy: Initiatives and the Undermining of Representative Government." In *Dangerous Democracy: The Battle over Ballot Initiative in America,* edited by Larry J. Sabato, Howard R. Ernst, and Bruce A. Larson, 33–61. Lanham, MD: Rowman and Littlefield.

"The California Ballot." *The Economist,* March 4, 2004.

Cameron, A. Colin, and Pravin K. Trivedi. 1998. *Regression Analysis of Count Data.* Cambridge: Cambridge University Press.

Chavez, Lydia. 1998. *The Color Bind: The Campaign to End Affirmative Action.* Berkeley: University of California Press.

Chong, Dennis. 1991. *Collective Action and the Civil Rights Movement.* Chicago: University of Chicago Press.

Coalition for a Better Ohio. 1998. www.ohiohemp.org (discontinued)

Colorado Citizens for Compassionate Cannabis. 1998. "Amendment 19: Medical Marijuana Ballot Initiative in Colorado: Is It Good Medicine?" Press release, December 10.

Cornell, Stephen, Joseph Kalt, Matthew Krepps, and Jonathan Taylor. 1998. "American Indian Gaming Policy and Its Socio-Economic Effects." A Report to the National Gambling Impact Study Commission. Cambridge, MA: Economics Resource Group.

Coughlin, Peter J., Dennis C. Meuller, and Peter Murrell. 1990. "Electoral Politics, Interest Groups, and the Size of Government." *Economic Inquiry* 28: 682–705.

Cronin, Thomas E. 1989. *Direct Democracy: The Politics of Initiative, Referendum, and Recall.* Cambridge, MA: Harvard University Press.

Dahl, Robert A. 1961. *Who Governs? Democracy and Power in an American City.* New Haven, CT: Yale University Press.

Dion, Douglas. 1997. *Turning the Legislative Thumbscrews: Minority Rights and Procedural Change in Legislative Politics.* Ann Arbor: University of Michigan Press.

Dombrink, John, and William N. Thompson. 1990. *The Last Resort: Success and Failure in Campaigns for Casinos.* Reno: University of Nevada Press.

Donovan, Todd, Shaun Bowler, and David McCuan. 2001. "Political Consultants and the Initiative Industrial Complex." In *Dangerous Democracy: The Battle over Ballot Initiative in America,* edited by Larry J. Sabato, Howard R. Ernst, and Bruce A. Larson, 80–108. Lanham, MD: Rowman and Littlefield.

———, and Ken Fernandez. 1998. "Contending Players and Strategies: Opposition Advantages in Initiative Campaigns." In *Citizens as Legislators: Direct Democracy in the United States,* edited by Shaun Bowler, Todd Donovan, and Caroline J. Tolbert, 80–108. Columbus: Ohio State University Press.

Downs, Anthony. 1957. *An Economic Theory of Democracy.* New York: Harper and Row.

Eadington, William R. 1999. "The Economics of Casino Gaming." *Journal of Economic Perspectives* 13: 173–92.

Ellis, Richard. 2002. *Democratic Delusions: The Initiative Process in America.* Lawrence: University of Kansas Press.

———. 2003. "Signature Gathering in the Initiative Process: How Democratic Is It?" *Montana Law Review* 64: 35–97.

Erikson, Robert S., Gerald C. Wright, and John P. McIver. 1993. *Statehouse Democracy: Public Opinion and Policy in the American States.* Cambridge: Cambridge University Press.

Ernst, Howard R. 2001. "The Historical Role of Narrow-Minded Interests." In *Dangerous Democracy: The Battle over Ballot Initiative in America,* edited by Larry J. Sabato, Howard R. Ernst, and Bruce A. Larson, 1–25. Lanham, MD: Rowman and Littlefield.

Everson, David. 1981. "The Effects of Initiatives on Voter Turnout: A Comparative State Analysis." *Western Political Quarterly* 34: 415–25.

Feld, Lars P., and John G. Matsusaka. 2003. "Budget Referendums and Government Spending: Evidence from Swiss Cantons." *Journal of Public Economics* 87: 703–24.

Gais, Thomas. 1996. *Improper Influence: Campaign Finance Law, Interest Groups, and the Problem of Equality.* Ann Arbor: University of Michigan Press.

Gamble, Barbara S. 1997. "Putting Civil Rights to a Popular Vote." *American Journal of Political Science* 41: 245–69.

George, Hunter T. 1998. "Marijuana Initiative on Track for Ballot." Associated Press, July 2.

Gerber, Elisabeth R. 1996. "Legislative Response to the Threat of Popular Initiatives." *American Journal of Political Science* 40: 99–128.

———. 1999. *The Populist Paradox: Interest Group Influence and the Promise of Direct Legislation.* Princeton, NJ: Princeton University Press.

———. 2001. "The Logic of Reform: Assessing Initiative Reform Strategies." In *Dangerous Democracy: The Battle over Ballot Initiative in America*, edited by Larry J. Sabato, Howard R. Ernst, and Bruce A. Larson. 143–71. Lanham, MD: Rowman and Littlefield.

———, Zolton Hajnal, and Hugh Louch. 2002. "Minorities and Direct Legislation: Evidence from California Ballot Proposition Elections." *Journal of Politics* 64(1): 154–77.

Gerber, Elisabeth R., and Arthur Lupia. 1995. "Campaign Competition and Policy Responsiveness in Direct Legislation Elections." *Political Behavior* 17: 287–306.

———, D. McCubbins, and D. Roderick Kiewiet. 2001. *Stealing the Initiative: How State Government Responds to Direct Democracy.* United States of America. Upper Saddle, NJ: Prentice Hall.

Glick, Henry R., and Scott P. Hays. 1991. "Innovation and Reinvention in State Policymaking: Theory and Evolution of Living Will Laws." *Journal of Politics* 53: 835–50.

Goebel, Thomas. 2002. *A Government by the People: Direct Democracy in America, 1890–1940.* Chapel Hill: University of North Carolina Press.

Goldberg, Carole. 1975. "Public Law 280: The Limits of State Jurisdiction over Reservation Indians." *UCLA Law Review* 22: 535–39.

Gray, Virginia, and David Lowery. 1996. *The Population Ecology of Interest Representation.* Ann Arbor: University of Michigan Press.

———. 1998. "State Lobbying Regulations and Their Enforcement: Implications for the Diversity of State Interest Communities." *State and Local Government Review* 30(2): 78–91.

Green, Donald P., and Ian Shapiro. 1994. *Pathologies of Rational Choice Theory: A Critique of Applications in Political Science.* New Haven, CT: Yale University Press.

Grenzke, Janet M. 1989. "PACs and the Congressional Supermarket: The Currency Is Complex." *American Journal of Political Science* 33: 1–24.

Griffith, Ernest S. 1939. *The Impasse of Democracy.* New York: Harrison-Hilton.

Hall, Richard L., and Frank W. Wayman. 1990. "Buying Time: Moneyed Interest and the Mobilization of Bias in Congressional Committees." *American Political Science Review* 84: 797–820.

Hansen, John Mark. 1991. *Gaining Access: Congress and the Farm Lobby, 1919–1981.* Chicago: University of Chicago Press.

Haskell, John. 2001. *Direct Democracy or Representative Government: Dispelling the Populist Myth.* Boulder, CO: Westview Press.

Hays, Scott P. 1996. "Controversy and Reinvention in the Diffusion of State Policy Innovation." *Political Research Quarterly* 49: 613–32.

Heckman, James J. 1979. "Sample Selection Bias as a Specification Error." *Econometrica* 47:153–61.

Heclo, Hugh. 1978. "Issue Networks and the Executive Establishment." In *The New American Political System,* edited by Anthony King, 87–124. Washington, DC: American Enterprise Institute.

Heinz, John P., Robert O. Laumann, Robert L. Nelson, and Robert L. Salisbury. 1993. *The Hollow Core.* Cambridge, MA: Harvard University Press.

Honaker, James, Anne Joseph, Gary King, Kenneth Scheve, and Naunihal Singh. 2001. Amelia: A Program for Missing Data (Windows Version). Cambridge, MA: Harvard University. http://gking.harvard.edu.

Hsiao Cheng. 1990. *Analysis of Panel Data.* Cambridge: Cambridge University Press.

Key, V. O., Jr., and Winston W. Crouch. 1939. *The Initiative and Referendum in California.* Berkeley: University of California Press.

Kim Jae-On and Charles W. Mueller. 1978. *Factor Analysis: Statistical Methods and Practical Issues.* Beverley Hills, CA: Sage Publications.

King, Gary. 1988. "Statistical Models for Political Science Event Counts: Bias in Conventional Procedures and Evidence for the Exponential Poisson Regression Model." *American Journal of Political Science* 32: 838–63.

———. 1989a. *Unifying Political Methodology: The Likelihood Theory of Statistical Inference.* Ann Arbor: University of Michigan Press.

———. 1989b. "Variance Specification in Event Count Models: From Restrictive Assumptions to a Generalized Estimator." *American Journal of Political Science* 33: 762–84.

———, James Honaker, Anne Joseph, Kenneth Scheve, and Naunihal Singh. 2001. "Analyzing Incomplete Political Science Data." *American Political Science Review* 95: 49–69.

———, Michael Tomz, and Jason Wittenberg. 2000. "Making the Most of Statistical Analyses: Improving Interpretation and Presentation." *American Journal of Political Science* 44: 341–55.

Kollman, Ken. 1997. "Inviting Friends to Lobby: Interest Groups, Ideological Bias, and Congressional Committees." *American Journal of Political Science* 41: 519–44.

Kollman, Ken. 1998. *Outside Lobbying: Public Opinion and Interest Group Strategies.* Princeton, NJ: Princeton University Press.

Kuehn, Bridget M. 2003. "Oklahoma Cockfighting Ban Faces Legal Challenges." *Journal of the American Veterinary Medical Association News,* March 15. http://www.avma.org/onlnews/javma/apr03/030415e.asp

Lascher, Edward L., Jr., Michael G. Hagen, and Steven A. Rochlin. 1996. "Gun behind the Door? Ballot Initiatives, State Policies, and Public Opinion." *Journal of Politics* 58: 760–75.

Lohmann, Susanne. 1993. "A Signaling Model of Informative and Manipulative Political Action." *American Political Science Review* 87: 319–33.

Long, J. Scott. 1997. *Regression Models for Categorical and Limited Dependent Variables.* Newbury Park, CA: Sage Publications.

Lowenstein, Daniel Hays, and Robert M. Stern. 1989. "The First Amendment and Paid Initiative Petition Circulators: A Dissenting View and a Proposal." *Hastings Constitutional Law Quarterly* 17: 175–224.

Lowery, David, Virginia Gray, Matthew Fellowes, and Jennifer Anderson. 2004. "Living in the Moment: Lags, Leads, and the Link between Legislative Agendas and Interest Advocacy." *Social Science Quarterly* 85(2): 463–77.

Lupia, Arthur. 1992. "Busy Voters, Agenda Control, and the Power of Information." *American Political Science Review* 86: 390–403.

Maddala, G. G. 1983. *Limited Dependent and Qualitative Variables in Econometrics.* Cambridge: Cambridge University Press.

Magleby, David B. 1984. *Direct Legislation: Voting on Ballot Propositions in the United States.* Baltimore: Johns Hopkins University Press.

Mason, W. Dale. 2000. *Indian Gaming.* Norman: University of Oklahoma Press.

Matsusaka, John G. 1995. "Fiscal Effects of the Voter Initiative." *Journal of Political Economy* 103: 587–623.

———. 2000. "Problems with a Methodology Used to Evaluate the Voter Initiative." *Journal of Politics* 63: 1250–56.

———. 2004. *For the Many or the Few: The Initiative Process, Public Policy, and American Democracy.* Chicago: University of Chicago Press.

———, and Nolan M. McCarty. 2001. "Political Resource Allocation: Benefits and Costs of Voter Initiatives." *Journal of Law, Economics, and Organization* 17: 413–48.

McAdam, Doug. 1988. *Freedom Summer.* New York: Oxford University Press.

McCuan, David, Shaun Bowler, Todd Donovan, and Ken Fernandez. 1998. "California's Political Warriors: Campaign Professionals and the Initiative Process." In *Citizens as Legislators: Direct Democracy in the United States,* edited by Shaun Bowler, Todd Donovan, and Caroline Tolbert, 55–79. Columbus: Ohio State University Press.

McCulloch, Anne. 1994. "The Politics of Indian Gaming: Tribe/State Relations and American Federalism." *Publius* 24: 99–112.

Meltsner, Michael. 1973. *Cruel and Unusual: The Supreme Court and Capital Punishment.* New York: Random House.

Miller, Carol. 1997. "Implementing Prop. 215." Sonoma Civil Rights Action Project press release, March 25. http://www.sonomacountyfreepress.com/scrap/implementing_215.html

Miller, Judith. 1996. "A Giver's Agenda: A Special Report: With Big Money and Brash Ideas, a Billionaire Redefines Charity." *New York Times,* December 17. http://www.sororstrading.com/art12_16_96.html

Mintrom, Michael. 1997. "Policy Entrepreneurs and the Diffusion of Information." *American Journal of Political Science* 41: 738–70.

———, and Sandra Vergari. 1998. "Policy Networks and Innovation Diffusion: The Case of State Education Reforms." *Journal of Politics* 60: 126–48.

Mitchell, William C., and Michael Munger. 1991. "Economic Models of Interest Groups: An Introductory Survey." *American Journal of Political Science* 35: 512–46.

Moe, Terry M. 1980. "A Calculus of Group Membership." *American Journal of Political Science* 24: 593–632.

Mooney, Christopher Z. 2001. "Modeling Regional Effects on State Policy Diffusion." *Political Research Quarterly* 54: 103–24.

———, and Mei-Hsien Lee. 1995. "Legislative Morality in the American States: The Case of pre-Roe Abortion Regulation Reform." *American Journal of Political Science* 39: 599–627.

———. 1999a. "Morality Policy Re-Invention: Death Penalty Policy in the American States." Working paper.

———. 1999b. "The Influence of Values on Consensus and Contentious Reform Policy: U.S. Death Penalty Reform, 1956–82." Working paper.

———. 1999c. "The Temporal Diffusion of Morality Policy: The Case of Death Penalty Legislation in the American States." Working paper.

Morrow, James D. 1994. *Game Theory for Political Scientists.* Princeton, NJ: Princeton University Press.

Morton, Rebecca. 1999. *Methods and Models.* Cambridge: Cambridge University Press.

Mowry, George E. 1951. *The California Progressives.* Chicago: Quadrangle Books.

Mueller, Dennis G., and Peter Murrell. 1986. "Interest Groups and the Size of Government." *Public Choice* 48: 125–45.

National Conference of State Legislatures. 2002. "Initiative and Referendum in the 21st Century: Final Report and Recommendations of the NCSL I&R Task Force." http://www.ncsl.org/programs/press/2002/pr020725I&R.htm

Nownes, Anthony J., and Patricia Freeman. 1998. "Interest Group Activity in the States." *Journal of Politics* 60: 86–112.

Olson, Mancur, Jr. 1965. *The Logic of Collective Action.* Cambridge, MA: Harvard University Press.

———. 1982. *The Rise and Decline of Nations.* New Haven, CT: Yale University Press.

Opheim, Cynthia. 1991. "Explaining the Differences in State Lobbying

Regulation." *Western Political Quarterly* 44: 405–21.

Ordeshook, Peter C. 1992. *A Political Theory Primer.* London: Routledge.

Pierce, Patrick A., and Donald E. Miller. 1999a. "Variations in the Diffusion of State Lottery Adoptions: How Revenue Dedication Changes Morality Politics." *Policy Studies Journal* 27: 696–706.

———. 1999b. "Roll the Dice: Internal Diffusion of Gambling Policy in the American States." Working paper.

———. 2004. *Gambling Politics: State Government and the Business of Betting.* Boulder, CO: Lynne Rienner Publishers.

Rogers, Everett. 1995. *Diffusion of Innovations.* 4th ed. New York: Free Press.

Romer, Thomas, and Howard Rosenthal. 1978. "Political Resource Allocation, Controlled Agendas, and the Status Quo." *Public Choice* 33: 27–44.

———. 1979. "Bureaucrats versus Voters: On the Political Economy of Resource Allocation by Direct Democracy." *Quarterly Journal of Economics* 93: 563–88.

Rothenberg, Lawrence S. 1992. *Linking Citizens to Government: Interest Group Politics at Common Cause.* Cambridge: Cambridge University Press.

Salisbury, Robert H. 1984. "Interest Representation: The Dominance of Institutions." *American Political Science Review* 78: 64–76.

Salt Lake Tribune. 2003. Editorial, "A Thousand Cuts." February 13.

Schattschneider, E. E. 1960. *The Semi-Sovereign People.* New York: Holtz, Rinehart and Winston.

Schildkraut, Deborah. 2001. "Official-English and the States: Influences on Declaring English the Official Language in the United States." *Political Research Quarterly* 54: 445–58.

Schlozman, Kay Lehman. 1984. "What Accent the Heavenly Chorus? Political Equality and the American Pressure System." *Journal of Politics* 46: 1006–32.

———, and John T. Tierney. 1986. *Organized Interests and American Democracy.* New York: Harper and Row.

Schmidt, David D. 1989. *Citizen Lawmakers: The Ballot Initiative Revolution.* Philadelphia: Temple University Press.

Schrag, Peter. 1998. *Paradise Lost: California's Experience, America's Future.* New York: New Press.

Sears, David O., and Jack Citrin. 1982. *Tax Revolt: Something for Nothing in California.* Cambridge, MA: Harvard University Press.

Shelley, Kevin. 2002. "A History of California Initiatives." Report prepared by the California Secretary of State's Office.

Shinkman, Ron. 1998. "Voters Back Pot Rights: Medicinal Use of Marijuana Approved in Four States." *Modern Healthcare* 28 (November 9): 6.

Simon, Herbert A. 1976. *Administrative Behavior.* New York: Free Press.

Skopek, Tracy A., Rich Engstrom Jr., and Kenneth N. Hansen. 2004. "All That Glitters . . . : The Rise of American Indian Tribes in State Political Behavior." Paper presented at the 2004 meetings of the Western Political Science Association, Portland, OR.

Smith, Daniel A. 1998. *Tax Crusaders.* London: Routledge.

———. 2001. "Homeward Bound?: Micro-Level Legislative Responsiveness to Ballot Initiatives." *State Politics and Policy Quarterly* 1: 50–61.

———. 2002. "Direct Democracy and Its Critics." In *American Politics: Core Argument/Current Controversy,* edited by Peter Woolley and Albert Papa. 2nd ed. Englewood Cliffs, NJ: Prentice Hall.

———. 2003. "Overturning Term Limits: The Legislature's Own Private Idaho?" *PS: Political Science and Politics* 36: 215–20.

———, and Joseph Lubinski. 2002. "Direct Democracy during the Progressive Era: A Crack in the Populist Veneer?" *Journal of Policy History* 14: 349–83.

———, and Caroline J. Tolbert. 2004. *Educated by Initiative: The Effects of Direct Democracy on Citizens and Political Organizations in the American States.* Ann Arbor: University of Michigan Press.

Smith, Mark A. 2001. "The Contingent Effects of Ballot Initiatives and Candidate Races on Turnout." *American Journal of Political Science* 45(3): 700–706.

Tolbert, Caroline J. 1998. "Changing Rules for State Legislatures: Direct Democracy and Governance Policy." In *Citizens as Legislators: Direct Democracy in the United States,* edited by Shaun Bowler, Todd Donovan, and Caroline J. Tolbert, 171–90. Columbus: Ohio State University Press.

———, John Grummel, and Daniel A. Smith. 2001. "The Effects of Ballot Initiatives on Voter Turnout in the United States." *American Politics Research* 29: 625–48.

———. 2003. "Enhancing Civic Engagement: The Effect of Direct Democracy on Political Participation and Knowledge." *State Politics and Policy Quarterly* 3: 23–41.

Tolbert, Caroline J., Daniel H. Lowenstein, and Todd Donovan. 1998. "Election Laws and Rules for Initiatives." In *Citizens as Legislators: Direct Democracy in the United States,* edited by Shaun Bowler, Todd Donovan, and Caroline J. Tolbert, 27–54. Columbus: Ohio State University Press.

Tomz, Michael, Jason Wittenberg, and Gary King. 2001. CLARIFY: Software for Interpreting and Presenting Statistical Results. Version 2.0. Cambridge, MA: Harvard University. http://gking.harvard.edu.

Truman, David B. 1951. *The Governmental Process: Political Interests and Public Opinion.* New York: Knopf.

U.S. Bureau of the Census. Various years. *Statistical Abstract of the United States.* Washington, DC: U.S. Government Printing Office.

Walker, Jack L. 1969. "The Diffusion of Innovations among the American States." *American Political Science Review* 63: 880–99.

———. 1983. "The Origin and Maintenance of Interest Groups in America." *American Journal of Political Science* 77: 390–406.

———. 1991. *Mobilizing Interest Groups in America: Patrons, Professionals, and Social Movements.* Ann Arbor: University of Michigan Press.

Wright, John R. 1990. "Contributions, Lobbying, and Committee Voting in the U.S. House of Representatives." *American Political Science Review* 84: 417–38.

———. 1996. *Interest Groups and Congress.* Boston: Allyn and Bacon.

Zimmerman, Joseph F. 1986. *Participatory Democracy: Populism Revisited.* New York: Praeger Publishers.

———. 2001. *The Referendum: The People Decide Public Policy.* Westport, CT: Praeger Publishers.

Index

www.ingramcontent.com/pod-product-compliance
Lightning Source LLC
LaVergne TN
LVHW091051080826
845145LV00002B/705

* 9 7 8 0 8 1 4 2 5 7 0 9 8 *